The Law of the Sea and the Planetary Crisis

This book examines the challenge of negotiating and implementing new legal regimes addressing contemporary ocean challenges in the context of uncertain planetary futures.

The book covers the themes of climate change, biodiversity loss, and pollution. Contributors examine a range of emerging, understudied issues, including the legal regulation of ocean acidification, the development of the mining code by the International Seabed Authority, the implementation of the 2023 Biodiversity Beyond National Jurisdiction (BBNJ) Agreement, and compliance mechanisms developed by the International Maritime Organization. Other chapters look at energy transition, green technology, and marine pollution from shipping.

Contributing to global discussions on sustainable development, this book will be of vital interest to scholars of the law of the sea, environmental law, and sustainable development.

LIU Nengye is associate professor of law at Yong Pung How School of Law, Singapore Management University, where he teaches and conducts research on law and sustainability.

Shirley V. Scott is professor of international law and international relations in the School of Humanities and Social Sciences at UNSW Canberra, Australia.

Routledge Research on the Law of the Sea

Available titles in this series include:

Law of the Sea and Maritime Delimitation
State Practice and Case Law in Latin America and the Caribbean
Angel Horna

Maritime Salvage Operations and Environmental Protection
Durand M Cupido

Peaceful Management of Maritime Disputes
James Kraska and Hee Cheol Yang

Global Governance and the International Law of the Sea
The Evolution and Practice of the Continental Shelf Regime
Shani Friedman

40 Years of the United Nations Convention on the Law of the Sea
Assessment and Prospects
Tomasz Kamiński and Karol Karski

The Law of the Sea and the Planetary Crisis
Edited by Nengye Liu and Shirley V. Scott

The Law of the Sea and the Planetary Crisis

Edited by Nengye Liu and
Shirley V. Scott

Routledge
Taylor & Francis Group
LONDON AND NEW YORK

First published 2025
by Routledge
4 Park Square, Milton Park, Abingdon, Oxon OX14 4RN

and by Routledge
605 Third Avenue, New York, NY 10158

Routledge is an imprint of the Taylor & Francis Group, an informa business

British Library Cataloguing-in-Publication Data
A catalogue record for this book is available from the British Library

Library of Congress Cataloging-in-Publication Data
Names: Liu, Nengye, editor. | Scott, Shirley V., editor.
Title: The law of the sea and the planetary crisis /
edited by Nengye Liu and Shirley V. Scott.
Description: 1. | New York: Routledge, 2025. |
Series: Routledge research in the law of the sea |
Includes bibliographical references and index.
Identifiers: LCCN 2024053700 | ISBN 9781032855325 (hardback) |
ISBN 9781032855349 (paperback) | ISBN 9781003518570 (ebook)
Subjects: LCSH: Marine resources conservation–Law and legislation. |
Marine pollution–Law and legislation | Law of the sea. | Environmental
law, International. | Ocean acidification–Law and legislation. |
Climatic changes–Law and legislation. | Biodiversity conservation–Law
and legislation.
Classification: LCC K3590.4 .L395 2025 | DDC 341.4/5–dc23/
eng/20241205
LC record available at https://lccn.loc.gov/2024053700

ISBN: 9781032855325 (hbk)
ISBN: 9781032855349 (pbk)
ISBN: 9781003518570 (ebk)

DOI: 10.4324/9781003518570

Typeset in Galliard
by Deanta Global Publishing Services, Chennai, India

Contents

List of Contributors

Gabriela Argüello is an associate senior lecturer in environmental law at the University of Gothenburg and a research fellow financed by the Royal Swedish Academy of Letters, History and Antiquities. Her expertise lies in the law of the sea and ocean governance, with a particular focus on interdisciplinary global environmental challenges related to the oceans that involve multiscale actors, including states, international organisations, industries, and civil society organisations. Gabriela has conducted extensive research and published on various topics, including waste management, pesticides, ship recycling, ship-source pollution, polar environments, ocean governance, and energy transitions. Additionally, she is a member of the European Marine Board Working Group on Marine Carbon Dioxide Removal (2024–2026) and a Fulbright Arctic Initiative IV Scholar (2024–2026).

Ana Flávia Barros-Platiau is an associate professor at the International Relations Institute, University of Brasilia, Brazil. She is also a researcher at the Superior Defence College, Brasilia, Brazil, and the director of the Brasilia Research Centre from the Earth System Governance Network (Utrecht University, Holland). Her research topics include ocean and polar governance. Professor Barros-Platiau holds a PhD in international relations from the Université de Paris I (Panthéon-Sorbonne, 2000).

Ethan Beringen is a PhD student and a member of the Centre for Environmental Law at Macquarie University in Sydney, Australia. He has also been a guest PhD researcher at the Norwegian Centre for the Law of the Sea at UiT the Arctic University of Norway. Ethan's research is focused on international environmental law and the law of the sea. Specifically, he is interested in the protection of marine biodiversity, with his PhD topic examining the interaction between international biodiversity law and international fisheries law. He has also published research on topics such as the negotiations for a new treaty instrument for conserving marine biodiversity beyond national jurisdiction, Australia's ocean governance, and middle power theory.

Harvey Mpoto Bombaka is a postdoctoral researcher at the University Centre of Brasilia and a senior researcher at the Research Group on the Law of Natural Resources and Sustainability (GERN-UNB), University of Brasilia. He holds a PhD in international law from the University of Brasilia and the Aix-Marseille University. Dr Bombaka was a visiting researcher at the Max Planck Institute for Comparative Public Law and International Law (2017), ITLOS – Nippon Fellow (2017–2018).

Kristine Elfrida Dalaker, PhD (Law), JD, BA, recently joined the Australian National Centre for Ocean Resources and Security (ANCORS) at the University of Wollongong in Australia as a lecturer. Previously, Kristine was a researcher at the Norwegian Centre for the Law of the Sea (NCLOS) at UiT the Arctic University of Norway in Tromsø, Norway, and prior to relocating to Norway, she was the associate director (administration and special projects) at the Centre for International Law (CIL) at the National University of Singapore. Kristine has presented, published, and taught on a wide range of the law of the sea topics, including the conservation and sustainable use of marine biodiversity (BBNJ), deep seabed mining, the historical development of the law of the sea, and the preservation of the marine environment.

Carina Costa de Oliveira is an associate professor of international and environmental law at the Law Faculty, University of Brasília, Brazil. She has been a visiting scholar at the Panthéon-Sorbonne; the C-EENRG at the University of Cambridge; the University of Adelaide, Australia; and the Centre d'Études et de Recherches Internationales et Communautaires (CERIC) at the University of Aix-Marseille, France. Professor Oliveira holds a PhD in international law from Panthéon-Assas, France. She is the coordinator of the Research Group on Law, Natural Resources and Sustainability (Gern-UnB – https://sites.google.com/ccom.unb.br/ndsr-gern/home) at the University of Brasilia.

Annika Frosch is a research fellow at the Bartlett School of Environment, Energy, and Resources, University College London. Her work centres on ocean governance and policy. She focuses on the debate on midterm measures in the International Maritime Organization, particularly the relationship between international and national governance. Additionally, Annika researches climate ocean change, with a special emphasis on ocean acidification. Annika completed her PhD at the European University Institute, funded by the German Academic Exchange Service, where her thesis focused on governance solutions for ocean acidification that can cater to the scientific reality of this complex problem. During her PhD, Annika was a visiting scholar at several academic institutions, including the National University of Singapore and the Bodega Marine Laboratory at UC Davis. Annika is also an assistant editor at Transnational Environmental Law. In addition to her academic work, she is an international policy consultant for the Ocean Acidification Alliance at the United Nations Foundation.

Nengye Liu (LLB and LLM, Wuhan, PhD, Ghent) is associate professor at Yong Pung How School of Law, Singapore Management University, where he teaches and conducts research on law and sustainability. Associate Professor Liu has taken the lead to edit three books; published 50+ refereed journal articles and book chapters in the fields of the law of the sea and international environmental law; and delivered 100+ presentations about his research findings across five continents. He is regularly covered by mainstream media around the world. He is on the editorial board of *Marine Policy* (Elsevier), *Ocean Development and International Law* (Taylor & Francis), and *Polar Record* (Cambridge University Press). Dr Liu is the founding chair of the steering committee of Asia Pacific Research Alliance on Law and Sustainability (2024–present).

David Leary is a professor of law at the University of Technology Sydney, Australia, where he teaches undergraduate and postgraduate courses in public international law, law of the sea, international environmental law, and private international law. With a wide range of research interests, he broadly describes his research as "Law at the frontiers of science and technology". He has published widely on issues associated with the law of the sea and deep-sea mining, marine genetic resources, international law and the Arctic and Antarctica, biotechnology, and offshore renewable energy, among other areas.

Rebecca Prentiss Pskowski is a civilian attorney-advisor at US Coast Guard headquarters in Washington, DC, and a WMU-Koji Sekimizu PhD fellow in maritime governance at the World Maritime University in Malmö, Sweden. Rebecca holds a BA, with honours, from the University of Chicago, a JD from Harvard Law School, and an LLM in admiralty, with distinction, from Tulane University Law School. She clerked for the Honorable Charles S. Haight, Jr. of the Southern District of New York. Prior to her legal career, Rebecca sailed as a merchant mariner for nine years. She is currently licenced as a mate of vessels less than 1,600 gross register tons on oceans and a master of vessels less than 200 gross register tons on coastal waters. Rebecca has published widely on maritime legal topics, including articles on ship recycling, bunker contamination claims, maritime arbitration, and maritime labour protections.

Shirley Scott is a professor of international law and international relations in the School of Humanities and Social Sciences at UNSW Canberra. Professor Scott's research lies at the intersection of international law and international relations. One of her most significant contributions to scholarship in international law has been her theory of international law as an ideology. She has also contributed widely on topics including the engagement of the United States with international law, Antarctic governance, Antarctica, climate change, and international security. In 2019, Professor Scott was elected president of the Asian Society of International Law (AsianSIL). She was also appointed a fellow of the Australian Institute of International Affairs.

Preface

Alexander Proelss[1]

The eight chapters collected in this volume, supplemented by the editors' introduction and conclusions, present the results of an international workshop titled "Developing Robust and Sustainable Ocean Regimes for Uncertain Futures", which was held in April 2023 at the Yong Pung How School of Law, Singapore Management University (SMU), under the direction of Professor Nengye Liu. The overarching topic of the contributions is the "triple planetary crisis" identified by the United Nations Environment Programme (UNEP), which consists of three core challenges for governance, politics, and law, namely climate change, biodiversity loss, and pollution. But how does public international law respond to the interconnection of these challenges? This question is particularly pressing because multilateral environmental agreements traditionally deal with separate environmental problems or specific cross-border challenges, respectively. Even though an increasing number of framework conventions has been negotiated since the 1992 Rio Summit, the fact remains that these conventions, like other activities aiming at the further development of public international law, have so far each related to a very specific field of environmental action, be it conservation and the sustainable use of biodiversity, climate change, the protection of the atmosphere, or the prevention of a specific type of pollution of the marine environment.[1]

Against this background, the question arises of how the traditionally static character of international treaty law can be supplemented with elements of an adaptive, flexible, and integrative approach. This question is not aimed at replacing existing international regimes with adaptive governance but rather at safeguarding their resilience, understood here as the ability to change under the influence of external circumstances while maintaining their essential contours and structures. For resilient legal frameworks are characterised by the fact that they meet the requirements of both stability and flexibility while taking into account the interrelations with other relevant regimes.

1 Professor Dr Alexander Proelss holds the chair in international law of the sea, international environmental law, public international law, and public law at the University of Hamburg.

As far as ocean uses and the protection and preservation of the marine environment are concerned, the United Nations Convention on the Law of the Sea (UNCLOS), the "constitution for the oceans" (TTB Koh), constitutes the normative starting point for assessing the resilience of the relevant rules and principles of international law. This agreement meets the requirements of a resilient regime if it provides legal certainty through the clear allocation of sovereignty, sovereign rights, and jurisdiction to individual states, contributes to the preservation of peace through a sophisticated regime of dispute settlement, and is based on strong institutional structures and procedures. At the same time, it also offers mechanisms for adapting to new and unforeseen challenges, and continues to comprehensively regulate all human activities in terms of a rules-based order for the ocean in all regions of the world. In principle, UNCLOS is ideally equipped to meet these requirements. On the one hand, it is difficult, if not impossible, to amend UNCLOS, and no general reservations or exceptions can be made to this convention by the states parties. It provides a system of binding dispute settlement and has created several institutions, even if no strong general institutional body has been established in which all states parties are involved (the Meeting of the States Parties [SPLOS] does not have powers comparable to the Conference of the Parties [COP] of a typical multinational environmental agreement). On the other hand, the provisions of UNCLOS allow for, and indeed require, further implementation, thus enabling its specification and adaptation. Such implementation can be achieved by concluding separate agreements, as recently occurred with the United Nations Agreement on Marine Biodiversity in Areas beyond National Jurisdiction (BBNJ Agreement), but especially by way of the numerous "renvoi" clauses codified in UNCLOS, which refer to "external rules." The conflict clauses contained in Articles 237 and 311 of UNCLOS can be understood as another mechanism that enables an integral approach. Finally, the widespread use of vague legal terms and concepts offers potential for dynamic interpretation. Against this background, it is not without reason that UNCLOS has been described as a "living instrument" by the International Tribunal for the Law of the Sea (ITLOS) in its recent advisory opinion submitted at the request of the Commission of Small Island States and International Law. But how far can this living instrument character be taken? Does it also include the central role of the ocean in facilitating energy transition? What is the relevance of new technologies in the context of the UNCLOS regime? And how can the risk of the deconstruction of the rules-based order for the oceans, which is arguably inherent in the concept of flexibility, be prevented?

This is where the contributions in this volume come in. They examine how UNCLOS, as the prime example of a global regime, addresses the uncertainties caused by the triple planetary crisis, and how it interacts with other treaty regimes to overcome this crisis. While related to the ocean and, in regulatory terms, taking UNCLOS as their starting point, the issues examined in this book focus on new technological approaches and current challenges, and they question the traditional uses of the sea in light of new scientific findings or partially altered perceptions. In doing so, they help to contextualise UNCLOS and to examine the future viability of the constitution for the oceans. In light of their topicality and the robust legal scholarship on which they are based, the chapters collected in this volume deserve widespread attention in international legal practice and academia.

Acknowledgement

The editors are grateful to the Chiang Ching-Kuo Foundation for International Scholarly Exchange and Baker McKenzie Wong & Leow for their support of this research project, which culminated in the present book. We would also like to thank Cheriya Chomrat and Michelle Chase for their excellent assistance.

Foreword

This volume arose out of a workshop held at the Yong Pung How School of Law, Singapore Management University in Singapore in April 2023 at which I was privileged to speak. It coincided with a crucial juncture in the law of the sea, with the simultaneous development of the Convention on Biological Diversity's Post-2020 Global Biodiversity Framework, the final stages of negotiation of the United Nations Agreement on Marine Biodiversity in Areas Beyond National Jurisdiction (BBNJ Agreement), and the adoption of the International Seabed Authority's Mining Code. The theme of "planetary crisis" arguably underpinned all the papers and subsequent chapters, which explore the themes of climate change, biodiversity loss, and marine pollution from the locus of the law of the sea. Linking all the chapters is the question of how rapidly and effectively the law of the sea can respond to a planetary crises.

As this volume demonstrates, the 1982 United Nations Convention on the Law of the Sea (UNCLOS) is a living instrument that can flex and evolve to meet new threats, opportunities and, to a more limited extent, changing values. This has been emphatically demonstrated in the recent advisory opinion of the International Tribunal for the Law of the Sea on climate change[1] and, to a lesser extent, by the objectives and modalities of the 2023 BBNJ Agreement. Whether such evolution will be embraced by the International Seabed Authority in respect of seabed mining remains to be seen at the time of writing. At the workshop and, as I have explored elsewhere,[2] I asked whether UNCLOS is truly capable of transformational change: change that is arguably a prerequisite for it remaining relevant and effective in the face of planetary crises. The chapters in this volume demonstrate authoritatively and eloquently the vitality of the law of the sea in responding to threats such as ocean acidi-

1 Request for an Advisory Opinion submitted by the Commission of Small Island States on Climate Change and International Law, Case Number 31, 24 May 2024.

2 Karen N. Scott, "The LOSC: A 'Constitution for the Oceans' in the Anthropocene?" 41 (2023) *Australian Yearbook of International Law* 269–298.

fication and climate change, new technologies, and novel ways of managing resources and sharing their benefits. *In toto*, this volume illustrates the emergence of a law of the sea for the Anthropocene, and, as such, makes a valuable contribution to modern law of the sea scholarship.

Professor Karen N. Scott
University of Canterbury, New Zealand

1 The "triple challenge" facing ocean law and governance

Nengye Liu and Shirley V. Scott

The Club of Rome was established in 1968 to investigate five major trends of global concern: accelerating industrialisation, rapid population growth, widespread malnutrition, the depletion of non-renewable resources, and a deteriorating environment.[1] Four years later, the resulting report concluded that "if the present growth trends in world population, industrialization, pollution, food production, and resources depletion continue unchanged, the limits to growth on this planet will be reached sometime within the next one hundred years".[2] Unfortunately, less than six decades later, the world has already entered a dangerous era, eloquently described by Singapore's President Tharman Shanmugaratnam in 2022 as a "long perfect storm".[3] President Shanmugaratnam highlighted foreboding clouds of rising inflation and economic recession, food and energy crises, climate change, mass extinction, pandemics, and geopolitical tensions.[4]

Prominent among the distinct yet interacting environmental crises that contribute to the "polycrisis" with which we are now faced,[5] is climate change. According to the United Nations Environment Programme (UNEP), "The world is not on course to fulfil the Paris Agreement to limit global warming to

1 Donella H. Meadows, Dennis L. Meadows, Jørgen Randers, William W. Behrens III, *The Limits to Growth, A Report for the Club of Rome's Project on the Prediction of Mankind* (Pan Books: London and Sydney, 1972), p.21.

2 Ibid 23.

3 SMU Ho Rih Hwa Lecture: Senior Minister Tharman Shanmugaratnam | 22 Sep 2022, https://www.youtube.com/watch?v=fdKY2jg3vAg

4 Ibid.

5 The word "polycrisis" was first used by Edgar Morin and Anne Brigitte Kern in 1999. They introduced the term to emphasise the concurrent nature of the multiple crises they identified, including, for example, "the ecological crisis", the "global crisis of development", "the uncontrolled and blind development of technoscience", "the rule of mechanistic and fragmented thinking", "the population surge", and "global economic disorder". This word became famous when then president of the European Commission, Jean-Claude Juncker, used it to refer to several challenges facing the European Union in 2016. Adam Tooze defined this term as a combination of distinct and interacting crises. See Eric Helleiner, Economic Globalization's Polycrisis, Theory Note, *International Studies Quarterly* (2024) 68, 1–3.

DOI: 10.4324/9781003518570-1

well below 2°C above pre-industrial levels, let alone meet the 1.5°C aspiration."[6] According to UNEP, "climate change, biodiversity loss and pollution add up to three self-inflicted planetary crises that are closely interconnected and put the well-being of current and future generations at unacceptable risk".[7] All three inter-related planetary crises need to be tackled together if human beings are to have a viable future on this planet. Uncertainties and risks caused by either climate change (extreme weather, for example), biodiversity loss (giving rise to, *inter alia*, mass extinction), or pollution (evidenced, for example, by marine plastics pollution) must be taken into consideration in developing international law to address any single one of these planetary crises.

Therefore, the ongoing evolution of international law cannot proceed other than in a context of complexity and associated uncertainty. This is nowhere more true than in respect of the international law governing the oceans. The international legal order that was established by the 1982 United Nations Convention on the Law of the Sea (UNCLOS),[8] its 1994 implementing agreement,[9] and the 1995 UN Fish Stocks Agreement[10] represented a significant achievement in human history for the breadth of issues covered and for having reconciled competing national claims to the resources and uses of the sea.[11] We are now in another critical period in the evolution of ocean governance. The agreement under the United Nations Convention on the Law of the Sea on Conservation and Sustainable Use of Marine Biological Diversity of Areas beyond National Jurisdiction (2023 BBNJ Agreement),[12] the Convention on Biological Diversity's Kunming–Montreal Global Biodiversity Framework (2022),[13] exploitation regulations of marine minerals

6 United Nations Environment Programme (2021). Making Peace with Nature: A scientific blueprint to tackle the climate, biodiversity and pollution emergencies. UNEP, Nairobi, p. 22.

7 Ibid https://www.unep.org/interactive/making-peace-with-nature/

8 United Nations Convention on the Law of the Sea, adopted 10 December 1982, 1833 UNTS 397 (entered into force 1 November 1994).

9 Agreement relating to the Implementation of Part XI of the United Nations Convention on the Law of the Sea of 10 December 1982, adopted 28 July 1994, 1836 UNTS 3 (entered into force 28 July 1996).

10 Agreement for the Implementation of the Provisions of the United Nations Convention on the Law of the Sea of 10 December 1982 relating to the Conservation and Management of Straddling Fish Stocks and Highly Migratory Fish Stocks, adopted 4 August 1995, 2167 UNTS 3 (entered into force 11 December 2001).

11 Tommy Koh, *Building a New Legal Order for the Ocean*, NUS Press, 2020, p. 9.

12 United Nations, Intergovernmental Conference on Marine Biodiversity of Areas beyond National Jurisdiction, https://www.un.org/bbnj/content/home?Is%20Featured=0&language=en&sort_by=created&sort_order=DESC&page=1

13 Convention on Biological Diversity, opened for signature 5 June 1992, 1760 UNTS 79 (entered into force 29 December 1993), Decision adopted by the Conference of the Parties, CBD/COP/DEC/15/4, 19 December 2022, https://www.cbd.int/doc/decisions/cop-15/cop-15-dec-04-en.pdf

in the Area[14] – seabed and ocean floor and subsoil thereof, beyond the limits of national jurisdiction,[15] and legally binding technical and economic measures to reduce greenhouse gas (GHG) emissions from shipping,[16] are simultaneously being developed and/or implemented by the relevant international bodies and the international community. Furthermore, following a request of the Commission of Small Island States (COSIS) in 2024, the International Tribunal for the Law of the Sea (ITLOS) delivered a historic advisory opinion on climate change and international law.[17] It is essential that the emergent regimes are individually and collectively adequate to address the triple planetary crisis of climate change, biodiversity loss, and pollution, and to contribute to a peaceful and sustainable future.

This volume brings together established and upcoming scholars from countries and organisations across the globe to assess the dimensions of this challenge. The book is divided into three parts, with the primary focus on climate change in Chapters 2–4; biodiversity in Chapters 5–7; and pollution in Chapters 8 and 9. As outlined below, the chapters encompass not only a range of substantive issue areas in respect of the oceans but also methodological and theoretical approaches by which to analyse and interpret developments underway.

Chapter 2 by Annika Frosch considers whether global experimentalist governance (GXG) is a suitable governance approach to tackle ocean acidification. GXG caters to problems surrounded by uncertainty and complexity, and it engages various governmental and non-governmental actors that operate on multiple levels. The chapter begins by explaining why ocean acidification is a serious issue and identifying problems with the existing governance landscape. The chapter then applies the theory of GXG to ocean acidification to assess whether the background conditions necessary for GXG to thrive are present. The chapter confirms the applicability of GXG to ocean acidification as a fast-developing, complex, and insufficiently understood ocean problem and considers the implications of the finding for progressing governance in respect of this issue.

The ocean is central to efforts to facilitate energy transition through a range of renewable energy technologies, including wind, tidal, wave, solar, and thermal. Chapter 3 by Gabriela Argüello engages in a comparative legal analysis of China, Germany, and Scotland, which are leading the development of offshore wind energy production. The analysis aims to determine the preconditions for the development of multi-use ocean spaces and the coexistence of multiple

14 International Seabed Authority, The Mining Code, https://www.isa.org.jm/the-mining-code/

15 Article 1 (1), UNCLOS.

16 International Maritime Organization, IMO's work to cut GHG emissions from shipping, https://www.imo.org/en/MediaCentre/HotTopics/Pages/Cutting-GHG-emissions.aspx

17 Request for An Advisory Opinion submitted by the Commission of Small Island States on Climate Change and International Law (Advisory Opinion) [2024] ITLOS, Case 31.

ocean users, in these examples, those engaged in fisheries and aquaculture. The author concludes that promoting multi-use ocean spaces through marine spatial planning can potentially contribute to the resilience of the international law of the sea by reducing conflicts among ocean users. In addition, the adoption of guidelines and best practices can support further collaboration between users and promote coexistence. Finally, strategic environmental assessments can play a vital role in identifying suitable locations for offshore renewable energy projects, potentially minimising their environmental impacts.

Next, David Leary explores the close relationship between the wicked problems of addressing climate change and regulating the environmental impact of deep-sea mining in Chapter 4. The chapter is divided into four parts. Following the introduction, the second part explores how technological solutions to climate change are driving renewed interest in deep-sea minerals. The third part examines the mandate of the International Seabed Authority (ISA) to regulate deep-sea mining. The fourth part considers its progress to date, while the final part offers some concluding thoughts on the challenges ahead.

By viewing the implementation of the BBNJ Agreement through Ostrom's analytical framework on robustness and adaptive governance, Kristine Elfrida Dalaker aims to assess the robustness of the treaty text and develop recommendations for the robust implementation of the agreement. In furtherance of this aim, Chapter 5 is organised as follows. First, it sets the stage by briefly discussing the background and context of the BBNJ process and the resulting agreement. The chapter then explores Ostrom's studies on robustness and adaptive governance and how they can form a framework of analysis from which the robustness of the treaty text can be assessed and recommendations for its robust implementation can be developed. The chapter ends with a presentation of the analysis, including recommendations and concluding remarks.

In Chapter 6, Ethan Beringen draws attention to the fact that the BBNJ Agreement has failed to substantively address commercial fishing, despite it being the greatest source of biodiversity loss in the high seas. The chapter examines how the BBNJ Agreement, as a key part of the international biodiversity regime, has been consciously and unconsciously kept separate from international fisheries law. He traces the process by which this came about, identifying the what, how, and who in the narrative of the biodiversity and fishing regimes, applying the framework developed by Ellen Hey. From this perspective, legal regimes are shaped by the narratives that have been developed, influencing not only the future evolution of the regime in question but also their interrelationship with regimes still under construction.

Chapter 7 by Carina Costa de Oliveira, Harvey Mpoto Bombaka, and Ana Flávia Barros-Platiau raises the question as to whether the principle of the common heritage of humankind (CHH), which has been promoted by developing countries from the UNCLOS negotiations to the BBNJ process, can help achieve sustainable development on the deep seabed. It first discusses the legal construction of the common heritage of mankind (CHM) principle in the law of the sea. The chapter then analyses the practical difficulties facing the

CHH, as well as its reinvigoration in recent negotiations of the Regulations on Exploitation of Mineral Resources in the Area (Mining Code) and the BBNJ Agreement. This chapter argues that through balancing mining interests and biodiversity conservation in the deep seabed, the CHH principle can contribute to the robustness of the international law of the sea to deal with global challenges and planetary crises.

Chapter 8 by Ethan Beringen and Nengye Liu analyses whether the current international legal framework on the prevention, reduction, and control of vessel-source pollution is sufficient and effective in dealing with greenhouse gas emissions from shipping and accelerating a transition to green shipping. This chapter aims to answer the question by conducting a comprehensive review of the current international legal regime on the prevention of vessel-source pollution. The first part assesses the relationship between UNCLOS and the International Marine Organization (IMO). The chapter then addresses the latest developments in the international legal framework for regulating vessel-source pollution. The last part is devoted to identifying gaps and examining possible future ways by which international law could facilitate a green shipping transition.

In Chapter 9, Rebecca Prentiss Pskowski continues the focus on the work of the IMO. Recent decades have seen challenges to the legitimacy of the IMO as the forum for international shipping regulation. Critics have questioned whether the organisation's treaties and the law of the sea jurisdictional principles undergirding those treaties are adequate to protect seafarers, the marine environment, and now the climate. In response, the IMO has developed and adopted novel institutional compliance mechanisms, including the STCW 95 List of Confirmed Parties and the IMO Member State Audit Scheme. This chapter asks what lessons these mechanisms hold, including for the ongoing negotiations over the IMO regulation of greenhouse gas emissions. In the face of uncertain futures, can institutional compliance mechanisms provide the IMO with the adaptability and dexterity it will need to continue to fulfil its role as shipping's global regulator?

The volume concludes with a final chapter in which the editors reflect on lessons learned and paths ahead. The editors hope that the collection will make a meaningful contribution to ameliorating the "long perfect storm" to which we have all been alerted by Singapore's President Tharman Shanmugaratnam.

2 Global experimentalist governance and ocean acidification

Annika Frosch[1]

Introduction

Our oceans are changing fast, and, in particular, human-induced climate change has negative effects on the ocean. Ocean acidification (OA), sea-level rise, and ocean warming are endangering oceanic ecosystems and ecosystem services simultaneously.[2] In addition, other human activities cause ocean stress at the same time, such as fishing or pollution. The research and understanding of these repercussions of climate change are growing, but not everything is understood. In particular, the interaction between different repercussions of climate change and other ocean stressors still requires research. Nevertheless, science is progressing fast; for example, nature-based solutions could be a helpful tool in the fight against these negative influences on the ocean.[3] As science advances, law and policy must also evolve to prevent changes in the ocean environment and avoid reaching critical tipping points. These tipping points mark significant and often irreversible shifts in the climate system, including the ocean.[4]

1 PhD candidate at the European University Institute, annika.frosch@eui.eu. The author would like to thank Professor Joanne Scott for her feedback and comments on this piece. The author would also like to thank the Ocean Climate Lab, UC Davis Bodega Marine Laboratory, and in particular Professor Tessa Hill and Meghan Zulian for answering many questions about ocean acidification and providing comments for the scientific section of this chapter. Lastly, the author wishes to thank the members of the Asia-Pacific Centre for Environmental Law and the Centre for International Law, National University of Singapore, for their questions and comments on this chapter.

2 IPCC, 'Summary for Policymakers' in HO Pörtner et al. (eds), *IPCC Special Report on the Ocean and Cryosphere in a Changing Climate: Special Report of the Intergovernmental Panel on Climate Change* (Cambridge University Press, 1st ed, 2022), for example see A2.1, A2.5, A3.

3 IUCN defines nature-based solutions as "actions to protect, sustainably manage and restore… ecosystems, which address societal challenges (e.g. climate change…) while simultaneously providing human well-being and biodiversity benefits". E. Cohen-Shacham et al. (eds), *Nature-Based Solutions to Address Global Societal Challenges* (IUCN International Union for Conservation of Nature, 2016) xii.

4 Cf. Egbert H Van Nes et al., 'What Do You Mean, "Tipping Point"?' (2016) 31(12) *Trends in Ecology & Evolution* 902.

DOI: 10.4324/9781003518570-2

As science and technology rapidly develop, the laws governing the oceans must be flexible and adaptable to keep up with these changes. Traditional law-making has been shown to involve lengthy processes with little room for ex-post adjustment to newly developed science or technology.[5] Hence, traditional law-making might stand in the way of a timely reaction to changing oceans.[6]

An alternative to these processes is global experimentalist governance (GXG).[7] This form of governance caters to problems surrounded by uncertainty and complexity, and it engages governmental and non-governmental actors that operate on multiple levels. Experimentalist actors from and within different levels review and learn from each other's experiences. Hence, learning and peer reviewing within GXG solves issues in real time without trying to find a one-size-fits-all solution. Following these reviews and in accordance with new scientific and technological knowledge, shared goals can be readjusted to tackle the problem. The process is coordinated by a central unit.[8] Therefore, GXG seems to offer the flexibility and adaptability needed to tackle complex problems surrounding fast-developing research and technologies.

Accordingly, this chapter investigates whether GXG is an effective governance method for addressing rapidly evolving marine environmental issues, using the example of OA. To better understand GXG's procedures, the so-called five steps for the ideal type of GXG are established. Once established, these elements are developed into tools that can, in future research, help identify whether GXG is present within the governance of an institution. OA has been chosen as an example, as it is caused by CO_2 as well as other compounds from different sources, which are discharged at different levels of governance (global to local level). These characteristics of OA, which are further explained below, make the problem complex and difficult to govern, and are thus an interesting case study. In addition, the pre-existing governance landscape for

5 Cf. J Pauwelyn, RA Wessel and J Wouters, 'When Structures Become Shackles: Stagnation and Dynamics in International Lawmaking' (2014) 25(3) *European Journal of International Law* 733, 742–744, 763.

6 Cf. ibid.

7 Chiara Armeni, 'Global Experimentalist Governance, International Law and Climate Change Technologies' (2015) 64 *International and Comparative Law Quarterly* 875; Gabrielle Goldstein and Christopher Ansell, 'Experimentalist Governance in Global Public Health: The Case of UNAIDS' (2018) 35 *Arizona Journal of International and Comparative Law* 219; Gráinne De Búrca, Robert O Keohane, and Charles Sabel, 'Global Experimentalist Governance' (2014) 44(3) *British Journal of Political Science* 477 ('Global Experimentalist Governance').

8 Cf. Robert O Keohane and Charles Sabel, 'New Modes of Pluralist Global Governance' (2012) 45 *New York University Journal of International Law and Politics* 723 ('New Modes of Pluralist Global Governance'); De Búrca, Keohane, and Sabel ('Global Experimentalist Governance') (n 7); Armeni (n 7); Goldstein and Ansell (n 7).

OA can be described as a regime complex, a governance landscape from which GXG often develops.[9]

Following this introduction, the chapter first introduces GXG. The chapter then outlines OA as a case study by describing the science behind OA and explaining the problem's already existing governance landscape. Then, the case (OA) and the theory (GXG) are matched. The chapter concludes that GXG can address OA, and can also accommodate the unique features of OA. Institutions that could function as a central unit to organise the governance of OA are also proposed.

Global experimentalist governance

GXG is a type of governance that is attempting to accommodate the rise of transnational problems and legal and institutional pluralism. To fulfil this goal, experimentalist governance attempts to solve problems based on learning with the engagement of various actors on multiple levels.[10] Thus far, experimentalist governance has been assessed and tested at the national, regional,[11] and less so, at the global[12] level. Nevertheless, Goldstein and Ansell have shown that, for instance, the United Nations Programme on HIV/AIDS (UNAIDS) is a working example of experimentalist governance on the global level.[13] Another example described by De Búrca, Keohane, and Sabel is global ozone layer protection through the Montreal Protocol.[14] In order to assess whether GXG is a suitable governance approach for OA, the chapter initially explains what GXG entails. This chapter defines GXG and provides the abstract definition with substance by establishing the five elements of the ideal type of GXG. Despite the repeated usage of these five elements in case studies, the literature fails to theoretically explain what these elements entail. Once established, these elements are developed into tools that can, in future research, help identify whether GXG is present within the governance of an institution. Therefore,

9 A regime complex, or as Eilstrup Sangiovanni calls it, a "global governance complex", can be defined by "rule sets and agents that assert overlapping authority claims to govern a specific global policy issue" Mette Eilstrup-Sangiovanni, 'Ordering Global Governance Complexes: The Evolution of the Governance Complex for International Civil Aviation' (2022) 17(2) *The Review of International Organizations* 293, 294.

10 Goldstein and Ansell (n 7) 220.

11 De Búrca, "New Governance and Experimentalism: An Introduction" (2010) 2010 *Wisconsin Law Review* 227; Charles F Sabel and Jonathan Zeitlin, 'Learning from Difference: The New Architecture of Experimentalist Governance in the EU' in Charles F Sabel and Jonathan Zeitlin (eds), *Experimentalist Governance in the European Union: Towards a New Architecture* (Oxford University Press, 2010); Jonathan Zeitlin (ed), *Extending Experimentalist Governance? The European Union and Transnational Regulation* (Oxford University Press, 1st ed, 2015).

12 Armeni (n 7); De Búrca, Keohane, and Sabel, 'New Modes of Pluralist Global Governance' (n 8); Goldstein and Ansell (n 7).

13 Goldstein and Ansell (n 7) 255.

14 De Búrca, Keohane, and Sabel, 'Global Experimentalist Governance' (n 7) 483.

this section outlines the definition of the notion of experimentalist governance and then discusses the five elements that imbue experimentalist governance in its ideal form.

Definition of global experimentalist governance

In a widely cited paper,[15] De Búrca, Keohane, and Sabel describe GXG as follows:

> an institutionalized transnational process of participatory and multi-level problem solving, in which particular problems (and the means of addressing them) are framed in an open-ended way, and subjected to periodic revision by various forms of peer review in light of locally generated knowledge.[16]

Based on this definition, five key elements of GXG are identified.[17] De Búrca, Keohane, and Sabel use these elements to assess the presence of this form of governance in an institution.[18] Even though this chapter will not test an institution against the elements, they are key to understanding GXG and its functioning. Without a deeper understanding of GXG, it will be difficult to evaluate whether this governance is suitable for OA. Furthermore, the literature explains that GXG and the operation of the five steps are coordinated through an umbrella institution, the so-called central unit. The central unit organises the interaction between actors participating in experimentalism. However, the role of the central unit does not reach further than that, as it should merely facilitate GXG.[19] The next section explains the five elements that constitute the core of GXG. Where relevant, the role of the central unit for the step in question is discussed.

The five elements of the ideal type of experimentalist governance

The literature distills five elements present in the ideal type of GXG.[20] As there is no one settled model of this type of governance,[21] an ideal type has been

15 See, e.g. Goldstein and Ansell (n 7) 220; Armeni (n 7) 876.

16 De Búrca, Keohane, and Sabel ('Global Experimentalist Governance') (n 7) 477.

17 De Búrca et al. refer to experimentalist governance as 'an "ideal type" in the sense used by Max Weber'. De Búrca, Keohane, and Sabel, 'New Modes of Pluralist Global Governance' (n 8) 727.

18 Armeni (n 7) 880; De Búrca, Keohane, and Sabel (n 8) 739; De Búrca, Keohane, and Sabel ('Global Experimentalist Governance') (n 7) 478; Goldstein and Ansell (n 7) 221.

19 Goldstein and Ansell (n 7) 220, 230–232.

20 Ibid 221; De Búrca, Keohane, and Sabel, 'New Modes of Pluralist Global Governance' (n 8) 738, 739; Sabel and Zeitlin, 'Learning from Difference: The New Architecture of Experimentalist Governance in the EU' (n 11) 3; Armeni (n 7) 879, 880.

21 Armeni (n 7) 879.

defined instead. Governance models can then be evaluated against this ideal type to determine whether the model in question resembles the ideal type.[22] If all the elements of the ideal type are at hand in a particular case, then one can speak of GXG. The elements can be considered the necessary features to be realised through various institutional arrangements.[23] In addition, by looking at the five elements, an in-depth understanding of what GXG entails and how it functions can be acquired. The five elements are as follows:

- The existence of a shared problem;
- Agreement on open-ended goals;
- Delegation to lower levels of governance;
- Mechanisms for gathering feedback and peer review; and
- Flexibility in the adjustment of overarching goals.

The five elements are usually mentioned and directly applied to a specific case. Therefore, the question of how to assess if an element is fulfilled remains open. The five elements are explained here as they are key to understanding GXG. Information about the five elements is inferred from what can be found in the literature and the existing case studies.[24] The five elements are discussed as follows: shared problem, open-ended goals, delegation to lower levels of governance, feedback and peer review, and adjustment of overarching goals.

Shared problem

The first element of the ideal type of GXG is the awareness among stakeholders that a shared issue needs to be addressed.[25] The literature has discussed GXG regarding a variety of concerns.[26] The kinds of problems that have been approached through this form of governance have a series of characteristics in common. The issues are often newly arising, creeping, or persistent.[27] An

22 Ibid.

23 Sabel and Zeitlin, 'Learning from Difference: The New Architecture of Experimentalist Governance in the EU' (n 11) 3.

24 Cf. Armeni (n 7); Goldstein and Ansell (n 7); De Búrca, Keohane, and Sabel (n 7); De Búrca, Keohane, and Sabel, 'New Modes of Pluralist Global Governance' (n 8); Sabel and Zeitlin, 'Learning from Difference: The New Architecture of Experimentalist Governance in the EU' (n 11); Vanessa C Pinsky, Isak Kruglianskas and David G Victor, 'Experimentalist Governance in Climate Finance: The Case of REDD+ in Brazil' (2019) 19(6) *Climate Policy* 725 ('Experimentalist Governance in Climate Finance'); Charles F Sabel and Jonathan Zeitlin (eds), 'Experimentalist Governance in the European Energy Sector' in *Experimentalist Governance in the European Union: Towards a New Architecture* (Oxford University Press, 2010).

25 De Búrca, Keohane, and Sabel ('Global Experimentalist Governance') (n 7) 478.

26 Goldstein and Ansell (n 7); De Búrca, Keohane, and Sabel, 'New Modes of Pluralist Global Governance' (n 8); Armeni (n 7); Pinsky, Kruglianskas, and Victor (n 24).

27 Armeni (n 7) 884; Sabel and Zeitlin, 'Experimentalist Governance in the European Energy Sector' (n 24) 72; Charles F Sabel and Jonathan Zeitlin (eds), 'Emerging Experimentalism

example of such a problem is climate change, whose effects have been slowly aggravating over several decades. If problems are new, creeping, or persistent, they also have low visibility, as did climate change a few decades ago, because an abrupt change from one environmental status to another is missing. In many cases, there is also a limited amount of scientific information available to understand the issue, which can lead to high uncertainty concerning causes, aggravating factors, and solutions.[28]

Another challenge is the global dimension that such problems usually exhibit.[29] Global dimension refers to the fact that problems can "only be addressed effectively by internationally coordinated measures".[30] In the face of political obstacles caused by questions of sovereignty or common but differentiated responsibilities and respective capabilities, these coordinated measures can be difficult to achieve.[31]

Further, the issues governed by GXG are considered complex.[32] High complexity means that "the sources of persistent problems are diffuse and involve a large number of actors, including important indirect contributors. In addition, cause and effect tend to be significantly delayed".[33] These characteristics make the problems at the centre of GXG seemingly impossible to solve, and compelling solutions are difficult to identify – at least ex-ante.[34]

To qualify as a "shared" issue, stakeholders should have started to reflect upon and discuss the problem in question.[35] This requirement implies that experimentalism may be suitable for governance situations without an overarching authority in charge that can define common goals.[36] Instead, it is up to the stakeholders to create a common perception of what the problem entails.[37] These stakeholders can be manifold and include governmental and non-governmental actors such as states, civil society representatives, or indigenous peoples.[38] Thus, part of the first step of the ideal type of GXG

in EU Environmental Governance' in *Experimentalist Governance in the European Union: Towards a New Architecture* (Oxford University Press, 2010) 127.

28 Cf. Pinsky, Kruglianskas, and Victor (n 24) 728; Sabel and Zeitlin, 'Experimentalist Governance in the European Energy Sector' (n 24) 65, 72.

29 Armeni (n 7) 884; Sabel and Zeitlin, 'Emerging Experimentalism in EU Environmental Governance' (n 27) 127.

30 Sabel and Zeitlin, 'Emerging Experimentalism in EU Environmental Governance' (n 27) 127.

31 Ibid.

32 Goldstein and Ansell (n 7) 230; Pinsky, Kruglianskas, and Victor (n 24) 728; Sabel and Zeitlin, 'Experimentalist Governance in the European Energy Sector' (n 24) 72.

33 De Búrca, Keohane, and Sabel ('Global Experimentalist Governance') (n 7) 479.

34 Goldstein and Ansell (n 7) 230.

35 Cf. De Búrca, Keohane, and Sabel ('Global Experimentalist Governance') (n 7) 478.

36 Charles F Sabel and Jonathan Zeitlin, 'Experimentalist Governance' in *Experimentalist Governance* (Oxford University Press, 2012) 169.

37 De Búrca, Keohane, and Sabel ('Global Experimentalist Governance') (n 7) 479.

38 Ibid 477; Pinsky, Kruglianskas, and Victor (n 24) 730; De Búrca, Keohane, and Sabel, 'New Modes of Pluralist Global Governance' (n 8) 741.

is identifying, phrasing, and defining the issue in a way that experimentalist actors can agree on. Ideally, this process should be informed by accurate data and ongoing monitoring.[39]

Open-ended goals

According to the second element of GXG, stakeholders should address the shared problem through the elaboration of open-ended and framework-like goals rather than prescriptive regulations.[40] These open-ended goals are necessary because uncertainty and disagreement prevent stakeholders from drafting detailed regulations.

Goals are set through consultation and collaboration between different stakeholders.[41] The actors involved are drawn from various governance levels and include civil society actors.[42] The outcome of these exchanges is an agreement on broad framework goals and provisional metrics to assess performance towards their attainment.[43] Metrics are tools designed to evaluate goal attainment and allow stakeholders to quantify the degree of success in reaching the goals.[44] While goals should be open-ended and framework-like in nature, both goals and metrics should be imbued with a provisional character.[45] This means that goals are likely to be loosely worded, without much detail, and often without specific timescales for their achievement.[46] A way to guarantee these features is by creating "living documents" open to review and update.[47] Provisionality is necessary as the goals and metrics need to be susceptible to adjustment in changing circumstances. Over time, they should be shaped through the experiences of actors at lower levels of governance in light of local contexts.[48] Newly discovered technological and scientific knowledge might lead to an alteration of goals and metrics in the future.[49] Examples of previously used open-ended goals are "good water quality", "adequate education", or "sustainable forests".[50]

39 Búrca (n 11) 235.
40 De Búrca, Keohane, and Sabel ('Global Experimentalist Governance') (n 7) 478; Goldstein and Ansell (n 7) 221.
41 Goldstein and Ansell (n 7) 230; cf. Joshua Cohen and Charles Sabel, 'Directly-Deliberative Polyarchy' (1997) 3(4) *European Law Journal* 313.
42 Goldstein and Ansell (n 7) 230; Sabel and Zeitlin, 'Experimentalist Governance' (n 36) 169.
43 Goldstein and Ansell (n 7) 230, 235.
44 Cf. Armeni (n 7) 880; Goldstein and Ansell (n 7) 236.
45 Goldstein and Ansell (n 7) 230, 235.
46 Ibid 236.
47 Sabel and Zeitlin, 'Experimentalist Governance' (n 36) 171.
48 Armeni (n 7) 880.
49 Ibid.
50 Sabel and Zeitlin, 'Experimentalist Governance' (n 36) 169; Sabel and Zeitlin, 'Learning from Difference: The New Architecture of Experimentalist Governance in the EU' (n 11) 3.

To fulfil the ideal type's second element, the described process should be steered and managed by a central unit.[51] The central unit should facilitate the consultation and collaboration of the multifarious stakeholders and establish framework goals while considering the different views voiced during the collaboration process.[52]

Delegation to lower levels of governance

The third element of the ideal type of GXG is delegation to lower levels of governance, including regional, national, and sub-national levels. These lower levels of governance develop solutions to achieve the open-ended goals through experience on the ground.[53]

More concretely, this means that finding solutions to the shared problem is, at least provisionally, delegated to lower-level units that are more familiar with local or regional conditions.[54] Lower-level actors have the discretion to experiment and adjust their practices and strategies over time.[55] This discretion derives from the framework-like nature of the goals.[56] Discretion reaches far, as actors can even depart from existing rules where they deem it counterproductive to follow them.[57] However, this discretion is not unlimited. Experimentalist actors must work transparently and justify their choices, which are subject to regular review by other actors on the lower level and the central unit.[58] If their judgment concerning the inappropriateness of the existing rules persists and is widely shared, this may prompt the reformulation of the old rules.[59] Solutions and strategies are thus explored which reflect localised, country, and region-specific needs and circumstances as they are created by actors familiar with the conditions prevailing within them.[60] Hence, experimentation and practical learning happen through a process on the national level and include trying different options through implementation and planning.[61] This experimentation at the lower levels provides the opportunity to "learn from differences".[62] Comparing the pool of diverse strategies and practices experimented with may

51 Goldstein and Ansell (n 7) 235.
52 Cf. ibid.
53 Pinsky, Kruglianskas, and Victor (n 24) 728.
54 De Búrca, Keohane, and Sabel ('Global Experimentalist Governance') (n 7) 478.
55 Goldstein and Ansell (n 7) 221, 230.
56 Cf. ibid 237.
57 Sabel and Zeitlin, 'Experimentalist Governance' (n 36) 174.
58 De Búrca, Keohane, and Sabel ('Global Experimentalist Governance') (n 7) 478; Goldstein and Ansell (n 7) 230; Sabel and Zeitlin, 'Experimentalist Governance' (n 36) 174.
59 Sabel and Zeitlin, 'Experimentalist Governance' (n 36) 174.
60 De Búrca, Keohane, and Sabel ('Global Experimentalist Governance') (n 7) 478.
61 Goldstein and Ansell (n 7) 235; De Búrca, Keohane, and Sabel ('Global Experimentalist Governance') (n 7) 478.
62 Goldstein and Ansell (n 7) 229; De Búrca, Keohane, and Sabel, 'New Modes of Pluralist Global Governance' (n 8) 740.

provide information about what does and does not work under certain conditions.[63] Ultimately, this can "establish processes that help us generate unimagined alternatives and improve our ability to choose among these alternatives by rigorously exposing each to criticism in light of the others".[64] Ideally, a broad range of stakeholders should be involved to generate knowledge and a variety of strategies from which to choose.[65] As it has been "observed empirically that enrolling diverse sources of knowledge in this process may also produce better solutions".[66] Thus, GXG provides a model through which transnational problems involving multiple stakeholders that may create a significant governance challenge can be managed.[67]

Experimentalist actors can be manifold, including states, municipalities, civil society representatives, academia, indigenous peoples, community-based organisations, national authorities, local communities, and scientists.[68] The composition of the actors working together at the lower level will vary in each geographical area.[69] Including a variety of actors may provide these different groups of people with a voice, build credibility, promote shared ownership, and encourage a shared future vision.[70] Such an open and transparent governance process involving diverse actors also increases accountability.[71] Decision-making in groups promotes accountability for two reasons. First, members operate under the scrutiny of their peers, which leads to informal pressure to avoid errors. Second, as giving reasons is essential for group decision-making and members come from various backgrounds, this ensures that matters taken for granted in homogeneous groups are clarified and questioned in more heterogeneous settings.[72] The operation of this element, for example, the communication of the shared problem and open-ended goals to the lower levels, is coordinated and organised by the central unit.[73]

63 Sabel and Zeitlin, 'Emerging Experimentalism in EU Environmental Governance' (n 27) 130.
64 De Búrca, Keohane, and Sabel ('Global Experimentalist Governance') (n 7) 484.
65 De Búrca (n 11) 235.
66 Goldstein and Ansell (n 7) 230; Burris Scott, Clifford Shearing, and Michael Kempa, 'Changes in Governance: A Cross-Disciplinary Review of Current Scholarship' (2008) 41(1) *Akron Law Review* 1, 11.
67 Goldstein and Ansell (n 7) 229.
68 De Búrca, Keohane, and Sabel (n 7) 477; Pinsky, Kruglianskas, and Victor (n 24) 730; De Búrca, Keohane, and Sabel, 'New Modes of Pluralist Global Governance' (n 8) 741.
69 Cf. Goldstein and Ansell (n 7) 238.
70 Ibid.
71 De Búrca, Keohane, and Sabel ('Global Experimentalist Governance') (n 7) 478, 484.
72 Sabel and Zeitlin, 'Experimentalist Governance' (n 36) 173.
73 Goldstein and Ansell (n 7) 230; De Búrca, Keohane, and Sabel, 'New Modes of Pluralist Global Governance' (n 8) 741.

Feedback and peer review

The fourth element of the ideal type of GXG is feedback and peer review. The literature identifies reporting, peer review, and feedback as core components of this element.

First, reporting refers to local units sharing information on their performance and, more precisely, on their achievement of the framework goals.[74] The information is shared with other local-level actors.[75] However, the exact information to be included in the report depends on the nature of the shared problem, metrics, and goals present.

Second, following the reporting, the information provided by the local units becomes subject to peer review.[76] During peer review, the local units' performances and experiences are compared to one another.[77] In other words, local actors compare their results from experimentation and evaluate each other's progress towards achieving the goals. Hence, information is pooled, and best practices can be identified, general lessons noted, and challenges acknowledged.[78] Therefore, fundamental to the process of information gathering and analysis is the collection, tracking, and dissemination of data, monitoring, and evaluation.[79] In addition, collecting case studies for future exemplification and learning can be helpful.[80] Accordingly, the process allows for the pooling of information gathered at the lower level, comparing results, identifying best practices, and communicating those to the central unit for consideration.[81]

As a last step, feedback on the results is then provided to the lower-level units by both their peers and the central unit.[82] As part of the feedback, lower units that are not making sufficient progress towards the agreed metrics or goals are expected to demonstrate that they are implementing appropriate adjusted measures.[83]

The feedback and review process can be facilitated in several ways. For example, initiatives can take the form of annual regional meetings, conferences, or

74 Goldstein and Ansell (n 7) 230; Armeni (n 7) 880.
75 Goldstein and Ansell (n 7) 230.
76 De Búrca, Keohane, and Sabel, 'New Modes of Pluralist Global Governance' (n 8) 739; De Búrca, Keohane, and Sabel (n 7) 478.
77 Goldstein and Ansell (n 7) 230.
78 Ibid 239, 240; Armeni (n 7) 762, 880.
79 Goldstein and Ansell (n 7) 239, 240.
80 Ibid 239.
81 Ibid 230, 238.
82 Ibid 230, 253; Armeni (n 7) 880; De Búrca, Keohane, and Sabel ('Global Experimentalist Governance') (n 7) 478.
83 Sabel and Zeitlin, 'Experimentalist Governance' (n 36) 170; Zeitlin (n 11) 2.

an active secretariat.[84] Accordingly, the otherwise considerable discretion of the lower levels is kept in check by the feedback and peer review process.[85]

Through these three components, experimentalist actors can learn from each other's experiences despite particular solutions not always being generalisable.[86] Therefore, GXG can be said to transform "diversity from an obstacle... into an asset".[87] Hence, feedback and peer review advance systematic learning from diversity while holding actors accountable for their work.[88] Thus, GXG is departing from the typical one-size-fits-all solution.[89] This form of governance is neither top-down nor bottom-up, as corrections happen both ways.[90]

Adjustment of overarching goals

The fifth element of the ideal type of GXG is the regular adjustment of overarching goals and metrics. Feedback and peer review constantly inform the substance of the framework goals and/or the metrics that are used to measure progress towards their attainment.[91]

It is a process of learning by doing.[92] Feedback and peer review uncover unforeseen details and unearth dead ends and new, generalisable solutions. This knowledge can raise questions about the previously agreed-upon open-ended goals and metrics.[93] Therefore, an approach predicated on provisionality applies in relation to goals, metrics, solutions, and even with regard to the problem definition itself.[94] Thus, over time, these should evolve in response to what has been learned from feedback and peer review.[95] In its entirety, the process can be considered a recursive learning process.[96] Similar to processes in "mathematics or computer science, whereby the output from one

84 Goldstein and Ansell (n 7) 239; Armeni (n 7) 762; An active secretariat plays '"focal point, hub and broker" role, including a key role as a "knowledge administrator for best practice information"'. Goldstein and Ansell (n 7) 239.
85 Sabel and Zeitlin, 'Experimentalist Governance' (n 36) 170; Sabel and Zeitlin, 'Learning from Difference: The New Architecture of Experimentalist Governance in the EU' (n 11) 3.
86 Sabel and Zeitlin, 'Experimentalist Governance' (n 36) 175.
87 Ibid.
88 De Búrca, Keohane, and Sabel ('Global Experimentalist Governance') (n 7) 479; Pinsky, Kruglianskas, and Victor (n 24) 728.
89 Zeitlin (n 11) 10, 11.
90 Charles F Sabel and David G Victor, *Fixing the Climate: Strategies for an Uncertain World* (Princeton University Press, 2022) 10.
91 De Búrca, Keohane, and Sabel ('Global Experimentalist Governance') (n 7) 478.
92 Goldstein and Ansell (n 7) 223.
93 De Búrca, Keohane, and Sabel, 'New Modes of Pluralist Global Governance' (n 8) 741.
94 Gráinne De Búrca and Joanne Scott, 'Introduction: New Governance, Law and Constitutionalism' in *Law and New Governance in the EU and the US* (Hart Publishing, 2006) 3; Sabel and Zeitlin, 'Learning from Difference: The New Architecture of Experimentalist Governance in the EU' (n 11) 3.
95 Goldstein and Ansell (n 7) 227, 235.
96 Ibid 220.

application of a procedure or sequence of operations becomes the input for the next, so that iteration of the same process produces changing results".[97] Recursive learning is considered the most crucial characteristic of experimentalist governance.[98] This feature allows for flexibility and adaptability in order to accommodate changing circumstances.[99] This is especially needed in issue areas characterised by uncertainty and a creeping complex character, as are many environmental issues.[100]

In conclusion, GXG is equipped to deal with problems that are typically complex, global in nature, newly arising, creeping, or persistent, and have low visibility. Along with these characteristics often comes a limited amount of scientific information and thus high uncertainty. As a result, the problems often have no obvious solution. To accommodate these features, GXG offers a recursive multilevel learning circle enabled through reporting, feedback, peer review, and provisionality. These elements can be realised through various types of institutional arrangements. While a central unit is envisioned, experimentalist governance includes many units on lower levels to maintain the ability to learn from one another.[101] A centre is mainly in charge of pooling information and organising peer evaluations.[102] That said, the centre can bring reluctant actors back into line through what has been labelled a "penalty default". A penalty default is a way of penalising non-cooperation.[103] Control is taken away from actors by threatening to impose alternative rules. More specifically, the central unit threatens that it will revert to traditional forms of rule-making that are out of the actors' control.[104] Usually, the loss of control is a less favourable option from an actor's perspective.[105] This threat should encourage actors to reconsider and remind them of the advantages of cooperation.[106] However, as discussing the penalty default is not necessary to match OA and GXG and is thus beyond the scope of this chapter, an in-depth discussion of what it is and how it functions is omitted here.

97 Sabel and Zeitlin, 'Experimentalist Governance' (n 36) 169.
98 Sabel and Zeitlin, 'Experimentalist Governance in the European Energy Sector' (n 24) 65.
99 Armeni (n 7) 883.
100 Sabel and Zeitlin, 'Emerging Experimentalism in EU Environmental Governance' (n 27) 128; De Búrca, Keohane, and Sabel, 'New Modes of Pluralist Global Governance' (n 8) 740.
101 Goldstein and Ansell (n 7) 230, 231.
102 De Búrca, Keohane, and Sabel ('Global Experimentalist Governance') (n 7) 478.
103 Goldstein and Ansell (n 7) 221; De Búrca, Keohane, and Sabel ('Global Experimentalist Governance') (n 7) 478.
104 Sabel and Zeitlin, 'Learning from Difference: The New Architecture of Experimentalist Governance in the EU' (n 11) 5; Sabel and Zeitlin, 'Experimentalist Governance' (n 36) 176; Zeitlin (n 11) 4.
105 Sabel and Zeitlin, 'Learning from Difference: The New Architecture of Experimentalist Governance in the EU' (n 11) 5.
106 De Búrca, Keohane, and Sabel ('Global Experimentalist Governance') (n 7) 478; De Búrca (n 11) 739.

The question remains: can GXG address marine environmental issues such as OA? Before identifying if GXG is a suitable theory and can tackle OA as a problem, one must look at what type of problem OA is. Without an in-depth understanding of the case of OA, it is difficult to analyse whether GXG can govern it. Hence, the next part provides the reader with an understanding of what OA is to match it with GXG as a theory.

Global experimentalist governance and the case of ocean acidification

Without understanding the case, here OA, first, it is difficult to identify if GXG is a suitable governance solution for this problem. Accordingly, this section introduces and describes OA as, on the one hand, a scientific problem and, on the other, from a governance perspective, as a regime complex. Together, these features lead to seven characteristics. Therefore, this section is split into two parts. The first summarises OA as a scientific problem and identifies four characteristics, while the second recaps OA as a regime complex and identifies the last three characteristics.

The scientific background

Despite a fast-developing body of research and literature, OA is still not understood well enough. Understanding the scientific background of OA, including its causes, stressors, and adaptation options, is an essential step to finding suitable governance solutions. Accordingly, this part provides a brief and simplified overview of OA for the non-scientist reader. The section first explains acidity and the difficulties that can occur when measuring it. Second, it explains how compounds that cause OA end up in the water. Third, activities leading to additional ocean stressors are discussed. Fourth, adaptation is briefly covered. To conclude, the characteristics of OA as a scientific problem are summed up.

Measuring acidity

Acidity is measured on a pH scale, and it is quantifiable. While this pH scale leads to a clear measurement, some characteristics of acidification should be kept in mind when it comes to interpreting the results. First, by nature, the acidity of seawater varies in accordance with different factors. Changes in acidity occur due to diurnal and seasonal cycles, on a geographic scale, and also depending on the water depth, meaning the water pH varies on the local, global, and even within the local level.[107] Hence, these natural variations can

107 Secretariat of the Convention on Biological Diversity et al., *An Updated Synthesis of the Impacts of Ocean Acidification on Marine Biodiversity* (2014) 7.

make it difficult to draw clear-cut conclusions and be certain about how acidification affects the oceans and the organisms they contain. OA is a rather young area of science, and to gain a fuller picture of the impacts on the oceanic ecosystem, only long-term experiments can provide answers.[108] Second, the reaction of the ocean to acidification triggers is delayed, particularly in relation to the discharge of anthropogenic emissions into the atmosphere. This means that the ocean chemistry does not change immediately after the release of CO_2. Thus, even if humanity stopped emitting today, acidification would continue for some years to come.[109]

The causes of ocean acidification and the compounds' pathways into the ocean

Three groups of compounds (CO_2, NO_x, SO_x) form acids that cause OA. This section focuses on how these compounds find their way into the ocean water and cause OA.

First, CO_2 enters or is formed in the ocean because of three different types of activities. These activities are anthropogenic CO_2 emissions, geoengineering, and coastal activities. Anthropogenic CO_2 emissions are the best-researched and the largest contributor of CO_2 to OA. After the generation of CO_2 emissions into the atmosphere, the ocean water absorbs the gas. The absorption occurs since the surface water tries to match its CO_2 level to that of the atmosphere, thereby obtaining a balance. Hence, the more CO_2 in the atmosphere, the more the ocean needs to absorb it to maintain an equilibrium.[110] These emissions are generated and have repercussions at the global level. In addition, reducing these emissions is a daunting task and is progressing slowly. Short-term solutions are unlikely; instead, solutions require long-term planning and actions.

Another set of activities that can have consequences leading to OA is geoengineering activities. Geoengineering is an umbrella term that includes a series of techniques to manipulate and intervene in the Earth's climate system, including the oceanic environment, to moderate global warming.[111] A way to remove CO_2 from the atmosphere is, for example, direct injections of carbon dioxide into the ocean water. Just as in the case of the natural absorption of

108 Sam Dupont and Hans-O Pörtner, 'A Snapshot of Ocean Acidification Research' (2013) 160(8) *Marine Biology* 1765, 1766.

109 Dan Laffoley et al. (eds), 'An Introduction to Ocean Acidification: What It Is, What We Know, and What May Happen' (International Union for Conservation of Nature and Natural Resources, 2017) 14.

110 Arctic Monitoring and Assessment Programme, 'AMAP Assessment 2013: Arctic Ocean Acidification' (2013) 1.

111 Intergovernmental Oceanographic Commission (IOC) et al., *Marine Climate Engineering 'Ocean Fertilization: A Scientific Summary for Policy Makers'* (IMO Report No. LC/SG 34/INF.3, International Maritime Organization, 10 February 2011) 1.

the gas by the water, this leads to OA.[112] Although these activities are only endangering the oceans when in use and are currently only in their infancy, they should not be omitted.[113] The danger of acidification through geoengineering can be prevented immediately. Since extensive geoengineering activities have not yet started, solutions and alternatives can be found in the short term. In addition, the effect of geoengineering is very localised, affecting only the areas where the activity is conducted.

The last group of activities that can cause OA are coastal activities. This group includes activities that occur on land but negatively influence the ocean, such as suboptimal coastal planning, land-based pollution, land use or land use change, and deforestation.[114] The consequences of these actions, such as soil erosion, runoff, and pollution, can then introduce organic matter and nutrients into the water.[115] These terrestrial anthropogenic disturbances disrupt the coastal ocean metabolism. Part of this metabolism is the death of plankton; once that happens, it sinks as organic matter towards the sea bottom. This organic matter, in addition to organic matter from coastal activities, is decomposed by bacteria. In this process, the bacteria dissolve the organic matter into inorganic substances, one of which is CO_2.[116] Coast-near waters, which suffer from consequences due to coastal activities, are called "hot spots".[117] However, measuring the exact impact of nutrients and organic matter on coastal waters is a difficult exercise, as discussed above. Thus, the exact significance of coastal activities for OA is not yet understood but is expected to be considerable.[118] Therefore, coastal activities are an important cause for OA on the local and up to the regional level. Solutions can be found in the short term, for instance, through the amelioration of coastal planning or the filtering of wastewater.

Second, NO_x and SO_x enter the ocean due to two types of activities. Just as with CO_2, the first type of activity is emissions, while the second type is

112 Dorothee Herr et al., *Ocean Acidification: International Policy and Governance Options* (2014) 8.

113 Elizabeth Kocs, 'The Global Carbon Nation: Status of CO 2 Capture, Storage and Utilization' (2017) 148 *EPJ Web of Conferences* 1, 4, 5, 6, 13 *('The Global Carbon Nation')*.

114 Ryan Kelly et al., 'Mitigating Local Causes of Ocean Acidification with Existing Laws' (2011) 332 *Science (New York, N.Y.)* 1036, 1036, 1037; *Report on the structured expert dialogue on the 2013–2015 review*, 42nd sess, UN Doc FCCC/SB/2015/INF.1 (4 May 2015) 159; Sverker C Jagers et al., 'Societal Causes of, and Responses to, Ocean Acidification' (2019) 48(8) *Ambio* 816, 818, 822; Laffoley et al. (n 109) 15.

115 Jagers et al. (n 114) 818; Kelly et al. (n 114) 1036, 1037.

116 Arctic Monitoring and Assessment Programme (AMAP), *AMAP Arctic Ocean Acidification Assessment: Summary for Policy-Makers* (Report, 2013) 4; Tyler Cyronak et al., 'Enhanced Acidification of Global Coral Reefs Driven by Regional Biogeochemical Feedbacks' (2014) 41(15) *Geophysical Research Letters* 5538, 5543, 5544; Wei-Jun Cai et al., 'Acidification of Subsurface Coastal Waters Enhanced by Eutrophication' (2011) 4 *Nature Geoscience* 766, 766.

117 Kelly et al. (n 114) 1036.

118 Cyronak et al. (n 116) 5544; Kelly et al. (n 114) 1036.

scrubber effluents. Both gases are emitted by the shipping industry.[119] Unlike CO_2, these gases have a short atmospheric residence time, which means they do not travel as far from the source as CO_2 could. Thus, the concentration of NO_x and SO_x is coupled with the amount and proximity of the sources of these gases.[120] This has led to the fact that highly trafficked shipping lanes, harbours, and coastal areas in proximity to the sources of these gases are particularly affected by acidification. Research in these areas indicates pH decreases of equal dimensions as CO_2-driven acidification.[121] Thus, as with geoengineering and coastal activities, the effect of this cause of OA is also local or regional. Attempts to regulate such emissions are already occurring in practice, as shown below.

The problem of scrubber effluents is a recent one and has started to occur since emissions, in particular NO_x and SO_x, from shipping have received more attention. Regulations were drafted to remedy the emissions problem through restrictions; therefore, exhaust gas cleaning systems such as scrubber technology have gained in popularity.[122] Scrubber technology is a tool to remove SO_x and sometimes NO_x from the exhaust gas released into the atmosphere and instead dispose of it as acid wash water in the ocean. The idea of scrubbers is to use seawater as a medium to clean, for instance, SO_x, out of exhaust gas since the alkaline water is supposed to neutralise the acids that form during this process. However, following this process, the water that is released back into the ocean has a very low pH.[123] A significant reduction in the pH of seawater is expected due to this technology, especially in highly trafficked areas of the sea.[124] The effect is localised to the area where the effluents are released. Stricter regulation with regard to scrubbers and, in particular, open-loop scrubbers might be a short-term solution. Alternatives such as closed-loop scrubbers are already available.

119 David R Turner et al., 'The Potential Future Contribution of Shipping to Acidification of the Baltic Sea' (2018) 47(3) *Ambio* 368; Ida-Maja Hassellöv et al., 'Shipping Contributes to Ocean Acidification' (2013) 40(11) *Geophysical Research Letters* 2731; Keith A Hunter et al., 'Impacts of Anthropogenic SO_x, NO_x and NH_3 on Acidification of Coastal Waters and Shipping Lanes: Acidification of Coastal Waters' (2011) 38(13) *Geophysical Research Letters* 54.

120 Turner et al. (n 119) 369; Robert Delmas, Dominique Serça, and Corinne Jambert, 'Global Inventory of NO_x Sources' (1997) 48 *Nutrient Cycling in Agroecosystems* 51, 1, 2.

121 Hassellöv et al. (n 119) 2731; Turner et al. (n 119) 369.

122 Turner et al. (n 119) 369, 370; Sonja Endres et al., 'A New Perspective at the Ship-Air-Sea-Interface: The Environmental Impacts of Exhaust Gas Scrubber Discharge' (2018) 5 *Frontiers in Marine Science* 139, 1, 2.

123 Endres et al. (n 122) 6; Turner et al. (n 119) 370; Valérie Dulière, Katrijn Baetens and Geneviève Lacroix, *Potential Impact of Wash Water Effluents from Scrubbers on Water Acidification in the Southern North Sea* (Royal Belgian Institute of Natural Sciences, 2020) 9.

124 Dulière, Baetens, and Lacroix (n 123) 8.

Activities leading to additional ocean stressors

There are activities that have consequences that stress the ocean and its organisms, making it less able to respond to changes such as OA. Activities that constitute additional stress partially overlap with those already analysed above. These activities include, for instance, anthropogenic emissions (from sea level rise, coral bleaching, and de-oxygenation), geoengineering, coastal activities, shipping, pollution, and fishing. By nature, ecosystems and their species can adapt to changes to which they are exposed.[125] However, if an ecosystem has to adapt to a variety of changes at the same time, this task becomes more difficult as stress increases. Thus, every influence that challenges an ecosystem makes it more difficult for it and its species to adjust to the next one.[126] Stress induced by different sources compounds each other and eventually leads to cumulative impacts and impaired resilience.[127]

Adaptation options

Three forms of adaptation are frequently discussed,[128] namely blue carbon, marine protected areas, and fisheries management. In the same vein, ways of mitigation apart from reducing CO_2 emissions are being considered. In the case of blue carbon, adaptation and alternative ways of mitigation overlap.[129] Therefore, in addition to being a tool that can facilitate adaptation, blue carbon can also be utilised for mitigation. More specifically, the term "blue carbon" refers to carbon fluxes, capture, and storage in marine systems such as marine and coastal ecosystems and species.[130] Using blue carbon ecosystems, carbon can be sequestered and stored from both the atmosphere and the ocean.[131] For instance, coastal blue carbon is captured and stored by rooted vegetation such

125 Laffoley et al. (n 109) 10.
126 Herr et al. (n 112) 8, 39; Structured Expert Dialogue (SED) (n 114) 153.
127 Kenneth RN Anthony, 'Coral Reefs Under Climate Change and Ocean Acidification: Challenges and Opportunities for Management and Policy' (2016) 41(1) *Annual Review of Environment and Resources* 59, 61.
128 Cf. Anne B Christianson et al., 'The Promise of Blue Carbon Climate Solutions: Where the Science Supports Ocean-Climate Policy' (2022) 9 *Frontiers in Marine Science* 851448; Dorte Krause-Jensen et al., 'Sequestration of Macroalgal Carbon: The Elephant in the Blue Carbon Room' (2018) 14(6) *Biology Letters* 20180236; Peter I Macreadie et al., 'Blue Carbon as a Natural Climate Solution' (2021) 2(12) *Nature Reviews Earth & Environment* 826; University of California, Santa Cruz et al., 'Planning for Change: Assessing the Potential Role of Marine Protected Areas and Fisheries Management Approaches for Resilience Management in a Changing Ocean' (2019) 32(3) *Oceanography* 116; George Hoppit et al., 'Are Marine Protected Areas an Adaptation Measure against Climate Change Impacts on Coastal Ecosystems? A UK Case Study' (2022) 2 *Nature-Based Solutions* 100030.
129 Christianson et al. (n 128) 2.
130 Ibid 2–3.
131 Dorothée Herr et al., 'Pathways for Implementation of Blue Carbon Initiatives' (2017) 27 *Aquatic Conservation: Marine and Freshwater Ecosystems* 116, 116.

as mangroves, seagrass, and salt marshes in coastal zones.[132] These types of vegetation have mitigation potential through rapid sequestration and storage, along with adaptation potential by, for instance, protecting coasts and enhancing fisheries.[133] Therefore, blue carbon ecosystems need to be conserved, restored, and protected to guarantee their mitigation/adaptation potential. Coastal degradation and annual emissions due to losses are comparable to up to 19% of GHG emissions per annum from global deforestation.[134]

The characteristics of ocean acidification as a scientific problem

There are three key takeaways from the science section above, which can be boiled down to four characteristics of OA as a scientific problem:

First, OA exhibits the elements of a complex problem. A problem can be considered complex when "the sources of persistent problems are diffuse..., including important indirect contributors. In addition, cause and effect tend to be significantly delayed".[135] Despite being a problem, the repercussions of which can mainly be seen in the ocean, the causes and stressors also derive from the atmosphere and land. Hence, similar to many environmental problems, there is an interaction between the Earth's spheres (ocean, atmosphere, and land),[136] and the problem does not play out in just one of them.[137] Furthermore, OA is not the only stressor the oceans are encountering; multiple stressors will most likely compound each other. The involvement of different environmental spheres and various stressors (indirect contributors) of OA makes it a diffuse problem. In addition, OA is a creeping process with repercussions only slowly becoming visible. There is a delay between cause and effect. It is thus clear that OA can be considered a complex problem.

Second, OA's causes and stressors can be traced back to global, regional, and local actions. In addition, the effects of OA show themselves on all these levels. Therefore, the search for solutions through mitigation and adaptation requires the engagement of actors at all these levels. However, beyond that, there is also a natural variation in pH between different levels (global/open ocean and local/in the vicinity of the coastline) and even within the same level. Hence, two points can be made here. First, in order to address OA, a multilevel approach is required. Second, a one-size-fits-all solution cannot be expected to work well, as a generalisation may sometimes be problematic even within the same level.

132 Christianson et al. (n 128) 5.
133 Macreadie et al. (n 128) 5–6.
134 Herr et al. (n 131) 117.
135 De Búrca, Keohane, and Sabel ('Global Experimentalist Governance') (n 7) 479.
136 Cf. figure 1 for Earth's spheres. Dahe Qin et al., 'Cryospheric Science: Research Framework and Disciplinary System' (2018) 5(2) *National Science Review* 255, 257.
137 Ibid, see figure 1 for Earth's spheres.

Third, techniques to address OA are still insufficiently researched, and behavioural changes may be required that are not considered feasible. For instance, concerning mitigation, the step that would lead to the most significant attenuation of the problem is the immediate cut in the emissions of all carbon dioxide gases. However, this is a daunting task and cannot be realised immediately. Research on OA mitigation and adaptation is being conducted, including on topics such as geoengineering and nature-based solutions, to provide more time for the demanding emission-cutting process. However, research is still needed before these alternatives can be employed. It can be expected that over time, OA, with its multifarious causes, stressors, consequences, and adaptation options, will be better understood. During this process, it is likely that some drivers can be controlled faster than others. For example, it may be less costly and politically feasible to clean wastewater from agriculture or urbanisation than to achieve a substantial cut in GHG emissions. It is down to single states or regions to control wastewater, which could otherwise lead to acidification in the vicinity of the coastline (local). Thus, while humankind is addressing the daunting task of reducing the emission of CO_2, it can eliminate other causes and stressors in the meantime. Starting to address some of the causes and stressors now can "buy time" in the process of addressing OA at large. Creating less stress through either causes or stressors can, for instance, give ecosystems and species time to adapt, and tipping points might not be reached as fast. In sum, this means that the governance framework needs to be flexible and easily adjustable to respond quickly to future progress in research.

In conclusion, four main elements can be identified which characterise OA as a problem:

- OA is a complex problem;
- Addressing OA requires a multilevel approach;
- No one-size-fits-all solution can be expected to work in relation to OA; and
- OA governance needs to be adjustable and flexible.

After understanding OA as a scientific problem and its four characteristics, the next section turns to OA from a governance perspective, namely OA as a regime complex. Together, these two parts, OA as a scientific problem and as a regime complex, lead to seven different characteristics. These seven characteristics will be matched with GXG below.

The governance landscape for ocean acidification

To ensure that GXG is a good match for OA, apart from underlining the characteristics of OA as a scientific problem, it should be further clarified whether GXG is able to build on the already existing governance landscape for OA. Governance of OA does not happen in a vacuum or from a clean slate, meaning that there are already actors and instruments in existence that touch upon areas relevant to OA.[138] In fact, it has already been identified elsewhere that OA as a problem is not governed by one "regime" but instead is governed by a so-called "regime complex".[139] Fittingly, GXG is a governance structure that is known to develop from a regime complex.[140] GXG can develop from a regime complex as it can cater to and accommodate a regime complex's characteristics, which is analysed in more detail below.[141] First, regime complexity is defined in the following paragraphs, and the regime complex for OA is described. Second, the main takeaways for OA as a regime complex are identified to later match them with GXG.

Ocean acidification as a regime complex

The term regime complex was originally coined by Raustiala and Victor in relation to plant genetic resources.[142] They define a regime complex as

> an *array* of partially *overlapping and nonhierarchical institutions* governing a particular *issue-area*. Regime Complexes are marked by the existence of *several legal agreements* that are created and maintained in *distinct fora* with participation of *different* sets of *actors*. These *rules* in these elemental regimes functionally *overlap*, yet there is *no* agreed upon *hierarchy* for resolving *conflicts* between rules.[143]
>
> [emphasis added]

In other words, the defining elements of a regime complex are the presence of non-hierarchical institutions that have a functional overlap as they govern the same issue area. However, this definition has been developed significantly over the years. Recently, authors have questioned the idea that regime complexes have to be non-hierarchical.[144] Newer understandings of regime

138 Cf. Raustiala and Victor make the point that 'the array of rules already in force channel and constrain the content' in their case of new elemental regimes within regime complexes. Kal Raustiala and David G Victor, 'The Regime Complex for Plant Genetic Resources' (2004) 58(2) *International Organization* 277, 280.

139 Karen N Scott, 'Ocean Acidification' in Elise Johansen, Signe Busch, and Ingvild Ulrikke Jakobsen (eds), *The Law of the Sea and Climate Change* (Cambridge University Press, 1st ed, 2020) 104, 109, 110.

140 De Búrca, Keohane, and Sabel ('Global Experimentalist Governance') (n 7) 479.

141 Cf. Christine Overdevest and Jonathan Zeitlin, 'Assembling an Experimentalist Regime: Transnational Governance Interactions in the Forest Sector: Assembling an Experimentalist Regime' (2014) 8(1) *Regulation & Governance* 22, 24, 25.

142 Raustiala and Victor (n 138).

143 Ibid 279.

144 Cf. Eilstrup-Sangiovanni (n 9); Jessica F Green, 'Hierarchy in Regime Complexes: Understanding Authority in Antarctic Governance' (2022) 66(1) *International Studies Quarterly* 1.

complexes claim that these complexes can vary in hierarchy.[145] Hence, they simply understand regime complexes to be "rule sets and agents that assert overlapping authority claims to govern a specific global policy issue".[146] As per this new definition, institutions that are part of a regime complex approach diverse delimited problems, which means that these complexes are at the "nexus" of different issue areas.[147] Therefore, institutions overlap as they not only have authority claims to govern a specific problem but are also part of adjacent governance systems. Independent of the exact definition, the regime complex literature can be helpful in describing a governance landscape.

Also, the regime complex for OA sits at the nexus of many different issue areas. Numerous existing institutions are dealing with diverse issues (oceans, atmosphere, biodiversity, etc.) that could approach OA. As has been seen above, OA is a problem that, for example, touches upon various Earth spheres[148] (land, air, and water) and is characterised by geographical differences (pH of open ocean vs. vicinity of the coastline). Due to these characteristics, diverse treaties such as the United Nations Framework Convention on Climate Change, the United Nations Convention on the Law of the Sea, or the Convention on Biological Diversity, could be relevant to tackle OA.[149] In the same vein, a variety of actors could take the lead, like the International Maritime Organization (IMO) or the United Nations Environmental Programme. Thus, it is obvious that OA governance does not begin with a clean slate, as actors and legal instruments that could address OA are already in existence. Hence, attempts to deal with OA are likely to exist across a multitude of institutions (actors and legal instruments). In addition, responses to the problem of institutions are and will be seen at different levels of governance. Present institutions likely to have the potential to address OA and its causes (anthropogenic CO_2 emissions, NO_x, SO_x) directly include the climate change regime or the International Convention for the Prevention of Pollution from Ships (Annex VI). Alternatively, institutions could mitigate factors that additionally stress the ecosystem, like the Regional Fisheries Management Organisations, which could prevent overfishing. In addition to dealing with causes and stressors, some institutions can also instigate adaptation, such as the Law of the Seas regime.

After understanding that the governmental landscape for OA can be described as a regime complex, the following outlines its characteristics to

145 Eilstrup-Sangiovanni (n 9) 296.

146 Ibid 294. More specifically, Eilstrup-Sangiovanni calls them 'global governance complexes' as she moves away from the original term 'regime complex'.

147 Ibid 297; cf. Amandine Orsini, Jean-Frédéric Morin, and Oran Young, 'Regime Complexes: A Buzz, a Boom, or a Boost for Global Governance?' (2013) 19 *Global Governance* 27, 30–31.

148 See figure 1 for Earth's spheres; Qin et al. (n 136) 257.

149 Cf. Scott (n 139) 109–110.

match them with GXG. Ideally, GXG should build on and make a virtue of the present regime complex for OA without necessitating a complete dismantling of it.

Takeaways for ocean acidification as a regime complex

Many actors could potentially be involved in OA governance, as is typical for regime complexes. Abbott, for example, identified that at the time of writing, 68 actors were relevant to the transnational regime complex for climate change.[150] In addition, these actors have different compositions. In the case that Abbott described, the 68 actors were a mix of public and private transnational actors.[151] Therefore, it is likely that, similar to other regime complexes, the regime complex for OA also includes public, private, and mixed actors.[152] Thus, two points can be made here: a large number of actors are involved and these actors are not homogeneous.

There seems to be increasing engagement and agreement among actors that OA is a problem that will endanger oceanic ecosystems and ecosystem services.[153] Nevertheless, because of varying interests and uncertainties, which are typical for a regime complex, it is unlikely that actors will engage in integrated governance solutions.[154] As indicated above, the regime complex for OA is composed of many non-homogeneous actors. If many non-homogeneous actors are addressing one issue, their interests can be expected to vary. These varying interests create uncertainty for actors regarding the future governance

150 Kenneth W Abbott, 'The Transnational Regime Complex for Climate Change' (2012) 30(4) *Environment and Planning C: Government and Policy* 571, 583; Kenneth Abbott, 'Strengthening the Transnational Regime Complex for Climate Change' (2013) 3 *Transnational Environmental Law* 57, 65.

151 Abbott, 'The Transnational Regime Complex for Climate Change' (n 150) 583; Abbott, 'Strengthening the Transnational Regime Complex for Climate Change' (n 150) 65.

152 See different types of actors raising concerns about OA: Inuit Circumpolar Council, 'Inuit at COP25 – Our Ice Is Melting, Our Oceans Are at Risk, Our Planet Is on Fire | Inuit Circumpolar Council Canada' (Web Page, 13 December 2019) <https://www.inuitcircumpolar.com/news/inuit-at-cop25-our-ice-is-melting-our-oceans-are-at-risk-our-planet-is-on-fire/>; Chile California Council, 'The Future of the Coast', *Chile California Council | Sitio Web Oficial* (Web Page, 2023) <https://chile-california.org/contenido-impacto/the-future-of-the-coast-2/>; Oceana, 'What Is Ocean Acidification?', *Oceana USA* (Web Page, 2023) <https://usa.oceana.org/what-ocean-acidification/>; OA Alliance, 'About Us', *OA Alliance* (Web Page, 2022) <https://www.oaalliance.org/about>.

153 See, e.g. OA Alliance, 'Action Plans', *OA Alliance* (Web Page, 2022) <https://www.oaalliance.org/action-plans>; IUCN, 'Climate Change and the Ocean', *IUCN* (Web Page, 7 October 2015) <https://www.iucn.org/theme/marine-and-polar/our-work/climate-change-and-ocean>; IAEA, OA-ICC, 'Ocean Acidification International Coordination Centre (OA-ICC)' (Web Page, 5 February 2018) <https://www.iaea.org/services/oa-icc>.

154 Cf. Robert O Keohane and David G. Victor, 'The Regime Complex for Climate Change' (2011) 9(1) *Perspectives on Politics* 7, 8–9, 13.

of that issue.[155] Apart from that, OA as a problem is already characterised by, for example, scientific uncertainty, which leaves actors in an uncertain situation. Thus, despite recognising OA as a problem, actors will likely struggle to agree on one joint approach because of the varying interests and many uncertainties at play. Hence, it is unlikely that there will be any agreed goals ex-ante.[156]

In conclusion, after reviewing different features in relation to the governance landscape of the problem, three main elements can be identified that characterise OA as a regime complex:

- A large number of actors are involved;
- Various types of actors are involved; and
- No agreement on how to address the problem concerned can be expected ex-ante.

With these three characteristics describing OA as a regime complex together with the four characteristics describing OA as a scientific problem identified above, one can now return to the question of whether GXG may be a useful governance framework to tackle OA. To decide whether the theory of GXG and the problem of OA align, it is necessary to consider whether the identified characteristics of OA can be accommodated by GXG. In other words, is there a "good match" between OA and its existing governance framework and GXG? This question is addressed in the next section.

Matching global experimentalist governance with the case of ocean acidification

Seven elements have been identified that characterise OA as a scientific problem and a regime complex. These points are examined one by one in the following paragraphs, and for each point, whether GXG is suitable to address the characteristic is discussed. First, the four points characterising OA as a scientific problem are discussed; then, those that characterise OA as a regime complex are addressed. To provide visual help, the match between the characteristics and GXG is presented in Tables 2.1 and 2.2.

Matching ocean acidification as a scientific problem and global experimentalist governance

The left side of Table 2.1 lists the characteristics of OA as a scientific problem and the right side lists different types of aspects of GXG. These different types of aspects were identified earlier in this chapter as the five elements of the ideal

155 Cf. ibid 9.
156 Cf. ibid 13.

Table 2.1 OA science and GXG

OA – Scientific Problem	*Global Experimentalist Governance*
Complex problem	• Newly arising • Creeping or persistent • Low visibility • Complex
Multilevel approach	• Global dimension • Goals set through discourse of stakeholders from various levels • (Multilevel) experimentation, comparison, feedback, and peer review
No one-size-fits-all solution/ diversity	• Delegation to lower levels of governance • Experimentation, comparison, feedback, and peer review
Adjustable and flexible governance/uncertainty	• Limited scientific information/uncertainty • No known solution – ex-ante • Provisionality of goals, metrics, solutions, and problem definition • Experimentation, comparison, feedback, and peer review

Table 2.2 OA regime complex and global experimentalist governance

OA – Regime Complex	*Global Experimentalist Governance*
Large number of actors	• Goals set through discourse of stakeholders from various levels • Finding solutions delegated to lower levels
Various types of actors	• Goals set through discourse of stakeholders from various levels • Finding solutions delegated to lower levels
No agreements ex-ante	• No known solution – ex-ante

type of GXG entail information about what type of problem the theory can deal with and how (see legend). In other words, Table 2.1 matches the characteristics with the relevant aspects of GXG to examine if this governance type is suitable for the problem of OA. The following sections discuss each of the four characteristics with regard to GXG.

Complex problem

OA is an emerging and complex problem. Its complexity derives from the fact that it is diffuse, involving different Earth spheres and various stressors. Its causes and effects are delayed, as it is creeping by nature with repercussions that become slowly visible. GXG is set up to address this exact type of issue. As noted above, the problems that the theory is intended to address are usually newly emerging, complex, and creeping, just like OA. In addition, as is typical for creeping problems, OA has gained limited public attention as it is silently emerging. This low visibility is typical of the type of problem that experimentalist governance approaches. Therefore, GXG may have the potential to address OA as a complex problem.

Multilevel approach

On the one hand, OA is a problem with a global dimension, and it needs international coordination to be addressed, as a large part of OA is caused by globally emitted CO_2. On the other hand, the causes, stressors, and repercussions of OA can be traced back and seen at the global, regional, and local level. In addition, there are natural pH differences at various levels, such as on the global level/open ocean and the local level/in the vicinity of the coastline. Therefore, it is only sensible that mitigation and adaptation are undertaken on all those levels. Thus, OA is a problem that is best addressed through a multilevel governance approach. GXG addresses problems that have a global dimension. GXG requires a multilevel approach to address complex and interconnected global problems. First, the theory requires that goals and metrics are set through collaboration between stakeholders of various kinds. These stakeholders are, additionally, from different levels of governance. Second, apart from the goal and metric setting, the recursive learning cycle involving experimentation, comparison, feedback, and peer review is also multilevel. Experimentation happens locally; results are compared, analysed, and communicated to higher levels for further review. Hence, in essence, GXG is conceived as a multilevel process, and a multilevel approach is a necessary part of GXG.

No one-size-fits-all solution/diversity

Along with the multilevel approach, it must be kept in mind that OA and, in particular, pH can be diverse even within a specific geographical locality, making one-size-fits-all and generalising solutions problematic. GXG accommodates this diversity and lack of generalisability by delegating the task of finding solutions to actors operating at a lower level of governance. These localised actors have the discretion and opportunity to experiment with solutions that are responsive to local circumstances. In the same vein, experimentation, comparison, feedback, and peer review guarantee that different strategies and solutions can be compared and critically analysed. Eventually, this may lead to a catalogue of best practices. This catalogue helps stakeholders choose practices that are likely to work under particular, for example, geographic circumstances. Thus, GXG can address problems that cannot have a one-size-fits-all solution.

Adjustable and flexible governance/uncertainty

OA is a relatively new environmental problem that has not been comprehensively researched. In addition, mitigation and adaptation responses will often be difficult to realise as they demand far-reaching and diverse behavioural changes. Mechanisms to address some of the drivers of OA will be more readily available than others as it is, for instance, less costly and politically more feasible to tackle drivers such as wastewater from agriculture or urbanisation as opposed to CO_2 emissions. Over time, scientific information will become available to better explain the causes, stressors, consequences, and adaptation options. At the same time, technology will advance and make possible new ways of tackling OA. This means that OA governance needs to be flexible and easily adjustable. GXG typically addresses problems with limited scientific information and a high level of uncertainty, like OA. Due to this lack of information, the problems that the theory approaches also have no straightforward solution ex-ante. The theory requires provisional goals, metrics, solutions, and problem definitions to accommodate this uncertainty. Provisionality allows for readjustment once new and additional scientific knowledge and technologies are discovered. Experimentation, comparison, feedback, and peer review facilitate the testing and evaluation of the discovered knowledge and technology. It allows for learning by doing in real time and customisation to new developments. Therefore, GXG is set up to deal with problems characterised by inherent uncertainty.

Regarding the key points in relation to OA as a scientific problem, it can be said that GXG is well adapted to accommodate them. This makes OA and GXG a "good match". The points relating to OA as a regime complex are discussed next.

Matching the regime complex for ocean acidification and global experimentalist governance

The previous section outlined three different characteristics of OA as a regime complex. The three characteristics are presented in Table 2.2, with the identical setup as Table 2.1. Hence, this section discusses whether GXG can accommodate and build on the characteristics of the regime complex for OA, the current governmental landscape. The following sections discuss each of the three characteristics with regard to GXG.

Large number of actors

As explained above, many actors are already involved in OA governance. OA sits at the nexus of different issue areas such as the ocean, land, and atmosphere. Thus, actors who work within these issue areas show interest in OA. As has been seen above, GXG entails setting provisional goals and metrics as a result of collaboration between different types of stakeholders on various levels across issue areas. The actual experimentation of strategies based on these goals and metrics is then delegated to the lower levels of governance. Hence, the theory facilitates and organises solution-finding, which includes many actors from different levels of governance. Therefore, GXG should be able to deal with the large number of actors potentially involved in OA governance.

Various types of actors

Apart from the multitude, there are also various types of actors that could be involved in the governance of OA. In particular, actors might have different compositions. They can be public, private, or mixed. In any case, these actors are not homogeneous. Within GXG, different stakeholders from various levels are involved in setting goals and metrics. Apart from that, the actors on the lower levels in charge of experimentation can be different types of stakeholders. Therefore, GXG not only enables but demands the inclusion of various actors.

No agreements ex-ante

Regime complexes deal with problems like OA for which no agreement can be found ex-ante. This probable disagreement can be traced to varying interests and uncertainties surrounding OA, which are characteristic of a regime complex. Despite growing engagement with the problem and an increasing number of actors voicing their concerns about OA, they will likely struggle to agree on one joint strategy to tackle OA due to the uncertainties and varying interests. Thus, it is unlikely that goals will be agreed on ex-ante. GXG is a theory that can address complex problems with high uncertainty. These types of problems often have no solution readily available. Thus, the theory can deal with problems for which a solution cannot be expected ex-ante, as is the case for OA.

After discussing these seven characterising points, it can be determined that the theory has the potential to address OA, both in view of its characteristics as a scientific problem and in view of the current existence of a regime complex. OA and its current governmental landscape are the type of problem that is typically addressed by GXG. Therefore, theoretically, GXG is a suitable governance approach for tackling OA. Nevertheless, for GXG to emerge and thrive, a number of conditions should ideally be present.

Concluding remarks

This chapter has shown that OA is a fast-moving issue that by its nature would be challenging to tackle using traditional law-making methods. Based on the scientific background of the problem and the identified regime complex for OA, this chapter has demonstrated that GXG is a mode of governance that appears to be a suitable match for OA. More precisely, GXG addresses the type of problem that OA is, namely, one that is complex and insufficiently understood. In addition, GXG can touch upon the features of OA. For instance, GXG can cater to the fact that OA needs a multilevel approach by involving actors or stakeholders from different governmental levels. As GXG caters to problems surrounded by complexity and uncertainty, this form of governance might be a sensible solution for OA and other problems endangering the ocean. Through its adaptability and flexibility, GXG facilitates finding solutions in real time and in accordance with developing science and technology. The question is if this type of governance can already be found within the operations of existing actors who, through pooling information and organising revision, can be considered as the centre. Arguably, the Paris Agreement, with its nationally determined contributions, could be seen as an example of experimentalist governance, albeit an imperfect one.[157] Other examples of GXG, such as UNAIDS and the global ozone layer regime, give hope that this form of governance can work.[158] However, regarding the governance of ocean issues, this topic requires further research. This chapter has developed and provided straightforward guidelines for five steps to the ideal type of GXG. These steps can be used as a test to identify patterns of GXG within the governance of institutions. As many institutions may be part of the regime complex for OA, one should aim to identify those that can approach the causes, stressors, and adaptation options to the problem. Institutions that have recently become more invested in ocean acidification are the United Nations Educational, Scientific and Cultural Organisation and, at the regional level, the Convention for the Protection of the Marine Environment of the North-East Atlantic. An additional area of research that needs to be further developed regarding GXG is the possible problems and shortcomings of the functioning of this type of governance at the international and local level.

157 Cf. Geng Qin and Hanzhi Yu, 'Rescuing the Paris Agreement: Improving the Global Experimentalist Governance by Reclassifying Countries' (2023) 15(4) *Sustainability* 3207.

158 Goldstein and Ansell (n 7); De Búrca, Keohane, and Sabel ('Global Experimentalist Governance') (n 7).

3 Multi-ocean spaces and offshore wind energy

Gabriela Argüello

Introduction

Climate mitigation calls for an energy system transition in which electricity generation is diversified with renewable energy sources.[1] In such diversification, the ocean is crucial for developing a wide range of renewable energy technologies, including wind, tidal, wave, solar, and thermal energy.[2] Undoubtedly, offshore wind power is the most developed technology with a significant deployment capacity and is widely considered environmentally friendly due to its ability to replace fossil fuel–based energy sources.[3] The European Union (EU), for example, considers offshore wind power a technology critical to its becoming carbon neutral by 2050.[4] China, one of the leading states in the development of offshore wind power, has the objective to become carbon neutral by 2060, and its national determined contributions (NDCs) under the Paris Agreement[5] include increasing "its total installed capacity of wind and solar power to over 1.2 billion kilowatts by 2030".[6]

Yet, the development of offshore wind power is riddled with trade-offs since the ocean is an already crowded space. According to Bogojević, while climate action is often presented positively, it does not always lead to win-win

1 IPCC, 'Summary For Policymakers' in HO Pörtner et al. (eds), *IPCC Special Report on the Ocean and Cryosphere in a Changing Climate: Special Report of the Intergovernmental Panel on Climate Change* (Cambridge University Press, 1st ed, 2022), 25.

2 Simon Neill and Reza Hashemi, *Fundamentals of Ocean Renewable Energy: Generating Electricity from the Sea* (Academic Press, 2018), chs 3–5.

3 International Renewable Energy Agency (IRENA), *Tracking the Impacts of Innovation: Offshore Wind as a Case Study* (Report, 2021) 17–21.

4 European Commission, *Communication from the commission to the European Parliament, the Council, the European Economic and Social Committee and the Committee of the Regions: An EU Strategy to harness the potential of offshore renewable energy for a climate neutral future* COM(2020) 741 final, 19 November 2020.

5 *Paris Agreement on Climate Change*, opened for signature (22 April 2016), [2016] ATS 24 (entered into force 4 November 2016).

6 The People's Republic of China, *China's Achievements, New Goals, and New Measures for Nationally Determined Contributions* (Report, October 2021).

DOI: 10.4324/9781003518570-3

scenarios.[7] In fact, climate action can often cause social, environmental, and economic conflicts. Offshore wind energy may be accompanied by conflicts between ocean users, such as fisheries and shipping. These are known as user–user conflicts. Furthermore, some evidence indicates that offshore renewable energy projects may impact the marine environment, which may cause a user–environment conflict.[8] Those impacts include species disturbance due to underwater noise, electromagnetic fields, and changes in the seabed and marine habitats during the construction and decommission phases.[9] From a legal perspective, such conflicts require devising legal pathways to balance climate action and marine environmental protection, and mechanisms to manage potential conflicts arising from competing uses of the same space.

Multi-use ocean spaces are a viable legal pathway to balance the competing uses of the marine space.[10] From a regulatory perspective, marine spatial planning (MSP) has been identified as a tool that can foster such coexistence.[11] It is worth noting that MSP evolved as a management alternative to existing sectoral management approaches (e.g. shipping, fisheries) or ad-hoc approval approaches, as in the case of offshore wind power.[12] Thus, the core of MSP is to "alleviate conflicts between human uses".[13] Yet, MSP has to be

7 Sanja Bogojević, 'Legal Dilemmas of Climate Action' (2023) 35(1) *Journal of Environmental Law* 1, 2.

8 Fatemeh Rezaei et al., 'Towards Understanding Environmental and Cumulative Impacts of Floating Wind Farms: Lessons Learned from the Fixed-Bottom Offshore Wind Farms' (2023) 243 *Ocean & Coastal Management* 1, 1–18; Uwe Stöber and Frank Thomsen, 'How Could Operational Underwater Sound from Future Offshore Wind Turbines Impact Marine Life?' (2021) 149(2) *The Journal of the Acoustical Society of America* 1791; Torben Kirchgeorg et al., 'Emissions from Corrosion Protection Systems of Offshore Wind Farms: Evaluation of the Potential Impact on the Marine Environment' (2018) 136 *Marine Pollution Bulletin*, 257.

9 Robin Pelc and Rod Fujita, 'Renewable Energy from the Ocean' (2002) 26(6) *Marine Policy* 471; Andrew Gill, 'Offshore Renewable Energy: Ecological Implications of Generating Electricity in the Coastal Zone' (2005) 42(4) *The Journal of Applied Ecology* 605; United Nations, *The First Global Integrated Marine Assessment: World Ocean Assessment I* (Cambridge University Press, 2017); Elina A Virtanen et al., 'Balancing Profitability of Energy Production, Societal Impacts and Biodiversity in Offshore Wind Farm Design' (2022) 158 *Renewable and Sustainable Energy Reviews* 112087.

10 Angela Schultz-Zehden et al., *Ocean Multi-Use Action Plan, MUSES project* (30 September 2008).

11 Coexistence is just one of many terms currently used in legal scholarship and marine spatial plans. Other similar terms refer to co-location, multi-use, or multisector planning.

12 Frank Maes, 'The International Legal Framework for Marine Spatial Planning' (2008) 32(5) *Marine Policy* 797; Jorge Viñuales, *The International Law of Energy* (Cambridge University Press, 2022); Aron Westholm, 'Divided Environments: Scalar Challenges in Sweden's Marine and Coastal Water Planning' in Irus Braverman (ed), *Laws of the Sea: Interdisciplinary Currents* (Routledge, 2022), 241.

13 Daud Hassan and Niko Soininen, 'Marine Spatial Planning as an Instrument of Sustainable Ocean Governance' in Daud Hassan, Tuomas Kuokkanen and Niko Soininen (eds), *Transboundary Marine Spatial Planning and International Law* (Earthscan, 2015), 3.

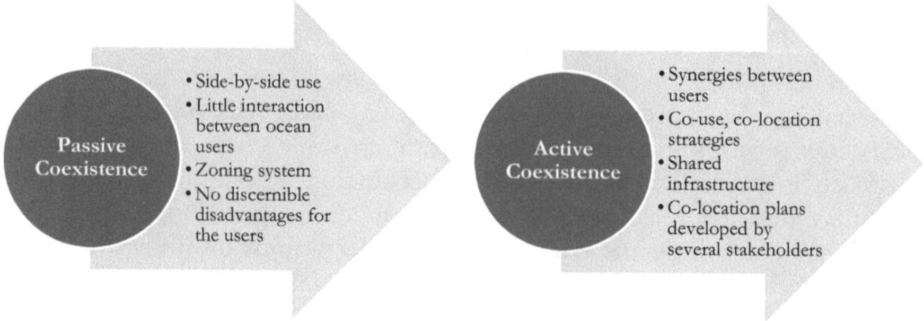

Figure 3.1 Coexistence levels

consistent with the 1982 United Nations Convention on the Law of the Sea (UNCLOS).[14]

From a broad perspective, multi-use ocean spaces are subject to several degrees of coexistence, as summarised in Figure 3.1.

This chapter analyses the preconditions necessary for developing multi-use ocean spaces, focusing on the interaction between offshore wind power and other marine activities such as fisheries and aquaculture. These uses were selected because fisheries have traditionally been displaced in areas where major offshore installations have been built, whereas aquaculture has been identified as a marine use with a high potential for coexistence. To this end, the chapter engages in a comparative legal analysis between China, Germany, and Scotland, which are leading the development of large offshore wind energy.

This chapter is structured as follows: first, the conditions contributing to the resilience of law are discussed, followed by an examination of the rights and obligations of coastal states regarding the establishment of offshore wind power structures within national jurisdiction. Additionally, there is a brief overview of marine spatial planning in relation to the law of the sea and its potential to foster a coexistence. The main challenges to the coexistence between offshore wind power, fishing, and aquaculture are then identified. National experiences of coexistence, specifically in China, Germany, and Scotland, are assessed. The chapter concludes with some closing remarks.

Towards a resilient law of the sea

Climate change, biodiversity loss, pollution, and spatial conflicts at sea are some of the challenges raising questions about the adequacy of UNCLOS

14 United Nations Convention on the Law of the Sea, opened for signature 10 December 1982, 1833 UNTS 396; 21 ILM 1261 (entered into force 16 November 1994) ('UNCLOS').

as a legal framework to address ocean complexities.[15] These challenges have prompted discussions about the resiliency of UNCLOS. However, what does it mean to be resilient? In common parlance, something or someone recovers and "returns to its original" form after experiencing a shock.[16] This definition is closely related to the concept of ecosystem resilience, which indicates the ability of the ecosystem to "return to its original state following a disturbance or other perturbation".[17] From a marine environmental perspective, resilience could refer to the fitness of UNCLOS to support the conservation of marine ecosystems while also supporting other goals, such as the transition to renewable energy or food security.

Yet, the resilience of law may have a different connotation. It refers to the ability to adapt and change in the face of external disruptions. In fact, from a theoretical perspective, resilience studies are related to adaptive governance.[18] Such adaptation may be necessary to fulfil legislative goals, for example, the conservation of the marine environment. If an instrument such as UNCLOS is incapable of change, it will become a "dead letter". In the words of Vining, law is "expressed in words spoken by responsible human beings to one another, who were listening to one another, and reexpressed and respoken over time".[19]

In a sense, law is constantly evolving and changing. References to "treaty evolution"[20] or "living instruments"[21] are not uncommon in the international law literature. Elsewhere, this author has described the formal and dynamic mechanisms for change in international law.[22] The former encompasses treaty amendment and customary law development, while the latter refers, for instance, to evolutive treaty interpretation, regime interaction, and normative

15 See e.g. a 2021 inquiry of the United Kingdom Parliament which explored to what extent UNCLOS remains fit for purpose in 2021; International Relations and Defence Committee, *UNCLOS: The Law of the Sea in the 21st Century – 2nd Report of Session 2021–22 London* (HL Paper 159, 2nd Report of Session 2021–22, 1 March 2022).

16 *Oxford Advanced Learner's Dictionary of Current English* (9th ed, 2018) 'resilient'.

17 Elsa Cleland, 'Biodiversity and Ecosystem Stability' (2011) 3(10) *Nature Education Knowledge* 14, 14.

18 Brita Bohman, *Legal Design for Social-Ecological Resilience* (Cambridge University Press, 2021), 8.

19 Joseph Vining, 'The Resilience of Law' (2008) *Law & Economics Working Papers Archive* 1–31, 3.

20 See e.g. Alan Boyle, 'Further Development of the 1982 Convention on the Law of the Sea: Mechanisms for Change' in David Freestone, Richard Barnes, and David Ong (eds), *The Law of the Sea: Progress and Prospects* (Oxford University Press, 2006). See also, Jill Barret and Richard Barnes (eds), *Law of the Sea: UNCLOS as a Living Treaty* (British Institute of International and Comparative Law, 2016).

21 See e.g. *Tyrer v United Kingdom* 1978 (Eur Court HR, Court Chamber, Application no. 5856/72, 25 April 1978) 1, [3]; *Request for an Advisory Opinion Submitted by the Sub-Regional Fisheries Commission (SRFC) (Advisory Opinion)* (ITLOS Reports 2015, Case no. 21, 2015) [18].

22 Gabriela Argüello, 'Opportunities for Protecting Biological Diversity in the Arctic Ocean' (2022) XIII *The Yearbook of Polar Law* 122.

developments carried out by international organisations.[23] Change alone is not adequate for legal resilience. Throughout this process, the changing instrument must remain authoritative, where it is both followed and relied upon.[24] In this chapter, reference to legal resilience means that law meets two criteria: it must adapt and respond to novel challenges and remain authoritative.

The international legal dimension of multi-use ocean spaces

This section examines the potential for and the challenges of coexistence from an international law perspective, exploring to what extent MSP can facilitate the spatial and temporal allocation of human activities at sea. It specifically concentrates on areas within national jurisdiction, where the majority of large-scale wind power expansion is taking place.

Territorial sea

UNCLOS is silent concerning the exploitation of wind power in the territorial sea. However, according to article 2 of the convention, coastal states enjoy territorial sovereignty over their territorial sea, the airspace above it, the seabed, and the subsoil subject only to the right of innocent passage. Based on the legal status of the territorial sea, one may conclude that sovereignty covers renewable energy resources in the same manner as on land. This means that the coastal state determines the procedures to build, operate, and decommission generating units and submarine infrastructure used to connect to the transmission grid.[25] Due to territorial sovereignty, the coastal state has full jurisdiction to implement MSP according to its socioeconomic and environmental goals. In the territorial sea, MSP has important potential to alleviate user–user and user–environment conflicts. To illustrate, the coastal state can designate priority zones for offshore wind power development, designate security zones, or establish protected areas where human activities are limited. Nonetheless, marine spatial plans are subject to the preservation of the regime of innocent passage.[26]

To prevent allisions with offshore structures, coastal states may require vessels exercising their innocent passage right to observe sea lanes and traffic

23 Ibid 128.

24 Vining (n 15) 9.

25 Mikhail Kashubsky, *Offshore Oil and Gas Installations Security: An International Perspective* (Informa, 2016) 202–204; Maria Madalena Das Neves, 'Offshore Renewable Energy and the Law of the Sea' in Elise Johansen, Signe Veierud Busch and Ingvild Ulrikke Jakobsen (eds), *The Law of the Sea and Climate Change: Solutions and Constraints* (Cambridge University Press, 2021) 206, 220–221; Olivia Woolley, 'Renewable Energy and the Law of the Sea' in James Kraska and Young-Kil Park (eds), *Emerging Technology and the Law of the Sea* (Cambridge University Press, 2022) 35, 38–39.

26 UNCLOS (n 14) art 24.

separation schemes, as outlined in article 22(1) of UNCLOS. Those mechanisms fall within "ship routing", such as deep water navigation lines, traffic separation schemes, two-way routes, areas to be avoided, no anchoring areas, inshore traffic zones, and precautionary areas.[27] Since the coastal state has sovereignty over the territorial sea, article 22(1) must not be interpreted restrictively. In fact, a coastal state has the legislative jurisdiction to designate any ship routing mechanism to secure the safety of navigation and to prevent the pollution of the marine environment in its territorial sea.[28] In contrast, the International Maritime Organization (IMO) has an advisory role in designing such ship routing mechanisms.[29] From a coexistence perspective, consultation with the IMO should not be overlooked since it provides an opportunity to engage, through the IMO, with other flag states and evaluate how the exercise of the rights established under UNCLOS may be affected.[30]

The exclusive economic zone

In the exclusive economic zone (EEZ), coastal states enjoy sovereign rights to explore and exploit energy from winds in accordance with article 56(1)(a) of UNCLOS and may implement such sovereign rights through MSP. Coastal states also have jurisdiction over the construction, operation, and decommissioning of structures and installations operating in the EEZ.[31] However, article 56(2) of the convention qualifies this right by requiring coastal states to "have due regard to the rights and duties of other states". Due regard obligations are relevant in the development of multi-use ocean spaces. In international law, due regard obligations are inherently open textured and substantively similar to other expressions found in UNCLOS, such as "taking into account", "with reasonable regard", and "taking into consideration".

It is apparent that due regard necessarily implies an intensification of cooperation obligations, particularly those of consultation and negotiation.[32] Such a process cannot be a mere formality but should be used to balance the rights of coastal and third states. Therefore, arguing a sovereign right to exploit energy from winds does not *ipso facto* give the coastal state an absolute priority

27 International Maritime Organization (IMO), *Resolution A.572(14) as amended: General Provisions on Ship's Routeing*, 14th sess, Agenda Item 10(b), A 14/Res.572 (20 January 1986, adopted 20 November 1985).

28 Julian Roberts 'Protecting Sensitive Marine Environments: The Role and Applications of Ships' Routeing Measurers' (2005) 20(1) *International Journal of Marine and Coastal Law* 135, 138; Gabriela Argüello et al., 'Regulation of Ships at Anchor: Safety and Environmental Implications' (2022) 140(105052) *Marine Policy* 1, 5.

29 UNCLOS (n 14) art 22(3)(a).

30 James Harrison, *Making the Law of the Sea: A Study in the Development of International Law* (Cambridge University Press, 2011) 180.

31 UNCLOS (n 14) art 60(1)(b).

32 *Chagos Marine Protected Area Arbitration (Mauritius v United Kingdom)* (Award) (Permanent Court of Arbitration, Case No. 2011-03, 18 March 2015) 1, [320].

to use a determined marine space in the EEZ, disregarding, for example, existing navigational routes.[33]

More specifically, a coastal state may not establish offshore wind power, installations and structures "where interference may be caused to the use of recognised sea lanes essential to international navigation".[34] UNCLOS does not provide a definition of essential sea lanes, nor does it clarify which states have jurisdiction to designate them.[35] It is also uncertain whether an essential sea lane refers to a specific volume of maritime traffic or if it is dependent on historic or customary shipping routes.

However, routing systems and traffic separation schemes established under the auspices of the IMO give some indications of areas to avoid when planning to construct offshore wind power structures.[36] IMO Resolution A.572(14), as amended, recommends that offshore structures are not established within routing systems or near their terminations. Yet, it provides for the temporary and permanent adjustment of traffic separation schemes for offshore rigs when drilling locations are found near the boundary of a traffic lane or separation zone. No such exception is made for offshore wind structures.[37] However, one could argue that other offshore structures, by analogy, should be subject to the same conditions. Mandatory routing schemes cannot be temporarily adjusted and, if required, could be suspended. Overall, in MSP, coastal states must consider the rights of other states and the safety of navigation when planning for the development of offshore wind power.

In situations where the coastal state has limited jurisdiction, MSP may not be able to resolve all relevant conflicts effectively. An example of this is the protection and preservation of the marine environment. According to article 56(b)(iii) of UNCLOS, coastal states have jurisdiction over the protection and preservation of the marine environment but lack sovereignty in this matter. Therefore, national environmental law may not automatically apply to the EEZ.[38] To prevent user–environment conflicts, environmental impact assessments (EIAs) are necessary prerequisites for the construction and operation of offshore wind power projects. As further elaborated in the following section, EIAs play a supportive role in MSP processes.

33 Julia Gaunce, 'On the Interpretation of the General Duty of "Due Regard"' (2018) 32(1) *Ocean Yearbook* 27; Tullio Scovazzi, '"Due Regard" Obligations, with Particular Emphasis on Fisheries in the Exclusive Economic Zone' (2019) 34(1) *The International Journal of Marine and Coastal Law* 56.

34 UNCLOS (n 14) art 60(7).

35 Woolley (n 25) 51–52.

36 IMO, *Ships' Routeing* (IMO Publications, 14th ed, 2019).

37 IMO (n 27); Secretariat of IMO, *Implications of the United Nations Convention on the Law of the Sea for the International Maritime Organization*, LEG/MISC.8. (30 January 2014).

38 Alexander Proelss and Chang Hong, 'Ocean Upwelling and International Law' (2012) 43(4) *Ocean Development & International Law* 371, 380.

Offshore wind energy and environmental impact assessment

At the heart of MSP is the coherent, integrative, and rational use of the ocean space while simultaneously preserving the marine environment. Over time, MSP became closely associated with ecosystem-based management (EBA),[39] a relationship further strengthened by the duty to carry out EIAs. The obligation to conduct an EIA is stipulated in various legal instruments, both binding and non-binding. These include the draft articles on the Prevention of Transboundary Harm from Hazardous Activities, the Convention on Environmental Impact Assessment in a Transboundary Context (Espoo Convention), UNCLOS, the Agreement on the Conservation and Sustainable Use of Marine Biological Diversity of Areas Beyond National Jurisdiction (BBNJ treaty), and the Convention on Biological Diversity.[40]

An EIA is a "national procedure for evaluating the likely impact of a proposed activity in the environment".[41] The obligation to perform an EIA is activated when a proposed activity, such as offshore wind energy development, has the potential, as per article 206 of UNCLOS, to result in "substantial pollution of or significant and harmful changes to the marine environment". From the wording of this provision, the obligation activates in light of foreseeable risk, while remote or speculative risks do not oblige the originating state to conduct an EIA.[42] The provision has been criticised for being weak since it is up to the originating state to decide the existence of this foreseeable risk and whether an impact is minor and transitory.[43]

39 UNESCO-IOC and European Commission, *MSP Global International Guide on Marine/Maritime Spatial Planning* (IOC Manuals and Guides no 89, 2021). See also, Fanny Douvere, 'The Importance of Marine Spatial Planning in Advancing Ecosystem-Based Sea Use Management' (2008) 32(5) *Marine Policy* 762, 763–765; Maes (n 12) 798. It is worth noting that the term ecosystem-based management does not have a clear-cut definition. The concept is also subject to terminological variability, including ecosystem approach, ecosystem approach to management, and ecosystem-based approach. Although some may use these terms interchangeably, others emphasise the differences between them. It is outside the scope of this chapter to discuss in detail ecosystem-based management. For a comprehensive analysis of the ecosystem approach, see Vito De Lucia, *The 'Ecosystem Approach' in International Environmental Law: Genealogy and Biopolitics* (Routledge, 2019).

40 International Law Commission, *Draft Articles on Prevention of Transboundary Harm from Hazardous Activities, with commentaries*, 53rd sess, A/56/10 (Report, 2001). Espoo Convention on Environmental Impact Assessment in a Transboundary Context, opened for signature 25 February 1991, 1989 UNTS 309; 30 ILM (entered into force 10 September 1997) ('Espoo Convention'). Agreement under the United Nations Convention on the Law of the Sea on the Conservation and Sustainable Use of Marine Biological Diversity of Areas Beyond National Jurisdiction, opened for signature 19 June 2023 (not yet in force) ('BBNJ').

41 Espoo Convention (n 40) art 1(iv).

42 *Pulp Mills on the River Uruguay (Argentina v Uruguay) (Judgment)*, 2010 ICGJ 425, [203] ('Pulp Mills').

43 Maki Tanaka, 'Lessons from the Protracted Mox Plant Dispute: A Proposed Protocol on Marine Environmental Impact Assessment to the United Nations Convention on the Law of the Sea' (2004) 25(2) *Michigan Journal of International Law* 350, 356; Alan Boyle and Cath-

The timing of an EIA is also crucial. While an EIA is usually carried out before granting an authorisation, the International Court of Justice (ICJ) in the *Pulp Mills* case[44] considered that an EIA must be conducted prior to the implementation of a proposed activity and that an environmental assessment will be continuously conducted during the whole lifespan of such a project. This means that several EIAs may be necessary.[45] In large-scale offshore wind energy projects, considerable time may pass from the authorisation and licencing until actual implementation. In that case, an EIA previously conducted should be revised or conducted again. From existing international case law, one can argue that an obligation to conduct an EIA is presumed in large-scale projects.[46]

The Convention on Biological Diversity

The 1992 Convention on Biological Diversity (CBD) is also relevant when assessing the impacts of offshore wind power structures in the marine environment. The scope of application of the CBD, concerning components of biological diversity, includes areas within national jurisdiction.[47] Those areas must be understood as comprising the marine environment, such as internal waters, territorial sea, EEZ, and the continental shelf. For processes and activities, the CBD applies to areas within and outside national jurisdiction. Article 14(a) prescribes that states will conduct an EIA when projects could "have significant adverse effects on biological diversity with a view to avoiding or minimising such effects". Arguably, such projects include offshore wind power. The wording of this article weakens the obligation to conduct EIAs by introducing the phrase "as far as possible and as appropriate". States have the discretion to decide if, for example, it is possible to conduct an EIA according to their technical and economic capacities. In 2012, the Conference of the Parties to the CBD adopted, through Decision XI/18, voluntary guidelines for the consideration of biodiversity in environmental impact assessments and strategic environmental assessments (SEAs) in marine and coastal areas.[48]

erine Redgwell, *Birnie, Boyle, & Redgwell's International Law and the Environment* (Oxford University Press, 4th ed, 2021) 197.

44 *Pulp Mills* (n 42) para 205.

45 Boyle and Redgwell (n 43) 193.

46 *Certain Activities Carried Out by Nicaragua in the Border Area (Costa Rica v Nicaragua) and Construction of a Road in Costa Rica along the San Juan River (Nicaragua v Costa Rica) (Judgment)*, 2015 ICJ Rep 665, [155].

47 Convention on Biological Diversity, opened for signature 5 June 1992, 1760 UNTS 79; 31 ILM 818 (entered into force 29 December 1993), art 4(a).

48 *Decision XI/18: Marine and coastal biodiversity: sustainable fisheries and addressing adverse impacts of human activities, voluntary guidelines for environmental assessment, and marine spatial planning*, UNEP/CBD/COP/DEC/XI/18, Eleventh Meeting of the Conference of the Parties to the Convention on Biological Diversity, Agenda item 10.2 (5 December 2012).

The Convention on the Conservation and Sustainable Use of Marine Biological Diversity of Areas Beyond National Jurisdiction

The deployment of renewable energy, including floating wind farms on the high seas, can potentially contribute towards mitigating the effects of climate change at sea.[49] Yet, large-scale offshore wind energy projects are likely to have impacts on the marine environment, making the EIA obligations established under the BBNJ treaty particularly relevant. EIA obligations are not only relevant for activities taking place in areas outside national jurisdictions. If activities within national jurisdiction are likely to cause substantial pollution or significant and harmful changes to the environment in areas beyond national jurisdiction (ABNJ), article 28(2) obliges state parties to conduct an EIA in accordance with the BBNJ or their national processes. If a party chooses to follow its national EIA procedure, it must provide information to the clearing-house mechanism. The scientific and technical body can provide comments to the party based on that information.

Article 27 of the convention includes several objectives of EIA procedures, such as the prevention, mitigation, and management of environmental impacts, the consideration of cumulative impacts, and the provision of strategic environmental assessments. The inclusion of cumulative impacts as one of the objectives of EIA is a positive step forward. According to article 1(6), cumulative impacts refer to the combined and incremental impacts resulting from different activities, as well as the consequences of climate change. The explicit reference to climate change within EIAs is unprecedented in international law. Thus, EIAs carried out under the BBNJ will be comprehensive in scope and include both the EIA process and the EIA reports.[50] The process is summarised in Figure 3.2.

The threshold for conducting an EIA is still related to the degree of harmful effects on the marine environment, which must be significant. Yet, even if the proposed activity has minor or transitory effects, or the impacts are still largely unknown, parties must still conduct the screening process described above to determine if a full EIA is required.[51] This is especially relevant for the development of new offshore renewable energy technologies and their large-scale deployment since their effects may be poorly understood. The screening process established under the BBNJ treaty can serve as a basis to foresee potential environmental impacts and support states during their MSP processes.

49 Karen Scott, 'The BBNJ Agreement: Strengthening the Oceans-Climate Nexus?' in James Kraska, Ronan Long, and Myron H Nordquist (eds), *Peaceful Maritime Engagement in East Asia and the Pacific Region* (Brill, 2022) 403, 415.

50 BBNJ (n 40) art 31, 32 and 33.

51 Ibid art 30(1).

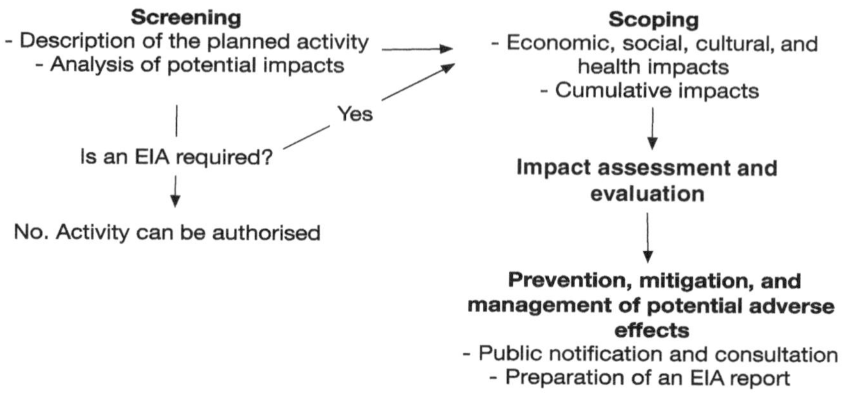

Figure 3.2 Process for EIA

Espoo Convention

According to article 2(2) of the Espoo Convention, activities that are likely to cause significant transboundary harm require an EIA. Appendix I of the convention lists the activities that fall under this category, including "major installations for the harnessing of wind power for energy production". Arguably, not all offshore wind energy projects should be subject to an EIA, only those falling under the category of "major". However, the meaning of "major installations" could be subject to debate. It appears that the originating state enjoys a certain amount of discretion when describing the scale of the project. It does not mean, however, that minor or medium-scale projects are exempt, *ipso facto*, from conducting an international EIA. Appendix III of the Espoo Convention includes criteria that states will observe to determine whether activities not listed in Appendix I should be subject to an EIA. The criteria include the size of the project, the location, and the effects. The location becomes particularly relevant if an offshore wind power farm is placed close to a frontier, near environmentally sensitive areas, or sites of archaeological, cultural, or historical relevance.

Overall, EIAs and SEAs play a vital role in identifying suitable locations for offshore renewable energy projects, potentially minimising their environmental impacts and conflicts. However, conflicts between users may still arise.

Challenges for coexistence between offshore wind power and fishing

The deployment of large-scale offshore wind power has gradually displaced fishing activities. The security of offshore wind structures and installations has been identified as a major factor driving this displacement of fisheries from their traditional grounds in Europe.[52] Notably, these conflicts also have temporal and stakeholder dimensions. Fisheries can be severely restricted during the construction, maintenance, and dismantling of offshore wind structures, while coexistence could be promoted during the operation of the wind farms.[53] This section evaluates the impact of protective measures on the coexistence of wind power and fisheries.

Protective measures of offshore installations in the territorial sea

Offshore wind power tends to occupy large areas of ocean space. It requires structures above sea level, in the water column, and on the seabed. These generating units are then connected to the transmission grid through submarine cables. Arguably, in the territorial sea, the coastal state can decide among various protective measures that safeguard offshore wind power structures and installations from accidental damage while simultaneously allowing the possibility of coexistence with fisheries to the maximum extent. For example, a coastal state may designate sea lanes, traffic separation schemes, or security zones. For this designation, article 22(3) of UNCLOS prescribes that the coastal state must take into account the following:

(a) the recommendations of the IMO;
(b) any channels customarily used for international navigation;
(c) the special characteristics of particular ships and channels; and
(d) the density of traffic.

From this provision, it becomes evident that the safeguard of navigation enjoys priority consideration.

Generally, fishing could still take place outside wind farms, provided that specific gear is used to prevent damage to submarine cables. In such cases, fisheries would coexist passively with offshore wind power. The coastal state may still permit fishing when security zones are established around offshore wind structures. This authorisation may be granted under certain navigation conditions, such as visibility and speed, and contingent upon the characteristics of the vessels, including their length and fishing gear.

Scientific evidence points out that wind power structures and installations may serve as artificial reefs. This means that offshore structures add new hard substrates for the colonisation of marine species that use these structures as

52 Clément Dupont, Frédérick Herpers, and Christophe Le Visage, *Recommendations for Positive Interactions Between Offshore Wind Farms and Fisheries: Short Background Study* (European Commission on Maritime Affairs and Fisheries No EA-03-20-493-EN-N, 2020), 1, 10–11; Gert Van Hoey et al., *Overview of the Effects of Offshore Wind Farms on Fisheries and Aquaculture* (European Commission, EASME/EMFF/2018/011 Lot 1, 2021), 1, 69.

53 Van Hoey (n 52) 26.

nursery areas. This results in an increase in the biological diversity and density of specific species in the area.[54] Even if scientific evidence points to the existence of the reef effect, not every stakeholder agrees with its potential benefit. In a report conducted on behalf of the Crown Estate Scotland, fishermen disagreed on the actual positive effects of offshore structures on fisheries activities.[55] In planning multi-use ocean spaces, stakeholders' perception of such an effect is also relevant. Marine planners should make explicit to fishing stakeholders the circumstances under which the reef effect may have spillover effects for fisheries.

Protective measures of offshore installations in the EEZ

In the EEZ, safety zones are available as protective measures to maintain the physical integrity of offshore installations. Around generating units, coastal states have the discretionary power to establish "reasonable" safety zones that must not exceed a distance of 500 m, as prescribed in article 60(4)-(7) of UNCLOS. Article 60 applies *mutatis mutandis* to the continental shelf.[56] Safety zones' limits could be extended if there are internationally accepted standards or by recommendation of the IMO,[57] and such assessment is done on a case-by-case basis.[58] According to article 60(4), the legislative jurisdiction in safety zones is limited to measures to ensure the safety of navigation and the offshore installation. Article 60(6) also makes reference to navigation taking place in the vicinity of safety zones: "All ships must respect these safety zones and shall comply with generally accepted international standards regarding navigation in the vicinity of artificial islands, installations, structures and safety zones."

This provision was drafted to prevent accidental allisions and damage to the infrastructure.[59] For this reason, some states prohibit fishing and navigation altogether or do not allow fishing with active gear. Others prohibit fishing even with passive equipment. Further temporal restrictions may occur while offshore structures and installations are built, maintained, and decommissioned. If fishing is allowed, one should consider vessel length, visibility, and gear. To ensure the safety of navigation, coastal states must keep their

54 Olivia Langhamer, 'Artificial Reef Effect in Relation to Offshore Renewable Energy Conversion: State of the Art' (2012) 2012 *The Scientific World Journal* 1, 2; Maria Glarou, Martine Zrust, and Jon Svendsen, 'Using Artificial-Reef Knowledge to Enhance the Ecological Function of Offshore Wind Turbine Foundations: Implications for Fish Abundance and Diversity' (2020) 8(332) *Journal of Marine Science and Engineering* 1, 10.

55 Mark Gray, Paige-Leanne Stromberg, and Dale Rodmell, 'Changes to fishing practices around the UK as a result of the development of offshore windfarms – Phase 1 (Revised)' (Report, 2016).

56 UNCLOS (n 14) art 80.

57 Ibid art 60(5).

58 Kashubsky (n 25) 187.

59 Ibid.

nautical charts[60] updated.[61] Regarding the safety of navigation around offshore installations and structures, the IMO recommends that coastal states examine shipping traffic patterns in areas relevant to resource exploitation (e.g. wind power) to determine potential interference with shipping transiting at an early stage close to or through identified areas.[62]

Protecting cables lying on the seabed is a challenge for the coexistence between offshore wind power and fishing. Accidental cable damage by fishing gear and anchors is a common source of conflict.[63] For example, the International Hydrographic Organization (IHO) recommends that vessels (including fishing fleets) avoid operating within 0.25 nautical miles on either side of submarine cables.[64]

Challenges for coexistence between offshore wind power and marine aquaculture

Unlike fisheries, which have been subject to progressive displacement due to the establishment and operation of offshore wind power, marine aquaculture has been identified as an ocean use with extensive active coexistence capacity since offshore wind structures and installations can be used to attach marine aquaculture systems. Despite this potential, this section examines the potential hurdles to the coexistence of offshore wind power and aquaculture.

Environmental and safety risks

Due to the territorial sovereignty that coastal states enjoy in internal waters and the territorial sea, marine aquaculture is subject to national regulation.[65] At the same time, in the EEZ, article 56(a) of UNCLOS provides for the sovereign right of coastal states to explore, exploit, and conserve natural resources. The introduction of invasive species and diseases is an area of special concern for the development of marine aquaculture projects. For instance, invasive algae may enter the marine environment through aquaculture and fishing equip-

60 Regulation 2(2) – Chapter V of the SOLAS Convention defines a nautical chart as "a special-purpose map or book ... issued officially by or on the authority of a Government ... designed to meet the requirements of maritime navigation". International Convention for the Safety of Life at Sea, opened for signature 1 November 1974, 32 UST 47; 1184 UNTS 278 (entered into force 25 May 1980).

61 Ibid Chapter V, Regulation 9.

62 IMO, *Resolution A.671(16): Safety Zones and Safety of Navigation around Offshore Installations and Structures*, Assembly – 16th session, Agenda item 1 (adopted 19 October 1989).

63 European MSP Platform, *Conflict fiche 2: Cables/pipelines and commercial fisheries/shipping* (Web Page) https://maritime-spatial-planning.ec.europa.eu/sites/default/files/2_cables_fisheries-revised_0.pdf ('European MSP Platform').

64 International Hydrographic Organization, *Resolutions of the International Hydrographic Organization* (Publication M-3, 2nd edn, updated August 2018).

65 UNCLOS (n 14) arts 2 and 3.

ment, including cages and ropes, while other species may escape aquaculture devices.[66] Thus, marine aquaculture planning needs to consider the species that, if introduced, will not endanger the functioning of such marine areas. In this regard, article 196(1) of UNCLOS places a twofold obligation on coastal states to

> control pollution of the marine environment resulting from the use of technologies under their jurisdiction or control, or the intentional or accidental introduction of species, alien or new, to a particular part of the marine environment, which may cause significant and harmful changes.

Although the CBD does not deal specifically with marine aquaculture, the convention establishes an obligation in article 8(h) to prevent the introduction of alien species. Furthermore, the Conference of the Parties to the CBD has made several decisions over the years recommending that the parties use native species while developing marine aquaculture.[67] The coexistence of offshore wind power and aquaculture in multi-use ocean spaces could lead to conflicts with shipping. Attaching aquaculture systems to offshore wind power infrastructure may also pose a risk to navigation safety, as the likelihood of collisions between supply vessels and allisions may increase.

Removal of offshore wind installations and structures

At the end of their operative life, offshore wind power structures and installations are to be removed to ensure the safety of navigation and prevent marine environment pollution. Decommissioning is not a standardised process and can be subject to several of the following operations:[68]

1. Complete removal of structures and installations found on the seabed and in the water column.
2. Clear seabed refers to removing structures and installations, including underwater transmission cables and debris, to allow fisheries, including trawling.
3. Partial removal refers to structures and installations left on the seabed or in the water column.

66 Sabine Rech et al., 'Dispersal of Alien Invasive Species on Anthropogenic Litter from European Mariculture Areas' (2018) 131 (Part A) *Marine Pollution Bulletin* 10.

67 Convention on Biological Diversity, *Decision IX/4: In-depth review of ongoing work on alien species that threaten ecosystems, habitats or species*, 9th mtg, Agenda item 3.3, UN Doc UNEP/CBD/COP/DEC/IX/4 (9 October 2008).

68 Ove Arup and Partners Ltd, *Review of Approaches and Costs of Decommissioning Offshore Wind Installations Edinburgh* (Report, 13 April 2018) 1, 11.

Yet, this obligation may conflict with marine aquaculture coexistence in cases where aquaculture systems are attached to these structures. For preserving aquaculture, one may argue that offshore structures are still being used as an "artificial reef". In this case, important legal questions remain to be addressed, including whether the aquaculture industry will become responsible for the maintenance of offshore structures and whether a partial decommission generates further conflicts with other ocean uses, including navigation and fisheries.

The procedure for decommissioning offshore wind power installations and structures in the territorial sea is left to national law. Arguably, safeguarding the safety of navigation in the territorial sea includes an obligation on the coastal state to regulate the removal of these installations and structures at the end of their operative life. Such regulation should also have procedures in cases where the structures and installations are abandoned.

In the EEZ, article 60(3) of UNCLOS prescribes that installations and structures abandoned or disused should be removed, taking into account international standards established, for example, by the IMO. The removal should "have due regard to fishing, the protection of the marine environment, and the rights and duties of other states".[69] The coastal state may consider a partial removal if marine aquaculture depends on existing offshore structures. One may argue that structures used for marine aquaculture cannot be considered abandoned or disused even if they can no longer generate electricity. The IMO Guidelines and Standards for the Removal of Offshore Installations and Structures on the Continental Shelf and in the Exclusive Economic Zone also consider the possibility of partial removal if the structure serves a subsequent new use.[70]

Although the convention allows partial removal, article 60(3) of UNCLOS explicitly mentions that coastal states are responsible for providing appropriate publicity of any remaining offshore infrastructure's depth, position, and dimensions. Any remaining infrastructure may continue supporting marine aquaculture but could exacerbate conflicts with fisheries. In this scenario, the role of marine planners and their relationship with diverse stakeholders are fundamental. Overall, under international law, there is no absolute obligation to conduct a complete removal unless the safety of navigation is at stake. Arguably, coastal states may allow partial dismantling to keep aquaculture and to preserve "the reef effect" of the offshore structures.

Additionally, states are obligated to prevent pollution of the marine environment from various sources, including dumping.[71] According to article 1(5) of UNCLOS, dumping refers to any deliberate disposal of wastes at sea.

69 UNCLOS (n 14) art 60(3).

70 IMO, *Resolution A.672(16) Guidelines and Standards for the Removal of Offshore Installations and Structures on the Continental Shelf and in the Exclusive Economic Zone,* 16th sess, Agenda item 10 (adopted 19 October 1989), para 1, sub para 1.2.

71 UNCLOS (n 14) arts 194 and 210.

Specifically, the abandonment of offshore structures at sea *for the sole purpose of deliberate disposal* is considered dumping under the 1996 London Protocol to the Convention on the Prevention of Marine Pollution by Dumping of Wastes and other Matter.[72] One may argue that under the dumping regime, states parties must completely remove offshore wind structures and installations at the end of their operative life to prevent pollution of the marine environment. However, partial removal is still possible because such remaining structures are left in the marine environment *not for disposal* but to continue an alternative use, such as aquaculture.

National experiences: coexistence between wind power and fishing

Establishment and licensing of offshore wind power structures and installations

Germany has a major offshore wind power market development where most of its structures are found in the EEZ. Currently, offshore wind power occupies around 1129 km^2 of its EEZ.[73] Offshore wind power has been considered within the national MSP. The Spatial Planning Act (ROG) constitutes the legal basis for planning the EEZ, and the latest plan entered into force in 2021.[74] In relation to the development of offshore wind power, the MSP process aims to facilitate co-use with other users of the sea.[75] For example, the plan requires that fishing vessels can navigate through offshore wind parks, while passive fishing is also allowed within safety zones.[76]

Germany has also enacted the 2017 Offshore Wind Energy Act (WindSeeG). Its scope of application is mainly the EEZ, where the federal government exercises jurisdiction. Specifically, the Maritime and Hydrographic Agency (BSH) oversees the planning and licencing activities. The Act applies incidentally to the territorial sea and the high seas.[77] In the territorial sea, jurisdiction

72 *Protocol to the Convention on the Prevention of Marine Pollution by Dumping of Wastes and Other Matter*, opened for signature 7 November 1996, 36 ILM 7 (entered into force 24 March 2006).

73 Maximilian Felix Schupp et al., 'Fishing within Offshore Wind Farms in the North Sea: Stakeholder Perspectives for Multi-Use from Scotland and Germany' (2021) 279(111762) *Journal of Environmental Management* 1, 2.

74 Verordnung über die Raumordnung in der deutschen ausschließlichen Wirtschaftszone in der Nordsee und in der Ostsee (AWZROV) Ordinance on Spatial Planning in the German Exclusive Economic Zone in the North Sea and the Baltic Sea 19 August 2021, BGBl. I S. 3886.

75 'Spatial Plan for the German Exclusive Economic Zone in the North Sea and in the Baltic Sea,' *Annex Volume to the Federal Law Gazette*, Part I, No 58, 26 August 2021, 9.

76 Ibid 11.

77 Gesetz zur Entwicklung und Förderung der Windenergie auf See (WindSeeG) Offshore Wind Energy Act (13 October 2016) BGBl. I S. 2258.

Figure 3.3 Relevant German legislation applicable to offshore wind power

is bestowed upon coastal *Länder*.[78] Other relevant legislation is illustrated in Figure 3.3.

The legislation evinces a choice to establish offshore wind power structures and installations in close proximity, also known as "clusters".[79] Yet, one should be cautious about placing critical infrastructure close together since the risks of major accidental and wilful damage increase.

From the WindSeeG and the planning process for constructing and operating wind power farms in Germany's EEZ, one may conclude that shipping and military activities are highly prioritised marine uses. The protection of the marine environment is also a legislative priority. However, the coexistence between offshore wind power and fisheries is not the main objective. Table 3.1 illustrates how WindSeeG gives special consideration to the protection of the marine environment, shipping, and the military.

China is the global leader in expanding its offshore wind power capacity,[80] with significant developments in the southeast region, specifically in Jiangsu, Zhejiang, Fujian, and Guangdong.[81] While most projects are located in the EEZ,[82] the future expansion of offshore wind power projects includes the high seas with investment in "large-scale high-altitude wind turbines".[83] The authority in charge of marine spatial planning in China is the State Oceanic

78 Anne Marie O'Hagan, 'Regulation of Marine Renewable Energy' in Robin Warner and Stuart Kaye (eds), *Routledge Handbook of Maritime Regulation and Enforcement* (Routledge, 2016) 295, 308.

79 Federal Maritime and Hydrographic Agency (BSH), *Spatial Offshore Grid Plan* (Web Page) <https://www.bsh.de/EN/TOPICS/Offshore/Sectoral_planning/Spatial-offshore-grid-plan/spatial_offshore_grid_plan_node.html>.

80 Rafael Monteiro de Vasconcelos et al., 'Environmental Licensing for Offshore Wind Farms: Guidelines and Policy Implications for New Markets' (2022) 177(113248) *Energy Policy* 1.

81 Energy Research Institute of Academy of Macroeconomic Research, *China Renewable Energy Outlook* (Report, 2019) 1, 75.

82 Ling Ou et al., 'Offshore Wind Zoning in China: Method and Experience' (2018) 151 *Ocean and Coastal Management* 99, 106.

83 Ibid 233.

Table 3.1 Wind farms and balance with other marine uses

Activity	*Shipping*	*Military*	*Environment*	*Other uses*
Site development plans	Cannot impair the safety of navigation or the efficiency of transport	Cannot impair the security or defence of Germany and the Alliance (NATO)	Should not endanger the marine environment and cannot be located in a protected area	Criteria for the stipulation of the sites should consider conflicts of use
	Section 5 (3.3)	Section 5 (3.4)	Section 5 (3.2 and 3.5(a))	Section 5 (4.4). Here, the interests of fisheries can be taken into account
Responsibilities for drawing up the site development plan	The site development plan must be produced by consensus between the BSH and the Federal Network Agency and in coordination with the Federal Agency for Nature Conservation, the Federal Waterways and Shipping Agency, and the coastal *Länder*. Section 6(7) Once again, the marine environment and shipping are explicitly considered in the site development plan			

Administration,[84] which, through marine function zoning (MFZ), aims to manage the ocean space comprehensively. MFZ identifies functional zones considering the area's socioeconomic and environmental conditions.[85] More specifically, MFZ has an adaptive governance perspective since it is an iterative process that started in the late 1970s. In 2021, the zoning system was consolidated into the National Territorial Spatial Planning framework for the period 2021–2035.[86] Potential coexistence between several marine uses is also considered in the MFZ process. As a result, offshore wind energy is included in two functional zones: marine renewable energy and fisheries zones.[87] Areas dedicated to offshore wind energy development also focus on the potential coexistence of wind energy and other marine uses.

84 About the institution, see (Web Page) <http://english.www.gov.cn/state_council/2014/10/06/content_281474992889983.htm>.

85 Xin Teng et al., 'Implementing Marine Functional Zoning in China' (2021) 132(103484) *Marine Policy* 1.

86 Charles Ehler, 'Two decades of progress in Marine Spatial Planning' (2021) 132(104134) *Marine Policy* 1, 8.

87 Ou et al. (n 82) 100.

The Renewable Energy Law of the People's Republic of China[88] applies to all maritime zones within the national jurisdiction,[89] and the Energy Administration Department is the authority responsible for renewable energy.[90] However, the legislation focuses solely on renewable energy and does not explicitly consider potential conflicts with other marine users nor provide mechanisms to prioritise among uses. Although the Renewable Energy Law does not prioritise marine uses, the Detailed Rules for the Implementation of the Interim Measures for the Management of Offshore Wind Power Development and Construction gives express priority to the environment, significant fishery areas, shipping, and military activities since offshore wind power cannot be planned in marine protected areas, nor can it hinder maritime safety and national defence.[91] Additionally, the 14th Five-Year Plan for marine economic development prioritises marine environmental protection in the planning process.[92] Yet, it is uncertain how this policy objective is translated into legislative acts. One may also argue that such a conflict assessment has already been carried out during MFZ since offshore wind plans must be consistent with the zoning process.[93] However, Huang argues that wind speed is the most relevant factor in identifying areas for offshore wind projects, followed by environmental considerations and coexistence with other uses.[94]

In Scotland, the licencing system for marine activities has been streamlined, with the Marine Licencing Operations Team (MS-LOT) as the central governmental body overseeing the entire process.[95] The 2010 Marine (Scotland) Act[96] is the relevant legislation for projects located in the territorial sea, while the 2009 Marine Coastal Access Act[97] is concerned with projects in the EEZ. The Acts introduced a simplified licencing process to support offshore wind

88 可再生能源法 Renewable Energy Law of the People's Republic of China adopted at the 14th Meeting of the Standing Committee of the Tenth National People's Congress on February 28, 2005; Amended according to the Decision of the 12th Meeting of the Standing Committee of the 11th National People's Congress of the People's Republic of China on December 26, 2009. The legislation is available at (Web Page) <http://www.npc.gov.cn/zgrdw/englishnpc/Law/2007-12/13/content_1384096.htm>.

89 Ibid art. 3.

90 Ibid art. 8.

91 See art. 5 of the Detailed Rules for the Implementation of the Interim Measures for the Management of Offshore Wind Power Development and Construction, available at (Web Page) <https://www.fao.org/faolex/results/details/zh/c/LEX-FAOC141039/> ('Detailed Rules').

92 Ruru Jia, Jinwu Gao, and Feng Gao, 'Robust Ocean Zoning for Conservation, Fishery and Marine Renewable Energy with Co-Location Strategy' (2022) 328(120166) *Applied Energy* 1, 2.

93 Detailed Rules (n 91) art 5.

94 Jie Huang et al., 'Evaluation of the Spatial Suitability of Offshore Wind Farm: A Case Study of the Sea Area of Liaoning Province' (2022) 14(449) *Sustainability* 1, 14.

95 O'Hagan (n 78) 310.

96 Marine (Scotland) Act, SS 2010.

97 Marine Coastal Access Act, RSUK 2009, c 23.

power development. A single marine licence substitutes licences required by several legislative acts concerning food, the environment, and coast protection.[98] In the case of offshore wind power, two permissions are required: a marine licence according to Part 4, Section 35 of the Marine (Scotland) Act and Part 4, Section 79 of the Marine and Coastal Access Act, and consent for the construction of generating stations as established under Section 36 of the Electricity Act. The applications can be made simultaneously and can be considered together.

In the decision to grant a marine licence, the Scottish ministers must have due regard to preventing interference with legitimate uses of the sea.[99] The reference to other marine uses is wide enough to include fishing and aquaculture. From the wording of this legislative Act, it is uncertain how interference should be prevented. The Scottish Government has actively assessed fisheries displacement by other licensed marine activities.[100] The use of a fisheries management and mitigation strategy (FMMS) has become standard practice during the application process. An FMMS is a condition to obtain a marine licence and consent for the construction of generating stations[101] since it allows for the development from an early stage of a co-location plan. An FMMS includes, for example, economic reparation for fisheries when their activities are halted during the construction and maintenance of offshore wind power installations and structures.[102] The Fishing Liaison with Offshore Wind and Wet Renewables Group (FLOWW) was adopted in 2002 as best practice to maximise the possibility of coexistence.[103] FLOWW fosters cooperation between the offshore and fishing industries from the earliest possible time in the planning phase.

In Scotland, maritime safety can affect the status of a marine licence. According to Part 4, Section 30(3.c) of the Marine (Scotland) Act, a marine licence can be subject to variation, suspension, or revocation in the "interests of safety of navigation". Consent for any offshore generating activities may not be granted if those activities interfere with the use of recognised sea lanes essential to international navigation.[104] Nonetheless, once consent for the construction of generating stations is given, shipping may be subject to several

98 O'Hagan (n 78) 310.
99 Marine (Scotland) Act (n 96) part 4, section 27(1.a.).
100 Marine Scotland, *Good Practice Guidance for assessing fisheries displacement by other licensed marine activities: Literature Review* (Report, June 2022).
101 Marine Scotland, *Guidance on preparing a Fisheries Management and Mitigation Strategy* (2020); F Nimmo, S MacNab, and T Huntington, *Co-existence of Capture Fisheries and Marine Aquaculture: Review of Measures for Improved Co-existence with Recommendations for Adoption in Scotland* (Report, May 2022).
102 Nimmo, MacNab, and Huntington (n 101).
103 Fishing Liaison with Offshore Wind and Wet Renewables Group (FLOWW), *Best Practice Guidance for Offshore Renewables Developments: Recommendations for Fisheries Liaison* (January 2014).
104 See Electricity Act, RSUK 1989, c 29, s 36B.

restrictions. Section 36A of the Electricity Act prescribes that navigation rights could be extinguished, suspended, or exercisable subject to conditions.

Safety zones

Since the international legal framework in an EEZ grants states the discretionary power to establish safety zones around installations and structures, some European states have taken regulatory steps to promote coexistence with fisheries. In the UK, fishing is only prohibited during the construction and maintenance of offshore structures. For example, during the construction phase, 500 m safety zones are placed around active building sites, where activities are physically taking place. Only those areas (not the whole project area) are fisheries excluded.[105] In Germany, safety zones can be established to ensure the safety of navigation. In this case, the agreement of the Federal Waterways and Shipping Agency is required. If safety zones are not established, fishing vessels may still operate in these zones. However, allision risks do exist. In China, safety buffers may also limit fisheries.[106]

In the UK, 50 m safety zones may be placed around offshore installations and structures during offshore wind farm operations. Apparently, fishing vessels may return to their fishing grounds, but some evidence points to the contrary. FLOWW clarifies that safety zones cannot be regarded automatically as exclusion zones. In general, safety zones should be temporary in nature, covering construction, maintenance, and decommissioning phases.[107] Even if fisheries are not prohibited from taking place inside offshore wind farms, UK fishermen pointed out that fishing in those areas diminishes because of safety and insurance considerations, including, for example, the risk of allisions with wind structures, and damage to seabed cables and fishing nets.[108]

Cable protection

To allow the coexistence of fisheries and offshore wind power, the German offshore grid plan in the EEZ includes the implementation of corridors for cables and pipelines. Based on the Energy Industry Act (Energiewirtschaftsgesetzes [EnWG]), such a task is exclusively trusted to the Federal Maritime and Hydrographic Agency.[109] Having only one authority in charge of planning expedites the process. A similar policy has been pursued in Scotland, where cable corridors are planned and fishing is allowed "along the offshore export cables".[110]

105 Dupont, Herpers, and Le Visage (n 52); Schupp et al. (n 73).
106 Ou et al. (n 82) 105.
107 Fishing Liaison with Offshore Wind and Wet Renewables Group (FLOWW) (n 103).
108 Gray, Stromberg and Rodmell (n 55); Van Hoey (n 52).
109 Federal Maritime and Hydrographic Agency (BSH) (n 79).
110 Schupp et al. (n 73) 3.

National experiences: coexistence between wind power and marine aquaculture

Large-scale marine aquaculture is yet to be realised and therefore legal progress is also scarce. Whether such development will take place is also dependent on national planning. Scotland has identified the possibility of expanding both shellfish and seaweed within an area of six nautical miles from the coast.[111] It has also been suggested that aquaculture activities need to formalise the use of guidelines similar to those developed with the fishing industry, such as the Fishing Liaison with Offshore Wind and Wet Renewables Group and the use of a fisheries management and mitigation strategy. Developing such guidelines for marine aquaculture as a best practice is still pending.[112]

Germany is also a pioneer in developing marine aquaculture and pursuing co-location with offshore wind farms. Pilot projects have taken place mainly at the German Bight.[113] Maritime safety is the main hindrance to developing offshore marine aquaculture because ample corridors to allow the navigation of commercial shipping must be available.[114] If marine aquaculture expands in those areas, not only will the corridors be reduced, but more supply and service vessels will operate in the offshore wind farm. Such expansion could increase collision and allision risks. A suggested alternative is prioritising extractive aquaculture, such as seaweed and bivalves, rather than feed aquaculture like fish. The former is low maintenance and will require fewer service vessels.[115]

China is interested in relocating aquaculture systems to deeper waters, and offshore wind power projects could be used to develop these aquaculture systems. According to Baiyu, an offshore wind power project built in Pingtan is co-used with aquaculture.[116] Of course, cages attached to offshore structures can negatively impact shipping and fisheries by increasing allision risks.

Conclusion

As human activities in the marine space intensify, so do user–user and user–environment conflicts. MSP is an area-based management tool that emerged as a potential solution to alleviate existing conflicts at sea. However, MSP must be implemented in accordance with the jurisdictional framework established

111 Nimmo, MacNab, and Hungtington (n 101) 3.

112 Ibid 13.

113 Bela Buck et al., 'The German Case Study: Pioneer Projects of Aquaculture-Wind Farm Multi-Uses' in Bela Buck and Richard Langan (eds), *Aquaculture Perspective of Multi-Use Sites in the Open Ocean: The Untapped Potential for Marine Resources in the Anthropocene* (Springer, 2017) 253, 25–26.

114 Ibid 339–342.

115 Schultz-Zehden (n 10) 18.

116 Gao Baiyu, 'Chinese companies explore joint wind and fish farms', *China Dialogue Ocean* (Blog Post) https://chinadialogueocean.net/en/fisheries/20062-chinese-companies-explore-joint-wind-and-fish-farms/.

under UNCLOS; planning cannot be used to extend coastal state jurisdiction at sea. While coastal states enjoy full sovereignty in internal waters and territorial seas, facilitating MSP, the EEZ presents challenges due to the functional nature of the zone.

The coexistence between offshore wind power and fisheries depends not only on how to use safety zones or cable routing efficiently. Even if fishing is not prohibited within offshore wind farms, the fishery industry is exposed to liability for collision and damage to submarine cables. It appears that the best available practices for fishing within offshore wind farms should be further developed. Additionally, liability and insurance systems for cable damage and allision/collision need further investigation.

The obligations to protect cables may limit the possibility of coexistence between wind power and fisheries. Several alternatives can be pursued to favour such coexistence, including cable routing, cable burial, shorter cable routes, best practices for fisheries within wind farms, non-anchoring areas or areas to be avoided, minimising trawling, and larger corridors between generating turbines.[117]

For cable routing, MSP can be used to initiate a co-creation process, including not only public authorities but also industry stakeholders. However, the International Cable Protection Committee (ICPC) is sceptical of the development of cable routing since the marine environment is increasingly crowded and such routes do not effectively provide sufficient space between submarine cables and fishing activities.[118] More importantly, grouping a growing number of critical seabed infrastructures in the same geographical location increases the risk of natural, accidental, and wilful damage. Further research is required concerning the protection of critical infrastructure.

The development of multi-use spaces should be seen as an iterative process that could provide resilience to the international law of the sea by promoting the development of adaptive and flexible legal frameworks. With the intensification of human use of the marine environment, conflicts between several marine users will become more common. Coexistence is a necessary first step to ensure that benefits and risks are distributed among different ocean users. However, significant issues remain to be tackled, such as how to balance various policy objectives, including energy security, environmental protection, and economic prosperity. It is also crucial to investigate the legal, political, and ethical aspects that are considered (or not) when prioritising marine uses.

117 Stephanie Moura, Andy Lipsky, and Molly Morse, *Options for Cooperation between Commercial Fishing and Offshore Wind Energy Industries: A Review of Relevant Tools and Best Practices* (November 2015); European MSP Platform (n 63); International Cable Protection Committee, *Government Best Practices for Protecting and Promoting Resilience of Submarine Telecommunications Cables* (Version 1.2.).

118 International Cable Protection Committee (n 117).

4 Regulating deep-sea mining for critical minerals

A "wicked problem" of the Anthropocene?

David Leary

Introduction

The challenges of climate change and the need to rapidly decarbonise our economy are driving massive investment in renewable energy generation for electricity, battery storage, and the electrification of the transport sector. The rapid uptake of these technological solutions to climate change, along with growth in the demand for minerals for a range of other technologies, such as smartphones and computers, is driving the increase in demand for minerals, especially nickel, cobalt, manganese, lithium, and rare earth minerals. Rare earth minerals include a group of minerals containing 17 metallic elements including lanthanum, lutetium, yttrium, scandium, and europium.[1] Contrary to their name, rare earth minerals are found in abundance in the Earth's crust, but are regarded as "rare" because they have only been found in a few locations in sufficient quantity, concentration, form, and setting to make mining economically viable.[2]

The available evidence suggests terrestrial sources of these minerals may be unable to meet the demands of current and projected future uses. However, these minerals are found in abundance on the deep ocean floor beyond national jurisdiction, in the part of the ocean known under the 1982 United Nations Convention on the Law of the Sea[3] (UNCLOS) and the subsequent 1994 Agreement relating to the Implementation of Part XI of the United Nations Convention on the Law of the Sea[4] (Part XI Agreement) as the "Area".[5] In addition to more common minerals such as nickel, copper, and magnesium, manganese nodules found in the Area have significant concentrations of cobalt,

1 The Geological Society of London, *Rare Earth Elements. A briefing note by the Geological Society of London* (Briefing note, December 2011) 2.

2 Ibid.

3 United Nations Convention on the Law of the Sea, 10 December 1982, 21 ILM 1245 (1982) ('UNCLOS').

4 Agreement relating to the Implementation of Part XI of the United Nations Convention on the Law of the Sea of 10 December 1982, 28 July 1994, 33 ILM 1309 ('Part XI Agreement').

5 Article 1(1) of UNCLOS defines the Area as "the seabed and ocean floor and subsoil thereof, beyond the limits of national jurisdiction".

DOI: 10.4324/9781003518570-4

lithium, molybdenum, rare earth elements, yttrium, and zirconium.[6] Cobalt crusts found in the Area also contain bismuth, molybdenum, niobium, potassium, rare earth elements, tellurium, thorium, titanium, tungsten, yttrium, and zirconium.[7] In volcanic arc environments, high concentrations of arsenic, cadmium, gallium, germanium, antimony, and selenium have also been identified.[8] Hence, the interest in mining in the Area.

Herein lies a dilemma. In addressing the significant threats and challenges of climate change, a major aspect of the technological solution involves expanding renewable energy sources and developing new technologies such as battery storage and electric cars. However, this expansion raises a whole new set of environmental challenges. In essence, dealing with climate change and regulating deep-sea mining are two wicked environmental challenges that are closely intertwined. While we focus on tackling climate change as one environmental challenge, our technological solutions are creating a new challenge: how to manage the environmental impacts of deep-sea mining.

This chapter explores the close relationship between the wicked problems of addressing climate change and regulating the environmental impact of deep-sea mining. The collision of the imperative of decarbonising the economy, driving the renewed interest in deep-sea mining, raises questions about the resilience of the law of the sea to navigate the challenges ahead and to facilitate those activities in an environmentally sustainable manner. In essence, climate change is fundamentally raising concerns about the resilience of the UNCLOS mining regime designed in the 1960s, 1970s, and early 1980s to respond to the environmental challenges of deep-sea mining in the present decade and beyond. The chapter argues that while many of the institutional mechanisms for regulating mining in the Area may be in place, the work of the International Seabed Authority (ISA) in developing effective regulation of the environmental impact of mining in the deep sea is very much falling behind where it should be, given that the first commercial mining is planned to commence in the next few years. This raises the question of how mining can proceed in the absence of appropriate environmental regulation. The chapter also focuses attention on the implications of Nauru's decision in 2021 to pull the "trigger" mechanism[9] and the resilience of the mining regime in the face of calls for a moratorium on deep-sea mining.

The chapter is divided into five parts. Following this introduction, the second part explores how our technological solutions to climate change are driving renewed interest in deep-sea minerals. The third part then examines the

6 James Hein, Kira Mizell, Andrea Koschinsky, and Tracey Conrad, 'Deep-Ocean Mineral Deposits as a Source of Critical Metals for High- and Green-Technology Applications: Comparison with Land-based Resources' (2013) 51 *Ore Geology Reviews* 1, 2.

7 Ibid.

8 Ibid 21.

9 Part XI Agreement (n 4) Annex, s 1, para 15.

mandate of the ISA. The fourth part considers the progress made by the ISA on the development of regulations for the management of the environmental impact of mining pursuant to that mandate. The final part of the chapter offers some concluding thoughts on the resilience of the law of the sea and its ability to navigate the challenges of an uncertain future.

Deep-sea minerals and the Anthropocene

Many social scientists and lawyers argue that we now live in the Anthropocene, an era in which human actions and activities have shaped our global climate and dramatically changed ecosystems.[10] While science still debates whether we are living in a new geological epoch called the Anthropocene, it is clear that human activities across the globe are dramatically impacting the world around us.[11]

Under the provisions of the Paris Agreement on Climate Change,[12] state parties have committed to "holding the increase in the global average temperature to well below 2°C above pre-industrial levels and pursuing efforts to limit the temperature increase to 1.5°C above pre-industrial levels".[13]

Despite this commitment, the combined pledges of 193 parties to the Paris Agreement are projected to steer the world towards temperature increases ranging from 2.1°C to 2.9°C by the end of the century.[14] More drastic cuts in greenhouse gas emissions need to be achieved to meet the 1.5°C goal and to avoid catastrophic climate change. Significant decarbonisation of both the electricity and transport sectors is imperative.[15]

Renewable energy, in conjunction with other measures such as energy efficiency, is projected to play a significant role in reaching the Paris Agreement goals. In order to achieve these goals, modelling by the International Renewable Energy Agency suggests that "the electricity sector will have to be thoroughly decarbonised by mid-century, with solar and wind leading the

10 On the Anthropocene and the law of the sea, see Davor Vidas, 'The Anthropocene and the International Law of the Sea' (2011) 369 *Philosophical Transaction: Mathematical, Physical and Engineering Sciences*, 909.

11 In relation to the Anthropocene among geologists, see Sid Perkins, 'Researchers Move Closer to Defining the Anthropocene' (2023) 120 (29*) Proceedings of the National Academy of Sciences of the United States of America*, 1.

12 *Paris Agreement on Climate Change*, opened for signature (22 April 2016), [2016] ATS 24 (entered into force 4 November 2016) ('Paris Agreement').

13 Ibid, Article 2(1)(a).

14 United Nations Framework Convention on Climate Change, *Nationally determined contributions under the Paris Agreement-Synthesis report by the secretariat*, UN Doc. FCCC/PA/CMA/2022/4 (26 Oct 2022), para 17.

15 International Energy Agency, *Energy sector is central to efforts to combat climate change* (Web Page) <https://www.iea.org/topics/climate-change>.

transformation".[16] The expanded use of low-carbon technologies such as electric vehicles (EVs) in the transport sector will also have a role to play in decarbonising transport systems. EV technology is now mature, and significant growth in EV sales is expected in the coming years. In 2021 alone, EV sales broke new records, with 10% of all new car sales globally being EVs, representing four times their market share in 2019.[17] The increased usage of EVs in conjunction with low-carbon electricity generation, such as renewable energy, will not only bring reductions in greenhouse gas emissions and other forms of pollution but also offer other environmental, societal, and health benefits.[18]

A further positive consequence of the growth of EVs is that it is enabling major cost reductions in battery technology that have a range of applications in other sectors such as electricity generation and storage.[19] A recent analysis by the International Renewable Energy Agency has observed that there is a very clear and synergistic link between the growth in EVs and the decarbonisation of the electricity system.[20]

The rapid growth in renewable energy generation for electricity, the growth in EVs in the transport sector, and the continual improvement in battery storage technology are all positive advancements towards decarbonisation. However, the increased demand for these technologies is leading to a greater need for key minerals essential in their manufacture. Put simply, these technologies require significantly more key minerals compared to existing energy systems. At present, EVs require three times as much copper as conventional vehicles.[21] For example, a single Tesla Model 3 lithium-ion battery requires 56 kg of nickel in nickel sulphate, 7 kg of cobalt in cobalt sulphate, 6.6 kg of manganese, and 85 kg of copper cathode.[22] That is approximately 155 kg of just these four minerals for one car.[23]

While we are currently unable to predict the exact quantity of these minerals required, it is clear that their demand will increase significantly. The International Energy Agency has recently estimated that the demand for key minerals in the manufacture of EVs, such as lithium and graphite, will grow by

16 International Renewable Energy Agency, *World Energy Transitions Outlook 2022: 1.5°C Pathway* (Report, 2022) 21.

17 International Energy Agency, *Global EV Outlook 2022* (Report, 2022) 33.

18 Ibid.

19 Ibid.

20 International Renewable Energy Agency, *Electricity storage and renewable: Costs and markets to 2030* (Report, 2017) 10.

21 Takuma Watari et al., 'Global Copper Cycles and Greenhouse Gas Emissions in a 1.5°C World' (2022) 179 *Resources, Conservation & Recycling* 106118.

22 Daina Paulikas et al., 'Life Cycle Climate Change Impacts of Producing Battery Metals from Land Ores versus Deep-Sea Polymetallic Nodules' (2020) 275 *Journal of Cleaner Production* 123822, 2.

23 Ibid, 40.

over 40 times and 20–25 times, respectively, by 2040.[24] The minerals utilised depend on the technology. Wind turbines, for example, require bulk commodities including iron ore, copper, aluminium, limestone, and carbon for the construction of their towers, and rare earth metals, including neodymium and dysprosium, for their drive magnets.[25] In the case of photovoltaic technology, such as solar cells, key minerals include silicon, silver, tellurium, indium, gallium, and selenium.[26] Minerals used in the manufacture of EVs include graphite, cobalt, nickel, manganese, copper, lithium, aluminium, and rare earths.[27] Rare earth elements, particularly neodymium and dysprosium, are important because of their use in magnets common in most EVs.[28]

Battery technology relies heavily on lithium, essential in lithium-based batteries, which dominates the battery market. Although used in a range of battery technologies, lithium is especially important in EV batteries, and continued access to lithium will be indispensable in scaling up EVs in the long run.[29]

However, many of these minerals are already used in a range of other applications. Hence, the existing uses of these minerals will compete with newer technologies. For example, lithium is particularly important in glass and ceramic manufacturing, and also in the production of aluminium and applications such as air conditioning.[30] Mobile phones also use metals such as tantalum, platinum, palladium, cobalt, gold, silver, and copper.[31] Computers utilise metals such as tellurium, bismuth, neodymium, and yittrium.[32] While platinum, yttrium, praseodymium, cerium, and terbium are utilised in common household appliances such as flat screen TVs.[33] Their use in existing applications will continue as demand increases in the renewable energy, EV, and battery storage markets.

24 International Energy Agency, *The Role of Critical Minerals in Clean Energy Transitions* (Report, 2022) 8.
25 Damien Giruco et al., 'Requirements for Minerals and Metals for 100% Renewable Scenarios' in Sven Teske (ed), *Achieving the Paris Climate Agreement Goals* (Springer, 2019), 437–457, 439.
26 The Institute for Sustainable Futures, *Renewable Energy and Deep-Sea Mining: Supply, Demand and Scenarios* (Report, July 2016) 18.
27 Buyung Agusdinata, Hallie Eakin, and Wenjuan Liu, 'Critical Minerals for Electric Vehicles: A Telecoupling Review' (2022) 17 *Environmental Research Letters* 1.
28 Damien Giruco et al. (n 25) 441.
29 Timothy Prior et al., 'Sustainable Governance of Scarce Metals: The Case of Lithium' (2013) 461–462 *Science of the Total Environment*, 786.
30 Steve Mohr, Gavin Mudd, and Damien Giurco, 'Lithium Resources and Production: Critical Assessment and Global Projections' (2012) 2 *Minerals* 65, 67.
31 James Hein et al., 'Deep-Ocean Mineral Deposits as a Source of Critical Metals for High- and Green-Technology Applications: Comparison with Land-Based Sources' (2013) 51 *Ore Geology Reviews* 1.
32 Ibid.
33 Ibid.

Furthermore, many of these minerals and metals, and especially rare earth minerals, are regarded as critical minerals for national security and defence applications. Some examples of existing applications include guidance and control systems for missiles and advanced munitions technology, defence electronic warfare, targeting and weapons systems, communication equipment such as satellites, radar technology, and optical equipment such as night vision goggles.[34]

Thus, maintaining supply chains of critical minerals and metals is now viewed by many governments as a matter of strategic concern at the heart of defence and national security policy.[35] Some states are particularly concerned about the dominance of only a few states in the mining, production, and export of some key minerals. For example, in 2020, China was estimated to control 55% of the global rare earths mining capacity and 85% of rare earths refining.[36] Likewise, in 2020, over 70% of the world's cobalt was mined in the Democratic Republic of the Congo.[37] Somewhere in the range of 50%–70% of cobalt is refined by China.[38]

In light of the geostrategic competition between China and the United States, countries including the United States and EU member states are increasingly looking for strategic alliances to diversify sources of critical minerals. The COVID-19 pandemic has also taught many nations the critical importance of reliable and resilient supply chains. Increasingly, policy debate in relation to critical mineral supply has turned to consider the merits of "friend-shoring" or sourcing critical minerals from reliable strategic partners, as well as stockpiling and investing in the domestic production and processing of such minerals and other strategically important products and commodities.[39] For example, the United States has formed the Minerals Security Partnership with key states including Australia, Canada, Finland, France, Germany, Japan, the Republic of Korea, Sweden, the United Kingdom, and the European Commission.[40] The aim of this partnership is to "develop and secure global supply chains

34 Dwayne Ryan Menezes, 'The case for a five eyes critical minerals alliance: Focus on Greenland' (March 2021) 14 <https://polarconnection.org/wp-content/uploads/2021/03/Report-The-Case-for-a-FVEY-CMA.pdf>.

35 G Campbell, 'Rare earth metals: a strategic concern' (2014) 27 *Mineral Economics* 21.

36 Carl Williams, 'China continues dominance of rare earth markets to 2030, says Roskill' (Web Page, 26 February 2021) <https://www.mining.com/china-continues-dominance-of-rare-earths-markets-to-2030-says-roskill/>.

37 Geneviève Theriault-Lachance and Anaïs Tobalagba, 'The road to ruin? Electric vehicles and workers' rights abuses at DR Congo's industrial cobalt mines' (Report, November 2021) 7.

38 International Energy Agency (n 24) 12.

39 For US policy, see The White House, *Building resilient supply chains, revitalising American manufacturing, and fostering broad-based growth* (Report, June 2021).

40 United States Department of State, 'Minerals Security Partnership' (Web Page) <https://www.state.gov/minerals-security-partnership/>.

for critical minerals that are crucial to clean energy technology and the global transition to clean energy".[41]

It is also worth noting that significant controversy surrounds some of the existing terrestrial sources for many of these minerals. For example, in the Democratic Republic of the Congo, which is one of Africa's poorest nations and currently the world's largest miner of cobalt, widespread reports of human rights violations and instances of child labour are common in the mining industry.[42]

Given the significant current use of critical and rare earth minerals and anticipated future needs as we decarbonise the global economy, projections differ on whether existing terrestrial resources are sufficient to meet demand. One study, for example, argues that existing critical and rare earth minerals can be met from known terrestrial resources.[43] Other more recent studies are less optimistic, projecting shortages of many of these minerals, especially lithium, cobalt, copper[44], nickel, neodymium, and dysprosium, over the next 10–15 years.[45]

Increased recycling rates could help alleviate part of the shortfall. For example, the International Energy Agency projects that 10% of the world's needs for copper, lithium, nickel, and cobalt could be met by recycling spent batteries used in electric vehicles by 2040.[46] However, the collection systems and infrastructure required to recycle metals used in renewable energy technology and electric vehicles are not well established.[47] For example, in the case of lithium-ion batteries, the current global capacity for recycling is only around 200 kt/year.[48] Currently, many of the minerals and metals vital for the decarbonisation of the global economy are not recycled.[49] Thus, it is unlikely that recycling will ever meet more than a fraction of the global need for these resources in the future should there not be significant changes to the scale of recycling.

As discussed above, the expected increased demand for critical and rare earth minerals as a result of the decarbonisation of the global economy, coupled with fulfilling current demands and the necessity to diversify mineral sources (particularly away from China), has triggered renewed interest in deep-sea minerals. Some mining companies, such as the Metals Company, now argue

41 The Hon Madeleine King MP, 'Australia joins global minerals security partnership' (Web Page, 12 July 2022) <https://www.minister.industry.gov.au/ministers/king/media-releases/australia-joins-global-minerals-security-partnership>.

42 Geneviève Theriault-Lachance, and Anaïs Tobalagba (n 37) 7.

43 Sven Teske, Nick Florin, Elisa Dominish, and Damien Giurco (n 26) 5.

44 International Energy Agency (n 24) 11.

45 International Renewable Energy Agency (n 16) 321.

46 International Energy Agency (n 24) 15.

47 Damien Giurco et al. (n 25) 454.

48 International Energy Agency, *Global Supply Chains of EV Batteries* (Report, July 2022) 25.

49 International Energy Agency (n 24) 179.

that mining in the deep sea is the way to achieve all these goals.[50] They argue that deep-sea mining can provide the minerals necessary to decarbonise our economy with reduced environmental impact and none of the social impacts associated with mining known terrestrial sources. The following discussion assesses the anticipated effectiveness of UNCLOS and the Part XI Agreement in regulating mining should it occur.

UNCLOS, the Part XI Agreement, and deep-sea minerals

Currently, 168 states have ratified or acceded to UNCLOS and 151 states have ratified or acceded to the Part XI Agreement.[51] Membership of the ISA is open to all state parties to UNCLOS. It is worth noting that, even though it was involved in the negotiation of both UNCLOS and the Part XI Agreement, the United States has not ratified either treaty to date, although it has signed the Part XI Agreement.[52] Regardless, it is clear that the provisions of UNCLOS and the Part XI Agreement create a regulatory regime in relation to the Area and its resources for all state parties to these treaties.[53]

By virtue of Article 136 of UNCLOS, the Area and its "resources" are regarded as the "common heritage of mankind". The ISA is the organisation through which state parties to UNCLOS and the Part XI Agreement organise and control activities in the Area.[54] The ISA exercises this mandate pursuant to the powers and functions expressly conferred on it by UNCLOS and the Part XI Agreement.

Minerals recovered from the Area may only be alienated in accordance with the provisions of Part XI of UNCLOS and the rules, regulations, and procedures to be put in place by the ISA.[55] No state or individual, whether natural or legal, may claim, acquire, or exercise any rights with respect to minerals recovered from the Area other than in accordance with those provisions.[56] However, the mandate of the ISA is limited to regulating "activities in the Area", which is defined as "all activities of exploration for, and exploitation

50 The Metals Company, 'A battery in a rock. Polymetallic nodules are the cleanest path toward electric vehicles' (Web Page) <https://metals.co/nodules/>.

51 Convention on the Law of the Sea, *Status of the United Nations Convention on the Law of the Sea, the Agreement relating to the implementation of Part XI of the Convention and the Agreement for the implementation of the provisions of the Convention relating to the Conservation and Management of Straddling Fish Stocks and Highly Migratory Fish Stocks as at 31 July 2021*, (Web Page) <https://www.un.org/Depts/los/reference_files/Los106UnclosStatusTableEng.pdf>.

52 On the United States, see K Willaert, 'Deep sea mining and the United States: Unbound powerhouse or odd man out?' (2021) 124 *Marine Policy* 104339.

53 Resources are defined in Article 133(a) of UNCLOS as "all solid, liquid or gaseous mineral resources *in situ* in the Area at or beneath the seabed, including polymetallic nodules".

54 UNCLOS (n 3) Article 157(1).

55 Ibid, Article 137(2)

56 Ibid, Article 137(3)

of, the [mineral] resources of the Area". Activities in the Area must be carried out for the benefit of all humankind, irrespective of the geographical location of states (including coastal and landlocked states), while also considering the particular needs of developing states and their economic progress as a result of decolonisation efforts.[57]

The ISA's predominant focus is the commercial exploitation of the mineral resources of the Area. Article 150 clearly articulates that the development of the mineral resources of the Area is the key reason for the creation of the ISA. However, in carrying out its responsibilities, the ISA must consider various other objectives, including fostering the healthy growth of the global economy and the balanced growth of world trade; promoting the interests of developing countries to ensure the development of the mineral resources of the Area; environmental objectives; increasing the involvement of developing country participants; facilitating technology transfer; ensuring a sufficient mineral supply for consumers; fairly remunerating producers and providing fair prices for consumers; preventing monopolisation and encouraging participation by all states; protecting developing economies that may be impacted by deep-sea mining; developing the common heritage for the benefit of humankind as a whole; and ensuring equal treatment of minerals from the Area with those mined on land.[58] The role ascribed to the ISA under Article 150 is thus complex, involving the balancing of numerous competing interests, in addition to its environmental protection obligations as discussed below. However, its primary function is to facilitate the exploitation of the mineral resources of the Area.

However, it should not go unnoticed that the ISA came from an idea born in the 1960s. This arguably reflects values of another era. The 1960s were an era when the exploitation of deep-sea minerals was viewed optimistically as a new economic opportunity, with little understanding of or regard for its environmental impacts. International environmental law and the law of the sea have progressed, and are now embracing new values of sustainability. Some argue that these changes raise doubts about the rationale behind creating the ISA. Nonetheless, the mandate of the ISA to facilitate and regulate mining is clear. How has the ISA progressed in fulfilling its mandate, especially with respect to the management of the environmental impacts of deep-sea mining?

The ISA Mining Code and regulation of the environmental impact of deep-sea mining

It is most likely that the first commercial deep-sea mining will be carried out by corporate entities sponsored by a sponsoring state party. The International

57 Ibid, Article 140(1).
58 Ibid, Article 150.

Tribunal for the Law of the Sea (ITLOS) has characterised the obligations of a sponsoring state to ensure compliance with the terms of contracts between a sponsored entity and the ISA and the obligations set out in the convention and related instruments, as obligations of due diligence.[59]

Commercial mining must be carried out in accordance with formal written plans approved by the Council of the ISA after review by the Legal and Technical Commission.[60] Since its inception and continuing to the present day, the ISA primarily carries out these functions through its constituent organs: the Assembly, the Council, the Secretariat, the Legal and Technical Commission, and the Finance Committee.[61] The Part XI Agreement sets out a range of steps that the ISA, acting through these organs, is required to carry out between the entry into force of the Part XI Agreement and the approval of the first plan of work for the exploitation of the minerals of the Area. These include the obligation of the ISA to adopt "rules, regulations, and procedures incorporating applicable standards for the protection and preservation of the marine environment" during this period.[62] This is consistent with the provisions of Article 145 of UNCLOS, which require necessary measures to be taken with respect to activities in the Area to "ensure effective protection for the marine environment from harmful effects which may arise from such activities".[63] Thus, the ISA is required to adopt appropriate rules, regulations, and procedures to prevent, reduce, and control pollution and other hazards in the marine environment, as well as protect and conserve natural resources and minimise damage to marine flora and fauna.[64]

The major focus of this work is to develop the ISA's Mining Code, which is a "comprehensive set of rules, regulations, and procedures issued by ISA to regulate prospecting, exploration, and exploitation of marine minerals in the... Area".[65] As such, the Mining Code encompasses more than just the rules, regulations, and procedures concerning the protection and preservation of the marine environment; it also addresses a range of other issues.

59 International Tribunal for the Law of the Sea, *Responsibilities and obligations of States sponsoring persons and entities with respect to activities in the Area (Request for Advisory Opinion submitted to the Seabed Disputes Chamber)*, ITLOS Reports 2011 (Advisory Opinion, 1 February 2011) ('Seabed Mining Advisory Opinion').

60 UNCLOS (n 3) Article 153(3).

61 Part XI Agreement (n 4) Annex, s 1(4) and Article 158 of UNCLOS create each of these organs. The composition, procedure, and voting of the Assembly are dealt with in Article 159 of UNCLOS; for the Council, see Articles 161, 162, and 163 of UNCLOS; the Legal and Technical Commission, see Article 165; and the Secretariat, see Articles 166–169.

62 Part XI Agreement (n 4) Annex, s 1, Article 5(g).

63 UNCLOS (n 3) Article 145.

64 UNCLOS (n 3) Article 145.

65 International Seabed Authority, 'The Mining Code' (Web Page) <https://www.isa.org.jm/mining-code>.

The initial work of the ISA focused on aspects of the Mining Code related to prospecting and exploration, including the adoption of regulations on prospecting and exploration in the Area for polymetallic sulphides in 2010,[66] cobalt-rich ferromanganese crusts in 2012,[67] and polymetallic nodules in 2013.[68] These regulations are supplemented with a number of recommendations for the guidance of contractors and sponsoring states.[69] To date, the ISA has issued a number of iterations of recommendations relating to exploration activities in the Area, of which five are currently in force.[70]

While no mining has occurred, the ISA has entered into 15-year contracts with 22 contractors for the exploration of polymetallic nodules, polymetallic sulphides, and cobalt-rich ferromanganese crusts.[71] Exploration in accordance with these contracts is governed by prospecting and exploration regulations adopted by the ISA, as mentioned above. Given the dual economic and strategic importance of these resources and concerns about China's dominance in the mining and processing of some of these minerals on land, it is worth noting that five of these contractors are sponsored by China.

In more recent years, the ISA has shifted its focus to developing aspects of the Mining Code relating to mining, a process that began in 2014 with

66 International Seabed Authority, *Regulations on prospecting and exploration of polymetallic sulphides in the Area*, Annex to International Seabed Authority-Assembly, 16th sess, UN Doc ISBA/16/A/12/Rev.1 (15 November, 2010).

67 International Seabed Authority, *Regulations on prospecting and exploration for Cobalt-rich Ferromanganese Crusts in the Area*, Annex to International Seabed Authority-Assembly, 18th sess, UN Doc ISBA/18/A/11 (22 October 2012).

68 International Seabed Authority, *Decision of the Assembly of the International Seabed Authority regarding the amendments to the Regulations on Prospecting and Exploration of Polymetallic Nodules in the Area*, 19th sess, UN Doc ISBA/19/A/9 (25 July 2013).

69 International Seabed Authority, 'The Mining Code' (Web Page) <https://www.isa.org.jm/mining-code>.

70 These are International Seabed Authority, *Recommendations for the guidance of contractors on the relinquishment of areas under exploration contracts for polymetallic sulphides or cobalt-rich ferromanganese crusts*, 25th sess, UN Doc ISBA/25/LTC/8 (27 July 2019); International Seabed Authority, *Recommendations for the guidance of contractors for the reporting of actual and direct exploration expenditure*, 25th sess, UN Doc ISBA/21/LTC/11 (14 April 2015); International Seabed Authority, *Recommendations for the guidance of contractors for the assessment of the possible environmental impacts arising from exploration for marine minerals in the Area*, UN Doc ISBA/25/6/Rev 2 (15 March 2019); *Recommendations for the guidance of contractors and sponsoring States relating to training programmes under plans of work for exploration*, 19th sess, UN Doc ISBA/19/LTC/14 (12 July 2013); and *Recommendations for the guidance of contractors on the content, format and structure of annual reports*, UN Doc ISBA/21/LTC/15 (August 2015).

71 See International Seabed Authority, 'Exploration Contracts' (Web Page) <https://www.isa.org.jm/exploration-contracts>.

a series of expert workshops,[72] expert studies,[73] and discussion papers.[74] Drawing on information from these and a process of stakeholder consultation from 2014 to 2022, the Legal and Technical Commission has developed a number of iterations of the Draft Regulations on Exploitation of Mineral Resources in the Area,[75] which will form part of the Mining Code. These draft regulations were considered at a meeting of the ISA Council between 16 and 31 March 2023. They were not adopted at this meeting and were instead further debated and revised. Four key aspects remain unresolved and, at the time of writing, are currently under ongoing negotiations: "i) a financial model and payment mechanism for deep-sea mining, ii) the protection and preservation of the marine environment, iii) inspection, compliance and enforcement, and iv) institutional matters".[76] Subsequently, at its 307th and 308th meetings on 21 July 2023, the ISA Council reached a decision regarding a timeline to finalise the draft regulations.[77] The timeline sets out a series of informal and formal meetings of working groups, along with meetings of the ISA Assembly and Council, throughout 2023 and 2024. The objective is to potentially adopt the draft regulations at the meeting of the council scheduled for 15–26 July 2024, "in the event they are ready for adoption".[78] Thus, the decision by the council is not a firm commitment to adopt the draft regulations at this meeting.

The draft regulations are quite detailed, covering a range of matters across 117 pages of provisions and associated annexes. A detailed examination of all of these provisions is beyond the scope of this chapter. For the purposes of this chapter, the key provisions are found in Part II and Part VI. Part II focuses on the requirements for applications for the approval of plans of work, setting out how they will be dealt with and assessed by the various organs of the ISA. This includes procedures for processing and reviewing

72 See International Seabed Authority, 'Draft Exploitation Regulations: Workshops' (Web Page) <https://www.isa.org.jm/mining-code/workshops>.

73 See International Seabed Authority, 'The Mining Code: Studies, Reports and Workshop Reports' (Web Page) <https://www.isa.org.jm/the-mining-code/studies-reports-and-workshop-reports/>.

74 See International Seabed Authority, 'Draft Exploitation Regulations: Discussion Papers' (Web Page) <https://www.isa.org.jm/the-mining-code/discussion-papers/>.

75 International Seabed Authority, *Draft Regulations on exploitation of mineral resources in the Area*, 25th sess, UN Doc ISBA/25/C/WP.1 (22 March 2019) ('Draft Regulations').

76 International Seabed Authority, 'ISA Council closes Part II of its 28th session' (Web Page) <https://www.isa.org.jm/news/isa-council-closes-part-ii-of-its-28th-session/>.

77 International Seabed Authority, *Consideration with a view to adoption of the draft regulations on exploitation of mineral resources in the Area-Decision of the Council of the International Seabed Authority on a timeline following the expiration of the two-year period pursuant to section 1, paragraph 15, of the annex to the Agreement relating to the Implementation of Part XI of the United Nations Convention on the Law of the Sea*, 28th sess, UN Doc ISBA/28/C/24 (21 July 2023).

78 Ibid, Annex 5.

applications,[79] public display and review of the environmental plans lodged with an application,[80] processes for the consideration of applications by the ISA Legal and Technical Commission,[81] and the consideration of an application by the ISA Council.[82]

Part VI deals with the protection and preservation of the marine environment. These provisions begin by restating general obligations with respect to the marine environment, including the application of the precautionary approach[83]; the application of the best available techniques and best environmental practices[84]; the integration of the best available scientific evidence in environmental decision-making[85]; the promotion of accountability and transparency in the assessment, evaluation, and management of the environmental effects from the exploitation of minerals in the Area[86]; the implementation and maintenance of environmental management systems[87]; the requirements for environmental impact assessments and statements[88]; pollution control and management of mining waste[89]; emergency response and contingency planning[90]; and provision for an environmental compensation fund.[91] The draft regulations also provide for the future development of standards relating to the environment.[92]

A series of annexes to the regulations then deal with a range of matters, such as the content of an application for approval of a plan of work[93]; mining workplans[94]; environmental impact statements[95]; emergency response and contingency plans; health and safety plans and maritime security plans[96]; environmental management and monitoring plans[97]; closure plans[98]; form of the

79 Draft Regulations (n 76) regs 9–10.
80 Ibid, reg 11.
81 Ibid, reg 12–15.
82 Ibid, reg 16.
83 Ibid, reg 44(a).
84 Ibid, reg 44(b).
85 Ibid, reg 44(c).
86 Ibid, reg 44(d).
87 Ibid, regs 46, 48, and 51–52.
88 Ibid, reg 47.
89 Ibid, regs 49 and 50.
90 Ibid, reg 53.
91 Ibid, regs 54–56.
92 Ibid, regs 45 and 94(1)(c).
93 Draft Regulations (n 76) Annex I.
94 Ibid, Annex II.
95 Ibid, Annex IV.
96 Ibid, Annex VI.
97 Ibid, Annex VII.
98 Ibid, Annex VIII.

exploitation contract and schedules[99]; and standard clauses for exploitation contracts.[100]

The draft exploitation regulations are comprehensive in scope and have been developed after careful consideration of many issues. They align with international best practices by incorporating the precautionary approach, the ecosystem approach, the polluter-pays principle, effective public participation, and best available scientific evidence, among other factors. However, even if they are finally adopted in 2024, the development of the Mining Code will continue as several key aspects of the regulations still require further development, especially concerning the protection and preservation of the marine environment. For example, under Draft Regulation 94, the Legal and Technical Commission is required to develop standards relating to exploitation activities in the Area. These include standards relating to operational safety, the conservation of resources, and the protection of the marine environment, which includes standards or requirements relating to the environmental effects.[101] Draft Regulation 45, in turn, requires that the ISA develop environmental standards that encompass environmental quality objectives, monitoring procedures, and mitigation measures.[102]

Continued effort is essential to ensure that a robust and effective regulatory regime is in place before the ISA can authorise the first commercial mining operations in the Area. Parallel to this, work will also be undertaken by state parties to further refine how they will implement their obligations under the 2023 Biodiversity Beyond National Jurisdiction (BBNJ) Agreement.[103] Assuming that the BBNJ Agreement enters into force, it would be desirable if the work by the ISA on the above standards is at least consistent with, if not exceed, the standards and/or guidelines to be developed by the Scientific and Technical Body under Article 38 of the BBNJ Agreement.[104] Although the BBNJ Agreement will largely regulate different activities, it is nonetheless desirable to maintain a level of consistency in approaches, especially concerning matters such as environmental impact assessments across UNCLOS, the Part XI Agreement, and the BBNJ Agreement.

However, while the work in developing the Mining Code is ongoing, two parallel developments have occurred which have increased the pressure on the ISA to conclude development of the Mining Code as soon as possible. The developments are the action taken by the Republic of Nauru and growing

99 Ibid, Annex IX.
100 Ibid, Annex X.
101 Draft Regulation (n 76) reg 94.
102 Ibid, 45.
103 *Agreement under the United Nations Convention on the Law of the Sea on the Conservation and Sustainable Use of Marine Biological Diversity of Areas beyond National Jurisdiction*, opened for signature 20 September 2023 (not yet in force).
104 The Scientific and Technical Body is constituted by Article 49(1) of the BBNJ Agreement.

international calls for a moratorium or a "precautionary pause" on deep-sea mining.

Nauru and the "two-year trigger"

Article 15(a) of Annex 1 to the Part XI Agreement provides that there is no time limit on when the ISA must finalise the development of the Mining Code. However, Article 15(b) of Annex 1 of the Part XI Agreement states that if a request is made by a state party for the ISA to finalise the development of the Mining Code, then the ISA Council must finalise the development and adoption of the provisions of the Mining Code within two years of the date of that notice. This is often referred to as the "two-year rule" or the "two-year trigger rule". In 2021, the Republic of Nauru effectively "pulled the trigger" on the "two-year trigger rule" by giving notice under Article 15(b) of Annex 1 to the Part XI Agreement. This meant that the ISA had two years from 30 June 2021 (later deferred to 9 July 2021) to finalise the adoption of the Mining Code and the associated environmental and safety standards discussed above. As noted above, the Mining Code was not finalised by the deadline of 9 July 2023.

The consequences of failure to meet this deadline are spelt out in Article 15(c) of Annex 1 to the Part XI Agreement which provides:

> If the Council has not completed the elaboration of the rules, regulations and procedures relating to exploitation within the prescribed time and an application for approval of a plan of work for exploitation is pending, it shall none the less consider and provisionally approve such plan of work based on the provisions of the Convention and any rules, regulations and procedures that the Council may have adopted provisionally, or on the basis of the norms contained in the Convention and the terms and principles contained in this Annex as well as the principle of non-discrimination among contractors.[105]

Thus, if a state such as Nauru were to lodge an application for approval of a plan of work for exploitation (i.e. a plan to mine), the ISA would be required to consider whether or not to approve it even without the Mining Code being in place. This, in turn, raises two unclear questions that would need to be resolved: (1) How should these applications be assessed? and (2) "What is the legal effect of a provisional approval by the [ISA] Council and what procedures should be followed?".[106] The applicability of the draft Mining Code

105 Part XI Agreement (n 4) Annex 1, Article 15(c).

106 K Willaert, 'Under Pressure: The Impact of Invoking the Two Year Rule within the Context of Deep Sea Mining in the Area' (2021) *The International Journal of Marine and Coastal Law* 505, 509.

remains uncertain; it is unclear whether, due to its draft status, it could be applied as is or if the council could outright reject such applications.[107]

State parties are currently divided regarding the legal obligations of the ISA to assess an application in the event that a sponsoring state lodges one for approval before the Mining Code is finalised. The ISA has established an informal intersessional dialogue that is considering a range of issues arising from these developments. At its meeting in March 2023, the ISA Council decided to continue these informal intersessional dialogues aimed at progressing discussions on several key areas: the legal basis for the council to postpone the consideration and/or provisionally approve a plan of work, along with the circumstances under which such actions may be taken; the necessity for the Legal and Technical Commission to review a plan of work and submit appropriate recommendations to the council as part of the process of consideration of such a plan; the guidelines or directives that the council may give to the commission, and/or the criteria the council may establish for the commission, for the purpose of reviewing a plan of work; and the considerations and procedures applicable after a plan of work has been provisionally approved and leading up to the conclusion of a contract for exploitation.[108]

However, it is difficult to see how the ISA could proceed to approve a plan of work prior to the Mining Code being adopted. The consequences for the entire deep-sea mining regime under UNCLOS, stemming from the failure to establish the Mining Code and required standards before considering whether or not to approve proposed plans of work, extend far beyond the consequences of any one proposal. As one author has correctly noted:

> Rushing to finalise the Mining Code without fully considering and addressing all the above matters can lead to very problematic outcomes. Once the regulations are in place and the first exploitation applications are subsequently approved, it would be hard for the ISA to preclude further applications or roll-back the conduct of exploitation activities. Hence, it is submitted that the entire system for exploitation, including environmental requirements and compliance mechanisms, must be ready and put in place before any exploitation activities are allowed to commence.[109]

107 Ibid.

108 International Seabed Authority, *Decision of the Council of The International Seabed Authority relating to the understanding and application of section 1, paragraph 15, of the annex to the Agreement relating to the Implementation of Part XI of the United Nations Convention on the Law of the Sea*, 28th sess, UN Doc ISBA/28/C9 (31 March 2023).

109 Pradeep Singh, 'The two-year deadline to complete the International Seabed Authority's Mining Code: Key outstanding matters that still need to be resolved' (2021) 134 *Marine Policy* 104804.

It is unclear whether Nauru will lodge an application for approval of a plan of work before the Mining Code is finalised. How then would a divided ISA proceed? This is unclear. This is further complicated by growing calls for a moratorium or a "precautionary pause" on mining pending the clarification of environmental impacts.

A moratorium or a "precautionary pause"?

While Nauru pushes for commercial mining to commence, several states and some institutions have been calling for either a moratorium or a "precautionary pause" on deep-sea mining. For example, on 16 January 2018, the European Parliament adopted a non-binding resolution on international ocean governance which called on the European Commission "to encourage Member States to cease subsidising licences for mining prospecting and extraction in areas beyond national jurisdiction and issuing permits for mining of their continental shelves".[110]

Critically, the resolution then goes on to call

> on the Commission and the Member States to support an international moratorium on commercial deep-sea mining exploitation licences until such time as the effects of deep-sea mining on the marine environment, biodiversity and human activities at sea have been studied and researched sufficiently and all possible risks are understood.[111]

Significantly, the resolution also expresses concern about the European Commission's insistence on deep-sea mining as a priority area for investment by the European Union.[112] It stressed

> that the precautionary principle must be applied to the emerging deep-sea mining sector, and that given the scientific warnings regarding significant and potentially irreversible environmental harm being implied, considers that the EU should not support the development of this industry but should, rather, invest in sustainable alternatives, and specifically in a transition to sustainable consumption and production.[113]

Likewise, in 2021, the Chilean Senate passed a resolution calling on the president of Chile and the Chilean Ministries of Foreign Affairs, Mining, and the Environment to advocate internationally for a moratorium on deep-sea

110 *European Parliament resolution of 16 January 2018 on international ocean governance: an agenda for the future of our oceans in the context of the 2030* [2018] OJ C 458/9, para 19.
111 Ibid, para 42.
112 Ibid, para 66.
113 Ibid, para 67.

mining, the issue of new exploration and exploitation contracts, and the adoption of the Draft Exploitation Regulations.[114] The senate resolution also, *inter alia*, called for greater transparency in decision-making by the ISA.

More recently, in June 2022, Palau and Fiji launched an "alliance" to call for a moratorium on deep-sea mining.[115] Subsequently, on 8 November 2022, French President Macron called for a moratorium on deep-sea mining and was the first head of state to do so.[116] Similar calls for a moratorium issued by Parliamentarians for Global Action have also been endorsed by 252 members of national and provincial parliaments from Vanuatu, Malawi, the Gambia, the Seychelles, Trinidad and Tobago, Cameroon, the Åland Islands, Pakistan, Switzerland, Zambia, Fiji, New Zealand, Bangladesh, the Republic of Cyprus, Belgium, Iceland, Spain, Papua New Guinea, Guam, Tuvalu, New Caledonia, the Maldives, Venezuela, Peru, France, the Netherlands, Australia, Nepal, Mozambique, Guinea-Bissau, Sao Tome & Principe, Samoa, Ireland, Norway, Austria, the Cook Islands Mexico, Canada, Jamaica, and the European Parliament.[117] Similar statements calling for a moratorium have also been issued by the Pacific Parliamentarians Alliance on Deep-Sea Mining and endorsed by members of parliament from New Zealand, Papua New Guinea, New Caledonia, Guam, Tuvalu, French Polynesia, Palau, and Vanuatu.[118] While the views of individual legislators do not bind their governments, these calls constitute evidence of significant and growing political support for a moratorium.

Likewise, at the World Conservation Congress held in Marseille in 2020, the International Union for the Conservation of Nature (IUCN) adopted a resolution on the protection of deep-ocean ecosystems and biodiversity through a moratorium on seabed mining.[119] A moratorium is also supported by environmental non-governmental organisations (NGOs) such as the Deep-Sea

114 'Senadores piden aplicar moratoria en la explotación minera de los fondos marinos' (Web Page, 29 November 2021) <https://www.mch.cl/2021/11/29/senadores-piden-aplicar-moratoria-en-la-explotacion-minera-de-los-fondos-marinos/> (English translation by the author).

115 Reuters, '"Not worth the risk": Palau, Fiji call for deep-sea mining moratorium' (Web Page, 28 June 2022) https://www.reuters.com/business/environment/not-worth-risk-palau-fiji-call-deep-sea-mining-moratorium-2022-06-27/.

116 Todd Woody, 'France Puts Future of Deep Sea Mining in Doubt', *Bloomberg* (Web Page) <https://www.bloomberg.com/news/articles/2022-11-10/france-puts-future-of-deep-sea-mining-in-doubt?leadSource=uverify%20wall>.

117 Parliamentarians for Global Action, *Global Parliamentary Declaration Calling for a Moratorium on Deep Seabed Mining* (Web Page) <https://www.pgaction.org/ilhr/oceans/call-for-moratorium-on-deep-seabed-mining.html>.

118 Pacific Parliamentarians Alliance on Deep-Sea Mining (Web Page) <https://www.pacificblueline.org/pacificparliamentarians>.

119 IUCN World Conservation Congress, *Protection of deep-ocean ecosystems and biodiversity through a moratorium on seabed mining*, WCC Res 122 (2020).

Conservation Coalition,[120] the World Wide Fund for Nature (WWF),[121] and Greenpeace,[122] as well as noted figures in the environmental movement such as Sir David Attenborough.[123] The NGO campaign against deep-sea mining has also included direct action by environmentalists such as Greenpeace. In May 2021, for example, Greenpeace activists operating from the Rainbow Warrior painted slogans on the hull of a Norwegian-flagged vessel involved in exploration activities in the Clarion–Clipperton zone.[124]

Corporations have also joined the campaign against deep-sea mining, with major companies including BMW, Volkswagen, Volvo, Samsung, Phillips, and Google signing a statement supporting a moratorium and committing not to use metals mined from the deep sea until environmental risks are "comprehensively" understood.[125] Likewise, banks and financial institutions including ABN AMRO, Lloyds Banking Group, NatWest, BBVA Bank, Standard Chartered, and the European Investment Bank have supported calls for a moratorium.[126]

Uncertainty as to environmental impacts of mining

Essentially, those calling for a moratorium are concerned about the environmental impact of deep-sea mining. These concerns are largely driven by a lack of knowledge about deep-sea ecosystems. A more detailed understanding of the deep-sea marine environment, the environmental baseline conditions, and the likely impact of mining is required to assess whether the Mining Code will be adequate or whether a moratorium is required.[127] There is also a lack of understanding of the environmental risks and how mining may impact pelagic

120 The Deep Sea Conservation Coalition (Web Page) <https://savethehighseas.org/>.

121 World Wide Fund for Nature, 'No Deep Seabed Mining' (Web Page) <https://wwf.panda.org/discover/our_focus/oceans_practice/no_deep_seabed_mining/>.

122 Greenpeace, 'Deep Sea Mining' (Web Page) <https://www.greenpeace.org/usa/issues/deep-sea-mining/>.

123 Fauna & Flora International, 'Sir David Attenborough urges halt to deep sea mining plans in wake of alarming new scientific report' (Web Page, 12 March 2020) <https://www.fauna-flora.org/app/uploads/2020/03/FFI_Deep-sea-mining_Press-release.pdf>.

124 Klaas Willaert, 'Protest at Sea against Deep Sea Mining: Lawfulness, Limits and Remedies', (2021) 36 *The International Journal of Marine and Coastal Law* 672, 673.

125 Environmental Justice Foundation, 'The rush to mine the deep sea will cause permanent damage to unique, fragile environments and worsen global inequalities: New Report', (Web Site) <https://ejfoundation.org/news-media/the-rush-to-mine-the-deep-sea-will-cause-permanent-damage-to-unique-fragile-environments-and-worsen-global-inequalities-new-report#:~:text=Major%20companies%20including%20BMW%2C%20Volkswagen,risks%20are%20%E2%80%9Ccomprehensively%20understood%E2%80%9D>. See also Reuters, 'Google, BMW, AB Volvo, Samsung back environmental call for pause on deep-sea mining' (Web Site) <https://www.reuters.com/business/sustainable-business/google-bmw-volvo-samsung-sdi-sign-up-wwf-call-temporary-ban-deep-sea-mining-2021-03-31/> .

126 Ibid.

127 Diva Amon et al., 'Assessment of scientific gaps related to the effective Environmental management of deep-seabed mining' (2022) 138 *Marine Policy* 105006.

and coastal ecosystems.[128] However, it is understood that most deep-sea ecosystems are pristine, particularly sensitive to anthropogenic disturbances, highly structured, diverse, and dominated by rare species that are threatened by the habitat removal involved in mining.[129] They are also sensitive to environmental impacts from light, noise, and electromagnetic disturbance.[130]

As evident from the discussion above, two broad approaches seem to emerge in international debates: (1) calls for a moratorium on deep-sea mining; and (2) calls for a "precautionary pause" until there is a greater understanding of the environmental impact of mining, and the formation of appropriate environmental regulations. These suggestions conflict with those who advocate for mining. They suggest that mining must be facilitated as soon as possible in response to climate change, despite the possibility of unknown environmental consequences.

Two key legal questions are raised here. The first is whether calls for a moratorium are consistent with the object and purpose of UNCLOS and the Part XI Agreement. As noted above, deep-sea mining managed by the ISA is lawful under international law. Calls for a moratorium on deep-sea mining challenge the legitimacy of the ISA and the entire Part XI regime. It is difficult to envision the legality of a moratorium in the absence of amendments to both UNCLOS and the Part XI Agreement. At present, obtaining international consensus to amend UNCLOS and the Part XI Agreement appears highly improbable. However, it is worth noting that such a scenario is not unprecedented in history. The clearest instance of this was the abandonment of the regulatory regime for mining in Antarctica as outlined in the Convention on the Regulation of Antarctic Mineral Resource Activites,[131] which was replaced by the ban on mining in Antarctica under the Madrid Protocol.[132] However, the ban on mining in Antarctica was far less complex to achieve than a moratorium on mining in the deep sea. UNCLOS and the Part XI Agreement deal with a range of complicated and interconnected issues and reflect compromises by numerous states on numerous issues. It is difficult to envision how the compromises made regarding mining can be reversed without causing ripple effects in other areas. There is simply no willingness among states

128 World Bank, *Precautionary Management of Deep Sea Minerals. Pacific Possible Background Paper No. 2.*, (Washington DC, World Bank, 2017), <https://openknowledge.worldbank.org/handle/10986/28298?show=full>, 9.

129 H Niner and J Ardon et al., 'Deep-sea Mining with no net loss of biodiversity-An impossible aim' (2018) 5(53) *Frontiers in Marine Science* 1, 2.

130 Ibid.

131 Convention on the Regulation of Antarctic Mineral Resource Activities, opened for signature 26 November 1988, 27 ILM No. 4 (1988) (not in force).

132 Protocol on Environmental Protection to the Antarctic Treaty, opened for signature on 4 October
1991, 30 ILM (1991) (entered into force 14 January 1998).

to undo the agreements reached throughout the entire treaty regime created by UNCLOS.

Given the unlikelihood of a moratorium, how compatible would a temporary "precautionary pause" be with UNCLOS and the Part XI Agreement? Following the advisory opinion rendered by the Seabed Disputes Chamber of the International Tribunal on the Law of the Sea in *Responsibilities and Obligations of States sponsoring person and entities with respect to activities in the area*,[133] it is clear that the "precautionary approach"[134] is central to the sponsoring states' obligation of due diligence under UNCLOS and the Part XI Agreement.[135] In the tribunal's opinion, such a conclusion was supported by earlier judgments, which include its own order in the *Southern Bluefin Tuna Cases* (*New Zealand v Japan*; *Australia v Japan*).[136] Similarly, ITLOS cited with approval the judgment of the International Court of Justice (ICJ) in *Case concerning Pulp Mills on the River Uruguay* (*Argentina v Uruguay*)[137] as to the role of the "precautionary approach" in treaty interpretation.[138]

In light of this, it is arguable that the ISA cannot approve a plan of work submitted by a sponsoring state without first finalising the Mining Code. Considering the limited scientific understanding surrounding potential environmental impacts, an application of the precautionary approach may result in the lack of approval of a plan of work pursuant to the Mining Code. Without a completed Mining Code and sufficient scientific understanding of the environmental impacts, the "precautionary pause" advocated by many is not only

133 *Responsibilities and obligations of States sponsoring person and entities with respect to activities in the Area (Request for Advisory Opinion submitted to the Seabed Disputes Chamber), Advisory Opinion of 1 February 2011*, available at https://www.itlos.org/fileadmin/itlos/documents/cases/case_no_17/17_adv_op_010211_en.pdf.

134 The author acknowledges that there is a significant debate on whether the "precautionary approach" or the "precautionary principle" is the correct terminology. Those debates are beyond the scope of this chapter. For consistency's sake, the author refers to the "precautionary approach" as this is the terminology used by ITLOS.

135 *Responsibilities and obligations of States sponsoring person and entities with respect to activities in the Area (Request for Advisory Opinion submitted to the Seabed Disputes Chamber), Advisory Opinion of 1 February 2011*, https://www.itlos.org/fileadmin/itlos/documents/cases/case_no_17/17_adv_op_010211_en.pdf, at para 131.

136 *Southern Bluefin Tuna Cases (New Zealand v Japan; Australia v Japan)*, ITLOS Reports 199, 274. See comments to that effect in *Responsibilities and obligations of States sponsoring person and entities with respect to activities in the Area (Request for Advisory Opinion submitted to the Seabed Disputes Chamber), Advisory Opinion of 1 February 2011*, https://www.itlos.org/fileadmin/itlos/documents/cases/case_no_17/17_adv_op_010211_en.pdf, at para 132.

137 *Case concerning Pulp Mills on the River Uruguay (Argentina v Uruguay), Judgment of 20 April 2010*, https://www.icj-cij.org/sites/default/files/case-related/135/135-20100420-JUD-01-00-EN.pdf.

138 This is discussed briefly by ITLOS in *Responsibilities and obligations of States sponsoring person and entities with respect to activities in the Area (Request for Advisory Opinion submitted to the Seabed Disputes Chamber), Advisory Opinion of 1 February 2011*, https://www.itlos.org/fileadmin/itlos/documents/cases/case_no_17/17_adv_op_010211_en.pdf, at para 135.

consistent with the obligations of states and the ISA under UNCLOS and Part XI but is also, in fact, mandated. It is not lawful for deep-sea mining to proceed until the Mining Code is finalised and the gaps in scientific knowledge about environmental impacts are addressed.

Transparency, compliance, and enforcement

These debates become even more challenging due to the difficulty of enforcing regulations related to mining in the Area, especially those relating to environmental impacts.[139] The deep sea presents an extreme environment, characterised by cold, darkness, and extreme pressure. As a result, specialised equipment is required to operate and monitor activities in the Area. Moreover, its remoteness adds to these challenges. Can we effectively monitor entities' compliance with contractual terms while mining in such a challenging environment, particularly regarding their compliance with environmental approval terms? How can we ensure that these terms are not violated? How will we detect environmental damage caused by these activities beyond the terms of their approval? Very few states or organisations have the necessary technology or capacity to thoroughly monitor such activities.

The challenges in monitoring and enforcement are compounded by a lack of transparency in certain aspects of the ISA's operations.[140] How can we trust the ISA to impartially oversee mining activities when its primary goal is to maximise returns for the international community, especially developing countries? This chapter does not provide definitive answers to these questions, but they are nonetheless legitimate questions to raise.

This is especially so considering the recent criticism by some member states of the secretary general of the Seabed Authority. They flagged the issue of the secretary general intervening in recent debates at the ISA concerning the "trigger mechanism" pulled by Nauru (as discussed earlier in this chapter). In an extraordinary intervention, the German Government wrote to the secretary general stating:

> the Federal Government recalls that the Contracting Parties to the Agreements have defined the tasks and competences of the organs of the International Seabed Authority in binding manner under international treaty law. The division of these tasks and competencies is not negotiable by the International Seabed Authority organs.
>
> It is not the task of the Secretariat to interfere in the decision-making of the other organs and subsidiary organs of the International Seabed

139 S Bräger et al. 'The current status of environmental requirements for deep seabed mining issued by the International Seabed Authority' (2020) 114 *Marine Policy* 103258.

140 J Ardon et al. 'Incorporating transparency into the governance of deep-seabed mining in the Area beyond national jurisdiction' (2018) 89 *Marine Policy* 58.

> Authority. This also applies to exchanges between members of the Council of the International Seabed Authority on the interpretation of Section 1, sub-section 15 of the Annex to the implementing agreement. The binding interpretation of the Agreements rests solely with the International Tribunal for the Law of the Sea.
>
> Notwithstanding the above, you used your introductory statement to the intersessional dialogue on 8 March 2023 to present your preferred interpretation of the Agreements as the supposed legal framework for delegation's decision-making.
>
> In the past, you have actively taken a stand against positions and decision-making proposals from individual delegations.
>
> The Federal Government is seriously concerned about this approach. All Contracting Parties to the Agreements must be able to trust that the Secretariat will respect its duty of neutrality.[141]

In reply to this letter, the secretary general commented:

> It may be useful to recall that Article 166 of the United Nations Convention on the Law of the Sea provides that the Secretary-General shall be the chief administrative officer of the Authority and shall act in that capacity in all meetings of the Assembly, of the Council and any subsidiary organ. This is also reflected in the Rules of Procedure of the Council which permit the Secretary-General, at any time, to make oral or written statements to the Council concerning any question under consideration by it.
>
> The principal role of the Secretary-General is to be a guardian of the integrity of the Convention and the 1994 Agreement and to ensure the good functioning of the Authority so that it fulfils its mandate. General principles of the law of international organisations recognise the implicit competence of the Secretary-General to discharge his or her responsibilities particularly as it relates to the respect by members of the legal framework. This is consistent with the role of the Secretariat as one of the principal organs of the Authority. Contrary to what is asserted in the letter, the opening remarks delivered by me at the intersessional dialogue on 8 March 2023 (attached) did not present any preferred interpretation of the Convention or the 1994 Agreement and did not refer to any specific proposal by any delegation. My remarks were fully consistent with the competences recognised to me, suggesting general and non-controversial considerations for evaluating all proposals and suggestions

141 Letter from Dr Framziska Branter, Parliamentary State Secretary, Federal Ministry for Economic Affairs and Climate Action, Germany, to Secretary-General, International Seabed Authority (Courtesy English translation) *New York Times*, <https://int.nyt.com/data/documenttools/0275-23-en-dh-international-seabed-authority/8db587d82e0eef75/full.pdf>

relating to the matter under consideration. They are remarks that I am not only entitled to make, but also expected to make in accordance with my responsibilities under the Convention.

What is of particular concern is that the letter goes on to make a bold and unsubstantiated allegation, without facts or evidence, that I have, in the past, actively taken a stand against positions and decision-making proposals from delegations. This is untrue and I reject such a baseless allegation.

I wish to take this opportunity to remind you of the provisions of Article 168 of the Convention and the obligation on each State Party to respect the exclusively international character of the responsibilities of the Secretary-General and the staff and not to seek to influence them in the discharge of their responsibilities.

I would suggest that circulating your letter to all members and observers of the Council would be ill-advised and unnecessary. Nevertheless, if Germany insists to circulate your letter, I respectfully request that you do so with my letter in response, and my remarks to the intersessional dialogue, attached.[142]

This correspondence is notably significant amid the ongoing debates at the ISA on the implications of Nauru's actions with respect to the "two-year trigger rule" previously mentioned. It raises pertinent questions about whether the secretary general will maintain the backing of states to perform his functions. Furthermore, there is uncertainty about how this instability may affect the progress of the Mining Code and its implications for the continued resilience of the mining regime.

Conclusion

When the ISA was first proposed in the 1960s, there was limited knowledge about the deep sea, mining's impact, and its consequences.[143] Similarly, little to no information was available about climate change at that time. Our efforts to address climate change and the technological solutions available for this purpose are conflicting with the imperative to protect and conserve the deep-sea marine environment. The dilemma presents us with some challenging decisions. Do we prioritise combating climate change while simultaneously

142 Letter from the Secretary-General of the International Seabed Authority, Michael Lodge, to Dr. Franziska Brantner, Parliamentary State Secretary, German Federal Ministry for Economic Affairs and Climate Action, available at *New York Post*, https://int.nyt.com/data/documenttools/2023-03-17-michael-lodge-letter-to-parliamentary-state-secretary-dr-brantner-germany/e3c8ac54bae32135/full.pdf

143 K Miller and K Thompson, et al., 'An overview of Seabed mining including the current state of development, environmental impacts, and knowledge gaps' (2018) 4 (418) *Frontiers in Marine Science* 1, 11.

mining in the deep sea to secure the mineral resources needed to decarbonise the global economy? Is it ethically and legally sound to allow mining in an environment about which we have limited knowledge, especially regarding its environmental impact? These are contradictory challenges that the law of the sea must grapple with in our current uncertain climate. They represent two critical challenges to both the resilience and the robustness of the international law of the sea in an uncertain future.

Decisions must be made on whether mining of the deep sea should progress on a commercial scale or if, as argued by some states, the uncertain and unknown environmental impact warrants a moratorium or a "precautionary pause" as the only feasible option. As has been argued in this chapter, a "precautionary pause" as opposed to a moratorium seems most consistent with international law.

Nevertheless, considering the potential scarcity of critical and rare earth minerals in the foreseeable future, should calls for either a moratorium or a halt to deep-sea mining succeed, there is an immediate necessity to find alternative sources. Failing to do so will jeopardise the transition towards a decarbonised future. Technological advancements are essential to improve the efficient utilisation of these minerals. We must develop technology components that can be easily disassembled and recycled, integrating existing supplies into the circular economy more effectively. Additionally, we need to invest in research and innovation in recycling, as well as in new infrastructure and technology to increase recycling rates.[144] Considering projected metal shortages, will these actions alone be sufficient to meet the demands of our technical solutions to climate change? If we opt not to mine the deep sea, could we find ourselves unable to implement the technology essential for tackling climate change? These are the wicked choices we face in the Anthropocene, where addressing intricate environmental challenges requires making challenging decisions. These technological solutions challenge the resilience of Part XI of UNCLOS and raise doubts about its continued relevance to our shared future.

144 T Watari and B McLellan et al., 'Environmental impacts and demand-supply balance of minerals for the transition to a low-carbon energy system' (2020) 9(1) *International Journal of Smart Grid and Clean Energy* 189, 196.

5 The case for using Elinor Ostrom's studies on robustness and adaptive governance to implement the BBNJ Agreement

Kristine Elfrida Dalaker

Introduction

Following the successful conclusion of the intergovernmental conference (IGC)[1] convened by the United Nations under the United Nations Convention on the Law of the Sea (UNCLOS)[2] for the negotiation of a treaty for the conservation and sustainable use of marine biological diversity[3] in areas beyond national jurisdiction (BBNJ Agreement),[4] it is timely to explore the next steps for bringing the agreement into force and implementing its provisions. With the adoption of the BBNJ Agreement on 19 June 2023, the challenging work of bringing the agreement into force can now begin. Article 68 of the BBNJ Agreement provides that it will enter into force 120 days after the sixtieth party deposits its instrument of ratification, approval, acceptance, or accession.[5] If the past is prologue (given that UNCLOS took 12 years to come into force and the UN Fish Stocks Agreement[6] took 6 years), this could be a lengthy process. Once the BBNJ Agreement comes into force, it will be the third implementing agreement under UNCLOS, with the Part XI

1 *International Legally Binding Instrument under the United Nations Convention on the Law of the Sea on the Conservation and Sustainable Use of Marine Biological Diversity of Areas Beyond National Jurisdiction*, GA Res 72/749, UN GAOR, UN Doc A/Res/72/249 (24 December 2017) ('*GA Res 72/249*'). The five individual sessions of the IGC are referred to numerically. For example, the first session is referred to as IGC-1.

2 *United Nations Convention on the Law of the Sea*, opened for signature 10 December 1982, 1833 UNTS 397 (entered into force 16 November 1994) ('*UNCLOS*').

3 The terms "marine biological diversity" and "marine biodiversity" are used interchangeably in this chapter.

4 See *Agreement under the United Nations Convention on the Law of the Sea on the Conservation and Sustainable Use of Marine Biological Diversity of Areas Beyond National Jurisdiction*, opened for signature 20 September 2023, A/CONF.232/2023/4 (not yet in force) ('*BBNJ Agreement*').

5 Ibid art 68.

6 *Agreement for the Implementation of the Provisions of the United Nations Convention on the Law of the Sea of 10 December 1982 Relating to the Conservation and Management of Straddling Fish Stocks and Highly Migratory Fish Stocks*, opened for signature 4 August 1995, 2167 UNTS 3 (entered into force 11 December 2001) ('*UN Fish Stocks Agreement*').

DOI: 10.4324/9781003518570-5

Agreement[7] and the UN Fish Stocks Agreement being the two other implementing agreements. This chapter assumes that the BBNJ Agreement will come into force; therefore, its scope is limited to how the implementation of the BBNJ Agreement can be achieved.

The implementation of the BBNJ Agreement will be a massive undertaking by the international community, one that will encompass a broad array of topics and detailed considerations. In preparing for the implementation, it is important to keep in mind what the agreement is trying to achieve. The general objective of the BBNJ Agreement is to ensure the conservation and sustainable use of BBNJ, for the present and in the long term, through the effective implementation of the relevant provisions of UNCLOS and further international cooperation and coordination.[8] Given the uncertainty regarding when the BBNJ Agreement will enter into force and the dynamic nature of the global commons that it governs, the agreement's robust implementation must be considered within the context of a framework of analysis that can adapt to an uncertain future amid the ongoing planetary crisis. To paraphrase Rachel Carson, this framework must be able to evolve alongside changing conditions.[9]

To develop a regime for the governance of BBNJ that can meet the agreement's general objective, this chapter looks outside the traditional law of the sea and draws inspiration from Elinor Ostrom's theory of polycentric governance. The reason for choosing Ostrom has much to do with the fact that numerous references were made during the BBNJ negotiations about the need for "robust" institutional arrangements. The issue of determining what robustness may mean in the context of BBNJ led this author to turn to Ostrom. By way of background, Elinor Ostrom, a renowned political economist, studied the governance of the commons and is the academic who further developed the theory of polycentric governance.[10] She was awarded the 2009 Nobel Memorial Prize for Economic Science for "her analysis of economic governance, especially the commons".[11] In developing her theoretical framework for polycentric governance, Ostrom focused on the robustness of institutional arrangements in managing common-pool resources (CPRs).[12] Ostrom found

7 *Agreement Relating to the Implementation of Part XI of the United Nations Convention on the Law of the Sea of 10 December 1982,* opened for signature 28 July 1994, 33 ILM 1309 (entered into force 28 July 1996) ('*Part XI Agreement*').

8 *BBNJ Agreement* (n 5) art 2.

9 Carson (n 1).

10 The focus of Ostrom's research arose in part out of a direct challenge to Hardin's 1968 'Tragedy of the Commons'. Garrett Hardin, 'The Tragedy of the Commons' (1968) 162(3859) *Science: New Series* 1243.

11 The Nobel Prize, 'Elinor Ostrom', (Web Page) <https://www.nobelprize.org/prizes/economic-sciences/2009/ostrom/facts/>.

12 Ostrom broadly defined "institutions" as follows: formal and informal mechanisms that shape social and individual expectations, interactions, and behaviour. Margaret M Polski and Elinor Ostrom, 'An Institutional Framework for Policy Analysis and Design' in Daniel H Cole and

that polycentric approaches can complement overarching global agreements in combating commons problems that require collective action at differing levels and scales, such as BBNJ.[13] Given that this chapter develops recommendations for the robust implementation of a treaty that governs a global commons from an institutional perspective, the use of Ostrom's theoretical framework as the point of departure is a natural fit.

Ostrom's research also informed the examination of the relationship between social and ecological considerations in managing CPRs, such as BBNJ, thereby contributing to the field of socio-ecological system (SES) studies. These studies explore the relationship between social actors and institutions within ecosystems and draw in part on the study of robustness. Academics in the SES field often explore how governance choices in SESs affect the robustness of those systems, i.e. their ability to result in sustainable (or successful) outcomes. This chapter follows in that same tradition by exploring which governance choices could be used to provide for the robust implementation of the BBNJ Agreement through its institutional arrangements, the constitutive documents for the subsidiary bodies established under the treaty, and other institutional arrangements necessary for its implementation.

Ostrom's later research in SES studies focused in part on the governance of CPRs in dynamic and diverse commons. In her studies on ocean fisheries, Ostrom used an adaptive governance approach. Adaptive governance is a concept from institutional theory that deals with the evolution of institutions for the management of CPRs.[14] This approach is uniquely suited for this chapter because it focuses on *how* institutional arrangements integrate adaptive management in conserving and sustainably using resources in diverse commons where change is omnipresent, such as in vast marine areas.

By viewing the implementation of the BBNJ Agreement through Ostrom's research on robustness and adaptive governance, the aim of this chapter is two-fold: (i) to use Ostrom's framework of analysis to assess the robustness of the treaty text; and (ii) from that analysis, to develop recommendations for the robust implementation of the agreement. In furtherance of this aim, this chapter is organised as follows. The first part of this chapter sets the stage by briefly discussing the background to and the context of the BBNJ process and the resulting agreement. The next part discusses Ostrom's studies on robustness and adaptive governance and how they can form a framework of analysis from which the robustness of the treaty text can be assessed and recommendations

---

Michael D McGinnis (eds), *Elinor Ostrom and the Bloomington School of Political Economy: A Framework for Policy Analysis* (Lexington Books, 2017), 13, 14.

13 Elinor Ostrom, 'Polycentric Systems for Coping with Collective Action and Global Environmental Change' (2010) 20(4) *Global Environmental Change* 550.

14 Steve Hatfield-Dodds, Rohan Nelson, and David Cook, 'Adaptive Governance: An Introduction and Implications for Public Policy' (Conference Paper, Australian Agricultural and Resource Economics Society Annual Conference, 13–16 February 2007).

for its robust implementation can be developed. This chapter then sets out the analysis and recommendations before closing with concluding remarks.

Setting the stage: the BBNJ process and Ostrom's theoretical framework

Marine areas beyond national jurisdiction (ABNJ), which comprise the Area and the high seas,[15] are a global commons where no state sovereignty exists under UNCLOS. The governance of CPRs within ABNJ poses unique challenges.[16] ABNJ are open access where anyone can enter and use the resources.[17] It is also difficult to define users of the resources and to exclude others from using them.[18] A further complicating factor is that one's use of the resources subtracts from the benefits and/or quantity of the resources enjoyed by others.[19]

In Ostrom's research, she examined the governance of "open access" common-pool resources, which she defined as those "common-pool resources that anyone can harvest, which are likely to be overharvested and potentially destroyed".[20] Within the context of the diverse commons of the oceans, Ostrom acknowledged that the "basic problem leading to massive overfishing in the oceans is the lack of any property rights for the many commercially valuable species in the open ocean", concluding that most ocean fisheries are open access common-pool resources.[21] Similarly, the location and nature of these resources in ABNJ make Ostrom's studies on open access CPRs particularly relevant to the framework for analysis used in this chapter.

Relevant background and context to the BBNJ process

The international community became aware of both the threats to and the importance of BBNJ in 2003, eventually leading to the convening of the IGC.[22] The conference negotiated four substantive elements (commonly referred to as the "package deal"): (1) marine genetic resources (MGRs), including questions on the sharing of benefits; (2) area-based management tools (ABMTs),

15 *UNCLOS* (n 3) arts 86, 89.

16 Ostrom and Dolšak found that the oceans are CPRs suitable for study and exploration using a polycentric approach. Nives Dolšak and Elinor Ostrom, 'The Challenges of the Commons', in Nives Dolšak and Elinor Ostrom (eds), *The Commons in the New Millennium: Challenges and Adaptations* (MIT Press Academic, 2003) 3.

17 Ibid.

18 Elinor Ostrom, 'The Challenge of Common-Pool Resources' (2008) 50(4) *The Environment* 10, 11 ('The Challenges of Common-Pool Resources').

19 Ibid.

20 Ostrom, 'The Challenges of Common-Pool Resources' (n 19) 11.

21 Ibid 12.

22 *Report on the Work of the United Nations Open-ended Informal Consultative Process on Oceans and the Law of the Sea*, 58th sess, UN Doc A/58/95 (9 June 2003).

including marine protected areas (MPAs); (3) environmental impact assessments (EIAs); and (4) capacity building and the transfer of marine technology (CBTT).[23]

The institutional arrangements needed to implement and operationalise the BBNJ Agreement were a cross-cutting issue that was the subject of great debate in the negotiations.[24] Some delegations sought to centralise and coordinate activities and conservation measures in ABNJ under the new regime. Other delegations expressed concerns with that approach, emphasising the IGC mandate that "the process and its result should not *undermine* existing relevant legal instruments and frameworks and relevant global, regional and sectoral bodies" (IFBs),[25] while still others took a middle-of-the-road position. In line with these positions, delegations proposed three approaches to the institutional arrangements during the IGC and its preparatory work: a global approach, a regional/sectoral approach, and a hybrid approach.[26] The IGC concluded with a treaty in line with the hybrid approach, whereby the BBNJ Agreement incorporates a global process to serve as a forum to conduct overall coordination and set international guidelines and standards that can be implemented at the regional/sectoral levels, among other functions enumerated in the agreement,[27] but do "not undermine" the IFBs.[28]

23 *GA Res 72/249* (n 2).

24 Kristine Dalaker Kraabel, 'The BBNJ PrepCom and Institutional Arrangements: The Hype about the Hybrid Approach', in Myron H Nordquist, John Norton Moore, and Ronan Long (eds), *The Marine Environment and United Nations Sustainable Development Goal 14 (Life Below Water)* (Koninklijke Brill, 2018) 137. See also International Institute for Sustainable Development, 'Conservation and Sustainable Use of Marine Biological Diversity Beyond Areas of National Jurisdiction – BBNJ', (Web Page) <https://enb.iisd.org/negotiations/conservation-and-sustainable-use-marine-biological-diversity-beyond-areas-national> and author's IGC notes (on file with author).

25 *GA Res 72/249* (n 2) para 7 (emphasis added). For a discussion on "not undermining", see Ethan Beringen, Nengye Liu, and Michelle Lim, 'Australia and the Pursuit of "Not Undermining" Regional Bodies at the Biodiversity Beyond National Jurisdiction Negotiations' (2022) 136 *Marine Policy*; Vito De Lucia, 'Rethinking the Conservation of Marine Biodiversity beyond National Jurisdiction: From "Not Undermine" to Ecosystem-Based Governance' (2019) 8(4) *ESIL Reflections*; Zoe Scanlon, 'The Art of "Not Undermining": Possibilities of Existing Architecture to Improve Environmental Protections in Areas Beyond National Jurisdiction' (2018) 75(1) *ICES Journal of Marine Science* 405–416.

26 *Chair's non-paper on elements of a draft text of an international legally-binding instrument under the United Nations Convention on the Law of the Sea on the conservation and sustainable use of marine biological diversity of areas beyond national jurisdiction*, (Non-Paper, 28 February 2017), 93–95 ('Chair's Non-Paper').

27 See Dalaker Kraabel (n 25).

28 *BBNJ Agreement* (n 5) art 5(2) ("[a]greement shall be interpreted and applied in a manner that does not undermine IFBs"), art 22(2) ("COP shall undermine IFBs in establishment of ABMTs"), art 22(5) ("decisions and recommendations adopted by the COP under Part III of the Agreement shall not undermine the effectiveness of measures adopted in respect of areas within national jurisdiction and shall be made with due regard for the rights and duties of all States, in accordance with UNCLOS").

Five sessions of the IGC were held between 2018 and 2023. The adoption of the final text was a lengthy process and took place over three time periods. The fifth session was first held from 15 to 26 August 2022 (IGC-5.1), a resumed fifth session was held from 20 February to 4 March 2023 (IGC-5.2), and a further resumed fifth session was held on 19 June 2023, at which the text of the BBNJ Agreement (IGC-5.3) was adopted.[29] The agreement opened for signature on 20 September 2023, and will come into force 120 days after the sixtieth ratification.[30]

From an institutional perspective, a preparatory commission will need to be established as soon as possible after the adoption of the BBNJ Agreement. The primary aim of the preparatory commission will be to lay the foundations for the establishment of the institutional agreements under the agreement, prepare for the first meeting of the conference of the parties (COP), and ensure that adequate funding is in place for the implementation of the agreement.[31] The necessary preparations for the institutional arrangements under the BBNJ Agreement are discussed in more detail below.

Ostrom and her work on polycentric governance

This section first explores Ostrom's studies on robust institutional arrangements, focusing specifically on nested enterprises. Then, the section turns to her work on adaptive governance within dynamic and diverse commons.

Ostrom on robustness

In Ostrom's research on polycentric governance,[32] she examined the relationship between the sustainability of institutions and the sustainability of resources.[33] She found that the success of a CPR was tied to the sustainability of its

29 *International Legally Binding Instrument under the United Nations Convention on the Law of the Sea on the Conservation and Sustainable Use of Marine Biological Diversity of Areas Beyond National Jurisdiction,* (GA Dec 76/564 to hold IGC-5, available as A/76/L.46), <https://documents.un.org/doc/undoc/ltd/n22/298/78/pdf/n2229878.pdf?token=DUqgSJPxncziP0BiIe&fe=true>. IGC-4 was held in March 2022, having been postponed due to the COVID-19 pandemic (*Intergovernmental conference on an international legally binding instrument under the United Nations Convention on the Law of the Sea on the conservation and sustainable use of marine biological diversity of areas beyond national jurisdiction*, GA Dec 74/543, UN Doc A/74/L.41 to postpone the Fourth Session of the Conference).

30 BBNJ Agreement (n 5) art 68.

31 Kristina Maria Gjerde et al., 'Getting beyond yes: fast-tracking implementation of the United Nations agreement for marine biodiversity beyond national jurisdiction' (2022) 1 *Ocean Sustainability* 6.

32 Elinor Ostrom, *Governing the Commons: The Evolution of Institutions for Collective Action* (Cambridge University Press, 1990) ('Governing the Commons').

33 Ibid. According to McGinnis, in contrast to adaptability, resilience, or sustainability, robustness is the appropriate criterion to use when evaluating human-designed systems. Michael D McGinnis, 'The IAD Framework in Action: Understanding the Source of the Design Princi-

institutions, thus allowing her to conclude that robust institutions are indeed integral to the sustainable management of CPRs.[34]

Ostrom's work resonated in the interventions made throughout the BBNJ process, where delegations proposed the inclusion of *robust* institutional arrangements for the agreement.[35] However, little indication of what "robust" meant was discussed in the negotiations.[36] This was not the first time that the term had been invoked within the context of the international community. The term was used at the 2022 climate change negotiations at COP26 in Glasgow, where the EU delegation defined the elements of a successful outcome of the negotiations as including *robust* rules for the cooperative approaches under Article 6 of the Paris Agreement.[37] Similarly, the European Commission underscored the need for a *robust* framework of rules for global carbon markets.[38] Recently, the term was used widely by the International Seabed Authority (ISA) in Jamaica, where negotiations were taking place to agree on deep seabed mining regulations. Several delegations called for a *robust* mining code, a *robust* framework for exploitation activities, and *robust* institutional arrangements, among others.[39]

The Cambridge Dictionary provides some guidance as it defines "robustness" as the quality of "being strong, and healthy or unlikely to break or fail".[40] Similarly, Ostrom ties the concept of robustness to the likelihood of success or failure of relevant institutions to achieve sustainable outcomes for CPRs.[41] Ostrom explained further that "[b]y 'successful' [CPR] institutions, [she

ples in Elinor Ostrom's Governing the Commons' in Daniel Cole and Michael D. McGinnis (eds) (2018) 3 *Elinor Ostrom and the Bloomington School of Political Economy: A Framework for Policy Analysis*, 87-108.

34 Elinor Ostrom, 'Beyond Markets and States: Polycentric Governance of Complex Economic Systems' (2010) 100 *American Economic Review* 641, 652–653 ('Beyond Markets and States').

35 The interventions were reflected in the chair's non-paper. Chair's Non-Paper (n 27) 93–95, 94 (n 690). See also this author's notes from the BBNJ Intersessional Work (on file with the author) ('Author's BBNJ Intersessional Work Notes') and author's IGC notes (n 25).

36 Ibid.

37 IISD Reporting Services, 'Glasgow Climate Change Conference: Sunday, 31 October 2021' (Report, 31 October 2021) 12(782) *Earth Negotiations Bulletin* 1.

38 IISD Reporting Services, 'Glasgow Climate Change Conference: Sunday, 1 November 2021' (Report, 1 November 2021) 12(783) *Earth Negotiations Bulletin* 2.

39 IISD Reporting Services, 'Summary of the Twenty-eighth Annual Session of the International Seabed Authority (First Part): 16-31 March 2023' (Report, 4 April 2023) 25(251) *Earth Negotiations Bulletin.*

40 *Cambridge Dictionary* (online as of 15 May 2024) 'robustness'.

41 Sustainable outcomes and productive outcomes are terms that are closely related to sustainability. In 1987, the United Nations Brundtland Commission defined sustainability (positively) as the ability to "meet… the needs of the present without compromising the ability of future generations to meet their own needs", while the BBNJ Agreement landed on a definition of "sustainable use" that defines it (negatively) as the "use of components of biological diversity in a way and at a rate that does not lead to a long-term decline of biological diversity, thereby maintaining its potential to meet the needs and aspirations of present and future generations".

meant] institutions that enable individuals to achieve productive outcomes in situations where temptations to free-ride and shirk are ever present".[42] This finding makes Ostrom's studies on robustness appropriate for exploration within the context of the conservation and sustainable use of BBNJ.

Ostrom's research on the robustness of institutions has contributed significantly to SES studies, which explore the relationship between social actors and institutions within ecosystems.[43] SESs are known to be both complex and adaptive. These systems require continuous monitoring and assessment for the purpose of developing knowledge and understanding for the protection and use of the resources within those systems.[44] The interdisciplinary field of SES research not only draws on the study of robustness, which serves as the focus of this chapter, but also involves the study of resilience, sustainability, and vulnerability.[45] Within the SES context, robustness is defined as follows: "[A SES] is robust if it prevents the ecological systems upon which it relies from moving into a new domain of attraction that cannot support a human population, or that will induce a transition that causes long-term human suffering".[46]

Ostrom's seminal research, *Governing the Commons*, comprises a meta-analysis of multiple cases where resource users organised themselves to protect a CPR from overuse.[47] To answer the question of what types of rules appear to be most successful in protecting CPRs from overuse, Ostrom collected and analysed the meta-data across these multiple cases. From that analysis, Ostrom distilled the institutional elements – or best practices – that were present within

BBNJ Agreement (n 5) art 1(13). Both definitions focus on the success or failure of the management of the use of the resource.

42 Ostrom, 'Governing the Commons' (n 33) 15.

43 See, e.g. Stefan Partelow, 'Co-evolving Ostrom's Social-Ecological Systems (SES) Framework and Sustainability Science: Four Key Co-Benefits' (2016) 11 *Sustainability Science* 399.

44 Steve R Carpenter and Lance H Gunderson, 'Coping with Collapse: Ecological and Social Dynamics in Ecosystem Management' (2001) 51 *BioScience* 451. The need for the continuous monitoring and assessment of these systems related to adaptive management is discussed above.

45 Eduardo Araral, 'What Makes Socio-Ecological Systems Robust? An Institutional Analysis of the 2,000 Year-Old Ifugao Society' (2013) 41 *Human Ecology* 859.

46 Graham R Marshall, 'Nested, subsidiarity, and community-based environmental governance beyond the local level' (2008) 2(1) *International Journal of the Commons* 75, 78, quoting John M Anderies, Marco A Janssen and Elinor Ostrom, 'A Framework to Analyze the Robustness of Social-Ecological Systems from an Institutional Perspective' (2004) 9(1) *Ecology and Society* 7.

47 Ostrom, 'Governing the Commons' (n 33); Ostrom, 'Beyond Markets and States' (n 35) 649–650.

robust[48] institutions and governance systems, describing these eight elements as "design principles".[49]

Of these principles, this chapter focuses on the eighth design principle, which applies to groups that comprise large-scale systems: nested enterprises.[50] In large-scale systems that govern CPRs, small-scale organisations tend to be "nested" within a large-scale organisation, allowing for rules to exist at multiple levels of governance, with some autonomy at each level.[51] The eighth design principle encompasses aspects of Ostrom's second to seventh design principles in that rules for appropriation, provision, monitoring, enforcement, conflict resolution, and decision-making are organised at multiple levels within such nested enterprises.[52] For that reason, Ostrom maintained that what differentiated robust nested enterprises from less robust governance systems was the presence of ***complete coordination*** of rules across the levels of governance.[53] The coordination of decisions across the system relies on collaboration between multiple decision-making centres, which relies in turn on the voluntary cooperation of its members.[54] Such complete coordination requires both vertical and horizontal coordination: vertical coordination within the nested enterprises and horizontal coordination across related governance systems.[55]

Some scholars have described nested enterprises as multiple levels of governance akin to Russian nesting dolls, where the rules at the lower levels of governance fit within the rules set at increasingly higher levels.[56] Other scholars

48 Ostrom engaged in the study of the robustness of systems. Elinor Ostrom, *The Future of the Commons: Beyond Market Failure and Government Regulations* (The Institute of Economic Affairs, 2012) 77 ('The Future of the Commons').

49 Ostrom, 'Beyond Markets and States' (n 35) 653; Ostrom, 'The Challenges of Common-Pool Resources' (n 19) 31–32. The design principles include: (1A and 1B) clearly defined user and resource boundaries; (2A and 2B) congruence with local conditions, both ecological conditions and local rules on appropriation and provision; (3) collective-choice arrangements; (4A and 4B) monitoring the resource and users; (5) graduated sanctions; (6) conflict resolution mechanisms; (7) minimal recognition of rights to organise; and (8) for "nested enterprises" (groups that are part of large-scale systems), appropriate coordination among relevant groups. Following the publication of *Governing the Commons*, Cox et al. improved Ostrom's design principles, and Ostrom adopted those improvements. Michael Cox, Gwen Arnold, and Sergio Villamayor Tomas, 'A Review of Design Principles for Community-based Natural Resource Management' (2010) 15(4) *Ecology and Society*.

50 Ostrom, 'Governing the Commons' (n 33) 101–102.

51 David Sloan Wilson, Elinor Ostrom, and Michael E Cox, 'Generalizing the Core Designs Principles for the Efficacy of Groups' (2013) 90S *Journal of Economic Behavior and Organization* S21; Ostrom, 'The Future of the Commons' (n 49) 82.

52 Ostrom, 'Governing the Commons' (n 33) 90.

53 Ibid 101–102.

54 Graham R Marshall, 'Nested, Subsidiarity, and Community-Based Environmental Governance beyond the Local Level' (2008) 2(1) *International Journal of the Commons* 75, 79.

55 Blake Hudson and Jonathan Rosenbloom, 'Uncommon Approaches to Commons Problems: Nested Governance Commons and Climate Change' (2013) 64 *Hastings Law Journal* 1273, 1314–1336.

56 Marshall (n 55) 77.

have criticised this description as being too simplistic and misconstruing Ostrom's view on nested governance as too top-down in its approach, for it presupposes that beginning with the highest level of governance – or the largest Russian nesting doll – each subsequent level of governance is smaller and fully encapsulated within the previous level.[57] Strict adherence to a "Russian nesting doll" approach to nested governance may not result in sustainable outcomes for CPRs.[58]

Two elements contribute to the robustness of institutional arrangements in nested enterprises: (1) the presence of a global coordinating body; and (2) decentralised decision-making centres that are sufficiently subsidiarised.[59] Regarding the first element, Ostrom emphasised the importance of large-scale organisations in nested enterprises to provide overall coordination, among other functions.[60] Other scholars support this view, contending that the lack of a legally binding global treaty or other arrangement for nested governance "has the potential to devolve into a tragedy".[61]

Regarding the second element, Ostrom found that decentralisation is essential to polycentricity, especially within nested enterprises. Even though decentralised systems may seem chaotic and fragmented, Ostrom found that their institutions may be more ordered and successful in achieving sustainable outcomes than they appear and may be preferable to centralised governance systems.[62] The decentralised nature of nested enterprises facilitates *subsidiarity* in which problems can be addressed at the most relevant and capable scale.[63] Subsidiarity means that "any particular task should be decentralised to the lowest level of governance with the capacity to conduct it satisfactorily".[64] Notably, subsidiarity does not require that such tasks be nested in strict accordance with a Russian nesting doll approach (as described above), but can in fact be assigned in keeping with the appropriate scope and scale relevant to

57 Prakash Kashwan and Robert Holahan, 'Nested Governance for Effective REDD+ Institutional and Political Arguments' (2014) 8(2) *International Journal of the Commons* 554, 560.
58 Ibid. Marshall (n 55) 80.
59 Ibid.
60 A large-scale organisation can add overall competence to help with higher level functions, such as monitoring performance, imposing sanctions, obtaining reliable information, and providing conflict resolution mechanisms to manage the resource. Ostrom, 'The Future of the Commons' (n 49) 81–82.
61 Hudson and Rosenbloom (n 56) 1301.
62 Ostrom, 'The Future of the Commons' (n 49); see also Robin Mahon and Lucia Fanning, 'Regional Ocean Governance: Integrating and Coordinating Mechanisms for Polycentric Systems' (2019) 107 *Marine Policy* 3.
63 Mahon and Fanning (n 63) 3; Cox et al. (n 50) 36.
64 Marshall (n 55) 80.

those tasks.[65] Decentralised decision-making that is sufficiently subsidiarised provides several benefits, particularly at the lower levels of governance.[66]

This chapter considers these two elements as part of the framework of analysis set out below.

Ostrom and the need for adaptive governance in diverse commons

Ostrom found that the governance of CPRs is highly dependent on the type and size of the resource involved, necessitating tailored governance choices.[67] In Ostrom's *The Challenge of Common-Pool Resources*, she turned her attention to the diverse commons of ocean fisheries.[68]

In reflecting on UNCLOS and its effect on the management of ocean resources, Ostrom recognised the limitations of UNCLOS to conserve and manage marine resources in ABNJ. She concluded that additional governance measures need to be taken to address commons problems in complex, uncertain, and fragmented systems.[69] She argued that *adaptive governance* is one such measure that should be considered.[70]

At the outset, *adaptive management*[71] should, however, be distinguished from *adaptive governance*, a related term with which it is often confused. Adaptive management focuses on the ecosystem and how to improve policy implementation in the face of changing circumstances within that ecosystem (i.e. regular monitoring by "learning through doing").[72] Due to its focus on the ecosystem, adaptive management is frequently integrated into an ecosystem approach.[73] In contrast, adaptive governance focuses on how institutional arrangements integrate adaptive management in conserving and sustainably using CPRs within diverse ecosystems where change is omnipresent, such

65 Kashwan and Holahan (n 58).

66 The benefits include: (1) improving access to local knowledge; (2) increasing the use of informal institutional arrangements to promote trust and reciprocity; (3) increasing reliance on disaggregated knowledge; (4) allowing for rules to be adapted to local conditions; (5) lowering the monitoring and enforcement costs by strengthening local perceptions of the legitimacy of rules; and (6) creating opportunities that allow for experimentation (and redundancy), thereby reducing the probability of failure for a large area. Elinor Ostrom, 'Coping with Tragedies of the Commons' (1999) 2 *Annual Review of Political Science* 493, 526.

67 Ostrom, 'The Challenges of Common-Pool Resources' (n 19) 10, 17.

68 Ibid.

69 Ibid.

70 Ibid.

71 See, e.g. Convention on Biological Diversity, *CBD Guidelines: The Ecosystem Approach* (Report, 2004), 1–2; the BBNJ Agreement includes an ecosystem approach as one of its guiding principles. *BBNJ Agreement* (n 5) art 7(f).

72 Lyndal Hasselman, 'Adaptive Management; Adaptive Comanagement; Adaptive Governance: What's the Difference?' (2017) 24(1) *Australasian Journal of Environmental Management* 31–46.

73 Ibid.

as marine resources.[74] Moreover, in adaptive governance, "[t]he legal and administrative arrangements need to enable flexibility and responsiveness; [and] institutions need to learn, problem-solve and connect across diverse stakeholders and knowledge bases".[75]

By employing an adaptive governance approach, this chapter next explores how to connect marine ecosystems in ABNJ with the institutions tasked with governing the management of them. Although legal scholars indicate that the management of marine ecosystems requires some semblance of adaptive governance,[76] there is little in the literature that dictates what adaptive governance specifically entails or looks like in practice for the high seas. Therefore, Ostrom's theoretical framework on adaptive governance may inform the way in which the BBNJ Agreement can be effectively implemented institutionally.

Numerous scholars (including Ostrom) have identified five requirements for adaptive governance from multidisciplinary studies of failed and successful regimes for governing diverse commons (such as the oceans). The requirements are closely aligned with Ostrom's design principles and were promoted by Ostrom with respect to ocean fisheries.[77] Adhering to these requirements increases the likelihood that robust institutions will result, and sustainable outcomes will be achieved. Ostrom's requirements for adaptive governance include: (i) obtaining accurate and relevant information for use in rule-making by focusing on the creation and use of timely scientific knowledge that is updated on a regular basis for monitoring CPRs; (ii) enhancing rule compliance by users through the monitoring of CPRs by the users themselves (rather than through centralised or external arrangements); (iii) dealing with conflict across multiple levels quickly and effectively; (iv) providing physical, technological, and institutional infrastructure to increase the effectiveness of internal operations, as well as to provide necessary linkages to other large regimes (i.e. coordination); and (v) an overall requirement of encouraging adaptation and change of the decision-making mechanisms in institutional arrangements to respond to errors and emerging developments.[78]

Assessment of the robustness of the BBNJ Agreement and recommendations for its robust implementation

Similar to the Part XI Agreement and the UN Fish Stocks Agreement, the BBNJ Agreement will be an implementing agreement under UNCLOS.

74 Ibid.

75 Ibid.

76 Froukje Maria Platjouw, *Environmental Law and the Ecosystem Approach* (Routledge, 2016); David Langlet and Rosemary Rayfuse, 'The Ecosystem Approach in Ocean Planning and Governance: An Introduction' in David Langlet and Rosemary Rayfuse (eds), *The Ecosystem Approach in Ocean Planning and Governance* (Brill Nijhoff, 2019).

77 Ostrom, 'The Challenges of Common-Pool Resources' (n 19) 17.

78 Ibid.

Therefore, the BBNJ nested enterprises examined in this chapter comprise UNCLOS as the overarching agreement, under which the BBNJ Agreement and its future related agreements are (and will be) "nested".

As such, this part first assesses the BBNJ Agreement from an institutional perspective using a framework of analysis that includes the two elements that contribute to robust institutional arrangements in BBNJ nested enterprises, together with five requirements for adaptive governance. In the discussion of each element and requirement, this part then extrapolates recommendations for the robust implementation of the BBNJ Agreement. As the point of departure, this part uses the BBNJ Agreement as adopted.[79] The view of delegations during the IGC was that the BBNJ Agreement should be both implementable and future-proof, where it includes sufficient detail to ensure that it can be implemented while retaining flexibility for future institutional development.[80] Therefore, this chapter's recommendations also include requirements for the constitutive documents of subsidiary bodies established under the BBNJ Agreement, and other institutional arrangements necessary to implement and operationalise the agreement.

The two elements that contribute to robust institutions in nested enterprises

First element: global coordination

Ostrom emphasised that the presence of a global coordinating body contributes to robustness because it provides the centralisation of key functions. Regarding the BBNJ nested enterprise where UNCLOS serves as the top of the nested enterprise, the institutional structure does not include a conference of the parties or other such global coordinating body. However, one could argue that the Meeting of States Parties (SPLOS) held in accordance with Article 319(2)(e) of UNCLOS and the Division for Ocean Affairs and the Law of the Sea (DOALOS) of the United Nations Office of Legal Affairs serve in this capacity either individually or in combination. Similarly, the UN Fish Stocks Agreement does not include a COP but does in fact conduct review conferences on a periodic basis.[81]

In a significant improvement as far as the robustness of the regime is concerned, the BBNJ Agreement includes the establishment of institutional arrangements that will provide overall coordination at the global level once

79 *BBNJ Agreement* (n 5).

80 Intersessional Work – Reports on the Four Thematic Issues of the BBNJ Conference and Cross-cutting Issues (September 2020 – March 2021) (on file with author), 25. At the 19 March 2021 session on cross-cutting issues that President Lee facilitated, she emphasised that the "first pillar of effectiveness" of the BBNJ treaty was its implementability. This view was echoed by several other delegations. 'Author's BBNJ Intersessional Work Notes' (n 36).

81 Article 36 of the UN Fish Stocks Agreement allows for the secretary general of the United Nations to convene a review conference. A review conference was first convened in 2006 and has been resumed periodically. *UN Fish Stocks Agreement* (n 7) art 36.

the agreement enters into force. The primary institutional arrangements established under the agreement include a COP,[82] a scientific and technical body (STB),[83] a secretariat,[84] and a clearing-house mechanism (ChM).[85] The BBNJ Agreement also establishes an access and benefit-sharing committee, a capacity building and transfer of marine technology committee, a funding mechanism (under which the COP will establish a finance committee), and an implementation and compliance committee (ICC), in addition to the option for the establishment of additional bodies.[86] The BBNJ Agreement includes the associated functions of all institutional arrangements established under the agreement.[87]

Although the final treaty text provides for a fairly centralised role for the COP,[88] the COP's functions have been weakened to some extent through the deletion of some obligations and the dilution of others.[89] The COP's functions were limited during IGC-5.1, particularly regarding monitoring, which had the effect of rendering the regime less robust at the global level (see below). Arguably, the COP's decision-making was also weakened by the inclusion of opt-out provisions in Article 23 of the BBNJ Agreement, which allow a state

82 *BBNJ Agreement* (n 5) art 47.
83 Ibid art 49.
84 Ibid art 50.
85 Ibid art 51.
86 *BBNJ Agreement* (n 5) art 15 (Access and benefit sharing committee), art 46 (CBTT committee), art 52 (Funding mechanism), art 52(14) (Finance committee), art 55 (Implementation and compliance committee).
87 See, e.g. BBNJ Agreement (n 5) art 15 (access and benefit sharing committee), art 16 (monitoring and transparency), art 18 (area of application), art 19 (proposals), art 21 (consultations on and assessments of proposals), art 22 (establishment of ABMTs, including MPAs), art 23 (decision-making), art 24 (emergency measures), art 28 (obligation to conduct EIAs), art 29 (relationships between the agreement and EIA processes under IFBs), art 33 (EIA reports), art 34 (decision-making), art 35 (monitoring of impacts of authorised activities), art 36 (reporting on impacts of authorised activities), art 37 (review of authorised activities and reporting on their impacts), art 38 (standards and/or guidelines to be developed by STB related to EIAs), art 39 (SEAs), art 44 (types of CBTT), art 45 (monitoring and review of CBTT), art 46 (CBTT Committee), art 47 (Conference of the Parties), art 48 (transparency), art 49 (Scientific and Technical Body), art 50 (Secretariat), art 51 (Clearing-house mechanism), art 52 (funding), art 54 (monitoring of implementation), art 55 (Implementation and compliance committee), art 72 (amendments), art 74 (annexes).
88 To aid the COP in its decision-making, the BBNJ Agreement permits the COP to request an advisory opinion from the International Tribunal on the Law of the Sea on a legal question on the conformity of the agreement with any proposal before the COP that falls within its competence. *BBNJ Agreement* (n 5) art 47(7).
89 See, e.g. *Revised draft text of an agreement under the United Nations Convention on the Law of the Sea on the conservation and sustainable use of marine biological diversity of areas beyond national jurisdiction*, 4th sess, UN Doc A/CONF.232/2020/3 (18 November 2019). This includes a proposed provision that would allow for the COP to monitor and keep under review the implementation of the agreement. This provision and similar provisions were not included in the final text that was adopted by the IGC.

party to opt out of any decision made under Part III of the agreement with respect to ABMTs, provided that one or more of certain conditions are met. While Article 23 includes safeguards to limit a party's ability to make an objection under this provision, opt-out provisions like these are prone to abuse in practice. This susceptibility could potentially affect the robustness/success of any measures taken in accordance with those decisions.

Given the mandate of the BBNJ Agreement and the several institutional arrangements that will be established under the agreement,[90] the key to the successful implementation of the agreement will be the funding mechanism established under Article 52. Funding for early ratification will be key to swift ratification and the long-term success of the agreement. Recognising the importance of such funding, the EU pledged 40 million euros for early ratification at IGC-5.2.[91] As adopted, the funding mechanism of the agreement initially comprises three funds: (i) a voluntary trust fund to facilitate participation by developing states parties in the meetings of the bodies established under the agreement; (ii) a special fund that will be funded by the contributions under Article 14 (fair and equitable sharing of benefits from activities involving MGRs and digital sequence information [DSI]) of the agreement; and (iii) the Global Environment Facility (GEF) trust fund.[92] This author's fear is that the agreement will not garner enough support to come into force. Alternatively, if the agreement does come into force, there might not be sufficient financial support from developed states in the form of assessed contributions to support its several institutions and to otherwise support the financial mechanism established by the agreement.

The effective implementation of the BBNJ Agreement requires that thorough preparations for the establishment of these institutional arrangements be conducted prior to the agreement entering into force. This can be achieved through the establishment of a preparatory commission as soon as possible following the adoption of the BBNJ Agreement. Its establishment will allow time to prepare for the first meeting of the COP and develop the institutional structure for the agreement through the establishment of working groups and the preparation of terms of reference for all institutional arrangements established under the agreement.[93]

90 *BBNJ Agreement* (n 5) art 52(2) (institutions established under the agreement will be funded through the assessed contributions of the parties).

91 Directorate-General for Maritime Affairs and Fisheries, 'An historic achievement: Treaty of the High Seas is adopted' (Web Page, 19 June 2023) <https://oceans-and-fisheries.ec.europa.eu/news/historic-achievement-treaty-high-seas-adopted-2023-06-19_en>.

92 *BBNJ Agreement* (n 5) art 52(4).

93 See Gjerde (n 32).

Second element: decentralisation and subsidiarity

For robust implementation, the BBNJ Agreement and its operationalising agreements and arrangements should promote the use of new and existing decentralised decision-making centres and arrangements. In accordance with Ostrom's studies, the assignment of functions across these decision-making centres and arrangements should be done in a way that is consistent with the principle of subsidiarity and takes into consideration the capacity of those who are performing the functions.

In this regard, the treaty text includes several provisions[94] that recognise existing arrangements and promote new ones.[95] The BBNJ Agreement also includes the concept of compatibility, which contributes to the "completeness" of the BBNJ regime as a robust nested enterprise. Specifically, the concept of compatibility was included in respect of ABMTs, where the COP may take decisions that are compatible with those adopted by relevant IFBs.[96]

During the implementation phase, consideration should be given to conducting a stocktake of the IFBs that may require consultation and coordination as part of the operationalisation of the BBNJ Agreement. Because the BBNJ Agreement includes several provisions that require the consideration of "relevant IFBs" in the consultation and due regard obligations outlined in the agreement, it will be essential for the parties to identify possible IFBs and consider their relevance to various aspects of the agreement.[97]

94 *BBNJ Agreement* (n 5) art 8 (international cooperation), art 19(2) (consultations on development of ABMT proposals), art 21 (consultation on and assessment of proposals), art 29 (taking into account the EIA processes of other relevant IFBs), art 32 (public notification and consultation), art 42 (modalities for CBTT), art 49 (STB should draw on advice from existing organisations), art 52(8) (funding should take into account existing funding mechanisms), art 55(4) (Implementation and Compliance Committee may draw on appropriate information from bodies established under the BBNJ Agreement, as well as relevant IFBs).

95 The promotion of the use of existing bodies, legal instruments, and frameworks takes into account the mandate of the IGC to "not undermine existing relevant legal instruments and frameworks and relevant global, regional and sectoral bodies". *International legally binding instrument under the United Nations Convention on the Law of the Sea on the conservation and sustainable use of marine biological diversity of areas beyond national jurisdiction*, GA Res 72/249, UN Doc A/RES/72/249 (19 January 2018), para 7.

96 *BBNJ Agreement* (n 5) art 22(1)(b) ("may take decisions on measures compatible with those adopted by…"). Complementarity and compatibility were discussed at length during the IGC, but no consensus was reached on a preferable term. Consensus was finally reached at IGC-5.2 on the term "compatible". Related discussions focused on "not undermining", resulting in the following language: decisions taken under Article 22 "shall respect the competences and not undermine relevant legal instruments and frameworks and relevant global, regional, subregional and sectoral bodies". *BBNJ Agreement* (n 5) art 22(2).

97 *BBNJ Agreement* (n 5) arts 15(5), 19(2), 21, 22(3), 22(5), 24(2), 32, 37(5) (IFBs "may be consulted"), 48(3).

Five requirements for adaptive governance

Monitoring the resource

Monitoring the resource is essential to the robust implementation of the BBNJ regime. While UNCLOS does not have an institutional body that has the primary task of monitoring marine resources,[98] the BBNJ Agreement, on the other hand, includes several such obligations, including Article 16 (monitoring of activities relating to MGRs and digital sequence data), Article 19 (ABMT proposal must outline proposal for monitoring), Article 26 (monitoring and review of ABMTs by STB), and Article 35 (monitoring of impacts of authorised activities under EIAs). Closely related to monitoring the resource is the compilation and dissemination of information to ensure that the best available science and scientific information and, where available, relevant traditional knowledge of Indigenous Peoples and local communities can be used for implementation.[99] The BBNJ Agreement provides that the ChM established under the agreement will serve as the portal for such compilation and dissemination.[100]

During the implementation phase, monitoring the resource should be subsidiarised and all information and reports should be fed into the ChM. In keeping with the need for decentralisation and subsidiarisation, existing organisations, bodies, and arrangements for monitoring the resource should be used wherever possible. The Ocean Biodiversity Information System (OBIS) is an example of a global open-access data and information clearing-house on a marine biodiversity platform that could support the BBNJ Agreement.[101] OBIS has been incorporated into a larger Ocean InfoHub (OIH) to be managed by the Intergovernmental Oceanographic Commission (IOC) of the United Nations Educational, Scientific, and Cultural Organization (UNESCO).[102]

98 Of its many functions, DOALOS also monitors and reviews developments in ocean affairs and the law of the sea and reports thereon to the General Assembly through annual reports on oceans and the law of the sea, as well as other reports as required on sustainable fisheries-related issues or on specific topics of current interest.

99 *BBNJ Agreement* (n 5) art 40(d) (increase the dissemination and sharing of information as an objective of CBTT), art 44 (types of CBTT, which include information dissemination and awareness-raising, including relevant traditional knowledge of Indigenous Peoples and local communities), art 48(3) (promotion of transparency, including through the public dissemination of information as part of the consultation process under the agreement).

100 *BBNJ Agreement* (n 5) art 51(3)(a) (ChM to serve as a centralised platform to enable parties to access, provide, and disseminate information with respect to activities undertaken under the agreement), art 51(5) (management of ChM shall fully recognise developing states parties, and all such information provided to those states on the activities taken under the agreement shall be provided with the aim of promoting dissemination).

101 Ocean Biodiversity Information System, 'SG-OBIS-VII' (Web Page) <https://obis.org/about/sg-obis-7/>.

102 Ocean InfoHub Project (Web Page) <https://oceaninfohub.org>. The OIH is an initiative that aims to improve access to ocean science data and information for management and sustainable development. The IOC, through the OIH, intends to merge OBIS, together with

The OIH focuses on *existing* global, regional, and national data, information, and knowledge resources by establishing a network of regional and thematic nodes that will improve access to these resources.[103] Although the IOC is included in Article 51(4) of the BBNJ Agreement as an organisation with which the ChM may cooperate,[104] formalising the role of the IOC (together with other organisations, including UNESCO, the International Maritime Organization [IMO], the International Seabed Authority, and the Food and Agriculture Organization of the United Nations [FAO]) in supporting the ChM would contribute to the robustness of the BBNJ regime.

Monitoring users

The BBNJ Agreement provides for the limited monitoring of users, which blurs the line between monitoring the resource and monitoring users.[105] "Users" can be defined as those who utilise MGRs, where the "utilization of MGRs" is defined under the agreement as the "means to conduct research and development on the genetic and/or biochemical composition of marine genetic resources, including through the application of biotechnology".[106] While some provisions call for the notification of the utilisation of MGRs,[107] other provisions obligate states parties to do little more than self-report their activities and the performance of their obligations under the BBNJ Agreement.[108]

The review of the implementation and effectiveness of the agreement is related to monitoring and is governed by Part VIII of the BBNJ Agreement.[109] Article 55 of the BBNJ Agreement provides for the establishment of an implementation and compliance committee to facilitate and consider the

its related online resources, including OceanExpert, OceanDocs, the Ocean Best Practices System, the World Ocean Database (WOD), and Ocean Data Portal (ODP). In addition, the OIH plans to develop the Ocean Data and Information System (ODIS) architecture to foster the interoperability of existing information systems.

103 Ibid. One of the webinars held during the BBNJ Intersessional Work focused on how the IOC, through the OIH, could support the ChM under the BBNJ Agreement, which included monitoring the resources.

104 *BBNJ Agreement* (n 5) art 51(4).

105 The monitoring of users by the COP was gutted during the later sessions of the IGC.

106 Article 1(14) of the BBNJ Agreement defines the "utilization of MGRs" as the means to conduct research and development on the genetic and/or biochemical composition of marine genetic resources, including through the application of biotechnology, and Article 1(3) defines "biotechnology" as "any technological application that uses biological systems, living organisms, or derivatives thereof, to make or modify products or processes for specific use".

107 *BBNJ Agreement* (n 5) arts 12(7), (8), 16.

108 *BBNJ Agreement* (n 5) arts 26, 35–37, 45(3), 54. An exception is Article 45(2), where the monitoring of CBTT shall be carried out by the CBTT Committee under the guidance of the COP.

109 Ibid art 25 (implementation of ABMT provisions), art 53 (implementation of the agreement).

implementation of, and promote compliance with, the provisions of the BBNJ Agreement.[110] Furthermore, the agreement provides that the ICC shall be "facilitative in nature and function in a manner that is transparent, non-adversarial and non-punitive".[111] These provisions contribute to the robustness of the regime and should be further elaborated upon in the terms of reference of the ICC. In addition, the COP is required to convene a review process to evaluate the adequacy and effectiveness of the BBNJ Agreement five years after the agreement's entry into force and on a periodic basis thereafter and may make recommendations for the strengthening of the agreement's implementation.[112] These are welcome inclusions and will contribute to the robustness of the BBNJ regime if implemented.

More extensive provisions for monitoring users, together with provisions for control and surveillance, should have been included in the BBNJ Agreement in order to ensure the robustness of the regime.[113] However, a couple of enabling provisions have been included in the body of the agreement, which could then be operationalised by the COP.[114] To ensure the completeness of the regime, these functions need to be sufficiently subsidiarised, with the focus on building trust and encouraging reciprocity at lower levels of governance. Doing otherwise would create a regime that is overly top-down and centralised in its approach and would not go far enough in ensuring that there are adequate "hooks" to create and maintain the vertical and horizontal linkages that will be necessary for the robust implementation of the BBNJ regime.

Dealing with conflicts

Regarding how the governance system for diverse commons deals with conflicts, both UNCLOS and the BBNJ Agreement obligate the parties to promote the peaceful settlement of disputes.[115] UNCLOS is unique in a treaty of broad acceptance in that it includes compulsory and binding dispute

110 Ibid art 55(1).
111 Ibid art 12(6).
112 Ibid art 47(8).
113 See, e.g. Klaudija Cremers, Glen Wright, and Julien Rochette, 'Strengthening Monitoring, Control and Surveillance of Human Activities in Marine Areas Beyond National Jurisdiction: Challenges and Opportunities for an International Legally Binding Instrument' (2020) 122 *Marine Policy*; Klaudija Cremers, Glen Wright, and Julien Rochette, 'Strengthening Monitoring, Control and Surveillance of Human Activities in Marine Areas Beyond National Jurisdiction' (2020) *STRONG High Seas Project*.
114 *BBNJ Agreement* (n 5) arts 35, 44(1)(h). Sophie Mirgaux, special envoy for the ocean for the Belgian Ministry of the Environment, made this suggestion in the following seminar: 'Strengthening Monitoring, Control and Surveillance of Human Activities in Marine Areas Beyond National Jurisdiction: Challenges and Opportunities for an International Legally Binding Instrument' (IDDRI Seminar, 17 November 2020).
115 *UNCLOS* (n 3) art 279; *BBNJ Agreement* (n 5) art 57.

settlement provisions under Part XV of the convention.[116] Likewise, the dispute settlement provisions of the UN Fish Stocks Agreement provided ample inspiration for the BBNJ Agreement because it adopts Part XV of UNCLOS *mutatis mutandis*. However, some delegations were hesitant to simply import the UN Fish Stocks Agreement's mandatory dispute resolution provisions in their entirety into the BBNJ Agreement.[117] Unlike the UN Fish Stocks Agreement, whose mandate is limited to specific fish stocks, the mandate of the BBNJ Agreement encompasses the broad subject matter of marine biodiversity and will likely also encompass and/or intersect with issues relating to environmental protection, sustainable use, climate-related issues, and intellectual property issues, among others.[118] Therefore, disputes are likely to arise under one or more treaties under the UNCLOS framework and/or other legal regimes, which could give rise to jurisdictional questions regarding the compulsory dispute settlement procedures under UNCLOS (if, as with the UN Fish Stocks Agreement, Part XV of UNCLOS were applied *mutatis mutandis* to the BBNJ Agreement) and voluntary dispute settlement procedures under another treaty.[119]

Going into the final negotiations at IGC-5.2, the provisions regarding the procedures for the settlement of disputes included two options: one which modelled the compulsory dispute resolution provisions of the UNFSA (i.e. adoption of Part XV of UNCLOS *mutatis mutandis*), and the other which provided for a voluntary mechanism.[120] The final formulation of Part IX of the BBNJ Agreement resulted in compromise provisions that differ from the two clear options considered at the start of the session. However, these provisions still include many of the same elements, such as compulsory and voluntary dispute settlement mechanisms, provisions relating to non-parties to UNCLOS, certain exclusions from jurisdiction, and "without prejudice" provisions, which prevent UNCLOS dispute settlement processes from superseding those under other agreements. For the purposes of this chapter, the fact that Article 60 of the agreement includes formal procedures for the resolution of disputes contributes to the robustness of the overall BBNJ regime. Thus, a

116 *UNCLOS* (n 3) pt XV.

117 For a discussion of proposals and considerations regarding the dispute resolution mechanism for the BBNJ Agreement, see Yubing Shi, 'Settlement of Disputes in a BBNJ Agreement: Options and Analysis' (2020) 122 *Marine Policy*; Joanna Mossop, 'Dispute Settlement in Areas Beyond National Jurisdiction' in Vito De Lucia, Alex Oude Elferink, and Lan Ngoc Nguyen (eds), *International Law and Marine Areas Beyond National Jurisdiction* (Brill Nijhoff, 2022).

118 Mossop (n 118); 'Author's BBNJ Intersessional Work Notes' (n 36).

119 Mossop (n 118). This issue of "parallel" jurisdiction was raised at the webinar on dispute resolution convened by President Lee during the BBNJ Intersessional Work. 'Author's BBNJ Intersessional Work Notes' (n 36).

120 *BBNJ Agreement* (n 5) pt IX (Settlement of Disputes). One delegation proposed a third option late in the negotiations.

legal analysis and commentary on the resulting BBNJ dispute resolution procedures are outside the scope of this chapter.[121]

For those conflicts that do not rise to the level of disputes, they are subject to the dispute resolution procedures. The resolution of such conflicts between and among parties to the BBNJ Agreement should be sufficiently subsidiarised. In addition, all such conflicts should be resolved expeditiously and in a cost-effective manner. In that regard, the BBNJ Agreement has been improved in significant ways. One, it includes provisions that promote the peaceful settlement of conflicts between and among parties through alternative means, including negotiation, inquiry, mediation, and conciliation, among others of their choice.[122] Two, like the UN Fish Stocks Agreement, the BBNJ Agreement uses *ad hoc* expert panel procedures for those conflicts of a technical nature.[123] Both of these improvements will contribute to the robust implementation of the agreement.

During the BBNJ negotiations, discussions on dispute resolution began to focus on dispute prevention, with several delegations noting the link between dispute resolution and compliance.[124] The BBNJ Agreement includes a provision that merely requires parties to cooperate to prevent disputes.[125] However, this dispute prevention provision is bolstered by the inclusion of a provision establishing the ICC.[126] The establishment of the ICC not only supports the requirement for adaptive governance when dealing with conflicts but also supports the requirement for monitoring users and contributes to the overall robustness of the regime.

Vertical and horizontal coordination and institutional linkages

Notably, the BBNJ Agreement includes several vertical linkages to UNCLOS, which strengthen the BBNJ regime.[127] Given the broad mandate of the BBNJ Agreement, the inclusion of general and specific vertical and horizontal linkages – both vertical coordination within the BBNJ regime and horizontal coordination across related regimes – will be critical to the successful implementation of the BBNJ Agreement. Even though Article 8 of the BBNJ Agreement obligates all states parties to cooperate between and among all relevant IFBs for

121 Another provision in Part IX of the agreement that was the subject of great debate is the addition of paragraph (7) to Article 60, which deals with the issue of non-parties to UNCLOS.

122 *BBNJ Agreement* (n 5) arts 57–58.

123 Ibid art 59. Some delegations sought to clarify that such disputes must be of a scientific rather than a technical nature but were not successful.

124 'Author's BBNJ Intersessional Work Notes' (n 36). These delegations encouraged the use of the COP, STB, performance review process, and a possible compliance committee to work together to prevent disputes.

125 *BBNJ Agreement* (n 5) art 56.

126 Ibid art 55.

127 Ibid Preamble, arts 2, 5, 7(b), 8, 11, 22, 23, 25, 27, 60.

the conservation and sustainable use of BBNJ and to promote international cooperation in marine scientific research and the transfer of marine technology, the agreement includes few specific horizontal linkages.[128]

To implement the provisions of the BBNJ Agreement related to horizontal linkages, it will be necessary for the relevant institution (e.g. COP, STB) under the agreement to enter into instruments with other IFBs. These instruments may take various forms, including but not limited to memoranda of understanding (MOU), memoranda of agreement, memoranda of cooperation, and data exchange agreements. Such instruments could provide for the exchange of data and scientific information, and the pursuit of issues of mutual interest, including collaboration on research efforts of common interest and the adequacy of conservation and management measures.

During the implementation of the agreement, consideration should be given to avoiding disputes and/or difficulties in operationalising the BBNJ Agreement.[129] It would also be incumbent on delegations to ensure that in formalising the horizontal linkages, they do not contravene Article 5(2) of the BBNJ Agreement, which states (consistent with the IGC mandate) that the interpretation and application of the agreement shall not undermine relevant IFBs.[130]

Discussions at the IGC negotiations underlie the level of coordination that will be required during the implementation phase in establishing and maintaining the vertical and horizontal linkages throughout the BBNJ regime. One such example shows that delegations have begun to focus on *how* to structure the management of the ChM such that the IOC would have a clear mandate for its support of the BBNJ Agreement and would not be subject to "two masters" – the COP and UNESCO.[131] A related question that has arisen is *how* to link the various existing clearing house mechanisms that could aid the implementation of the BBNJ Agreement, either through its ChM, regional nodes, or other means.[132] Article 51(3)(c) of the BBNJ Agreement obligates the ChM to consider this very question and provide links to such existing databases and clearing house mechanisms. This can and should be achieved during the implementation phase of the BBNJ Agreement.

128 Ibid art 8.

129 See Article 5(3) of the BBNJ Agreement, which provides that the legal status of non-parties to UNCLOS or any other related agreements is not affected by the agreement. This language was included to further the universal acceptance of the agreement.

130 Ibid art 5(2).

131 See *BBNJ Agreement* (n 5) art 51(4) where although the BBNJ Agreement refers to the IOC as a possible institution for cooperation, the logistical arrangements for such cooperation remain undetermined. Furthermore, the BBNJ Agreement leaves the specific modalities for the operation of the ChM to the COP, ibid art 51(2). See also 'Author's BBNJ Intersessional Work Notes' (n 36).

132 Ibid.

Successful implementation and ability to respond to future challenges

Good governance principles underlie this requirement of adaptive governance and appear to be present within the BBNJ Agreement. For example, Article 12 of the BBNJ Agreement requires the COP to promote transparency in the decision-making processes and activities under the agreement.[133]

The BBNJ Agreement includes provisions that allow temporary measures to be taken in the event of an emergency caused by a natural phenomenon or a human-made disaster that has caused, or is likely to cause, serious or irreversible harm to BBNJ.[134] To allow for such measures to be taken on an emergency basis, the agreement provides that such measures may be proposed by parties or recommended by the STB, and adopted intersessionally.[135] Such measures are considered temporary and would be re-evaluated at the next meeting of the COP.[136]

The BBNJ Agreement includes several "future-proof" provisions, which allow its institutional arrangements to respond and adapt to new information and challenges.[137] For example, Article 47(6)(d) of the agreement provides that the COP may respond to emerging challenges by establishing subsidiary bodies as necessary to support the implementation of the agreement.[138] Also, terms such as "best available science" and "best practices" have been included throughout the BBNJ Agreement[139] to allow for future advances in scientific

133 Other provisions in the BBNJ Agreement that promote transparency include: art 15(1) (access and benefit sharing committee), art 16 (monitoring and transparency in MGR activities), art 21 (ABMT proposals), art 24(5) (ABMT emergency measures), art 32(4) (public notification and consultation in CBTT), art 42 (CBTT modalities), art 48 (transparency), art 51(3)(e) (ChM), art 52(14)(c) (funding), art 52(14) (finance committee), art 55(1) (ICC). Ibid.

134 Ibid art 24.

135 Ibid art 24(3).

136 Ibid art 24(3).

137 Ronan Long presented a paper at a Nordic online conference hosted by the University of Gothenburg Department of Law in which he made several specific recommendations for future-proofing the BBNJ Agreement. Ronan Long, 'Future-Proofing the BBNJ Agreement: Techniques for Future Normative Development', *Bioprospecting, Biodiversity and Novel Uses of Marine Resources – New Approaches in International Law* (Webinar Presentation, 30 March 2021).

138 *BBNJ Agreement* (n 5) art 47(6)(d).

139 Examples of the use of terms "best available science", "best practices", and "best available information" are already included in the BBNJ Agreement: art 7(i) (best available science), art 13 (STB shall collect information on current international best practices relating to MGRs in ABNJ), art 19(3) (identification of ABMTs using best available science), art 24(3) (measures taken on an emergency basis shall be based on the best available science), art 26(5) (use of best available science in the monitoring and review of ABMTs), art 31 (use of best available science in screening and scoping EIAs), arts 33(6), 33(7), 36, 38 (use of EIA reports to develop guidelines, including identification of best practices), art 39 (SEAs shall be used to collate and synthesise best available information about a region, assess impacts, and identify data gaps and priorities), annex II (ChM shall serve as repository of best practices, among other functions).

knowledge and technological development in the collection and dissemination of such knowledge.[140] The term "global minimum standards" in the context of EIAs had been included in a previous draft of the treaty text in IGC-5 but was deleted from the BBNJ Agreement as adopted. This deletion was unfortunate because its inclusion would have allowed for standardisation.

A positive inclusion in the BBNJ Agreement is the use of annexes to future-proof the BBNJ Agreement, where it is proposed that the indicative criteria for the identification of ABMTs and types of CBTT will be set out in annexes to the treaty and updated periodically.[141] The BBNJ Agreement also uses "indicative and non-exhaustive lists" for this purpose in another provision.[142]

It will be challenging to achieve the BBNJ Agreement's general objective of conserving and sustainably using BBNJ for the present and long term.[143] However, when viewed through the lens of Ostrom's design principle on nested enterprises and the associated requirements of adaptive governance, the BBNJ Agreement renders recommendations that provide an essential guide for the robust implementation of the agreement.

Concluding remarks

Lawyers and policymakers like certainty and predictability. In making governance choices for the management of CPRs, they often seek a solution that is set in stone – a blueprint that can be used in other circumstances without alteration in design or consideration of differences in the ecology, the resource, or the stakeholders.[144] Diverse commons, such as the ocean commons, are confounding, for they simply do not lend themselves to a cookie-cutter approach to governance. Ostrom acknowledged this fact in her later research, recognising that large-scale systems require more than basic adherence to her eight design principles, particularly the eighth one, which requires decentralisation and coordination in nested enterprises.[145]

The governance systems for diverse commons must, in fact, be able to change and adapt over time. For this reason, Ostrom promoted the investment by the global community in adaptive governance for the institutional architecture for the management of open access CPRs.[146] In keeping with Ostrom's work on diverse commons, if the BBNJ Agreement is to succeed in meeting its objective of ensuring the long-term conservation and sustainable use of

140 See Long (n 138).
141 *BBNJ Agreement* (n 5), arts 19, 44. Presumably, the Annex would be amended in the procedure set out in Article 74.
142 Ibid art 38(2)(a); the use of "indicative, non-exhaustive lists" that can be reviewed, assessed, and amended periodically is included in the agreement with respect to EIAs.
143 Ibid art 2.
144 Polski and Ostrom urged against a blueprint approach; Polski and Ostrom (n 13) 13, 15.
145 Ostrom, 'The Future of the Commons' (n 49).
146 Ostrom, 'The Challenges of Common-Pool Resources' (n 19) 19.

BBNJ, it must be built on an institutional foundation that is sufficiently robust to ensure its successful implementation as recommended in this chapter. In doing so, the BBNJ Agreement would serve as an example of a regime that can meet Rachel Carson's mandate for conservation in that it "must be dynamic, changing as conditions change, seeking always to become more effective".[147]

To close, in an important piece written by Nilufer Oral, the director of the Centre of International Law in Singapore, she reflected on the 1972 Stockholm Conference and its fiftieth anniversary and wrote in words that could have been mistaken for Ostrom's: "Where there is a *robust* legal framework and collective action, success can be achieved".[148]

147 Carson (n 1).

148 Nilufer Oral, 'A Fifty-Year Stocktaking and Achieving Transformative Change through the Rule of Environmental Law', *Pathway to the 2022 Declaration* (Blog Post, 9 May 2021) <https://www.pathway2022declaration.org/article/a-fifty-year-stocktaking-and-achieving-transformative-change-through-the-rule-of-environmental-law/> (emphasis added).

6 International fisheries as the "whale in the room" at the negotiations for a new instrument for biodiversity beyond national jurisdiction

Ethan Beringen

Introduction

The "elephant in the room" is an idiom referring to an obvious and significant subject of discussion that everybody is aware of but avoids acknowledging.[1] The "whale in the room" could be a fitting marine synonym. Throughout the negotiations for a new legally binding instrument to conserve and sustainably utilise Biodiversity beyond national Jurisdiction (BBNJ instrument), state delegates steadfastly avoided addressing a particularly large and controversial topic that loomed in the background. This was, of course, the issue of high seas fisheries and how the complex system of regional bodies and instruments related to fisheries would interface with the new convention. While the issues of conserving high seas biodiversity and managing international fisheries would seem to have significant overlap, this chapter examines whether this overlap is part of a broader pattern of separation between the legal regimes designed to address these goals.

The BBNJ instrument is an implementing agreement to the 1982 United Nations Convention on the Law of the Sea (UNCLOS), designed to fill gaps left in the "constitution for the oceans".[2] It is the third such implementing agreement, with the first two being the 1994 Agreement relating to the Implementation of Part XI of UNCLOS,[3] and the 1995 United Nations Fish

1 Mirriam-Webster Dictionary (online at 15 May 2024) "an elephant in the room".

2 See, e.g. Tommy Koh, "A Constitution for the Oceans' Remarks by Tommy B. Koh, of Singapore President of the Third United Nations Conference on the Law of the Sea" (Speech, Final Session of the Third United Nations Conference on the Law of the Sea at Montego Bay, 6 and 11 December 1982); *Development of an international legally-binding instrument under the United Nations Convention on the Law of the Sea on the conservation and sustainable use of marine biological diversity of areas beyond national jurisdiction*, GA Res 69/292, UN Doc A/RES/69/292 (6 July 2015, adopted 19 June 2015).

3 *Agreement relating to the Implementation of Part XI of the United Nations Convention on the Law of the Sea of 10 December 1982*, opened for signature 28 July 1994, 1836 UNTS 3 (entered into force 28 July 1996).

DOI: 10.4324/9781003518570-6

Stocks Agreement (UNFSA).[4] The BBNJ instrument has been through a process of extensive negotiation and planning, with the inception of the first working group on the issue dating back to 2004.[5] While its conclusion at the second session of the fifth intergovernmental conference in 2023 is undoubtedly a significant achievement,[6] the role that this instrument will play with regard to international fisheries law has been left relatively unaddressed in the final treaty text.

The apparent solution to this dilemma has been the much-discussed directive to interpret and apply the instrument in a way that "does not undermine relevant legal instruments and frameworks and relevant global, regional, subregional and sectoral bodies and that promotes coherence and coordination with those instruments, frameworks and bodies".[7] State parties have persistently argued for the exclusion of fisheries from the agreement entirely.[8] The final agreement includes only one provision directly addressing fisheries, which is to remove them from the scope of provisions on marine genetic resources (MGR).[9] Often cited is the UNFSA, accompanied by the argument that the matter of high seas fisheries is adequately settled.[10] However, the lack of clarity surrounding the meaning of the term "undermine",[11] coupled with the

4 *Agreement for the Implementation of the Provisions of the United Nations Convention on the Law of the Sea of 10 December 1982 relating to the Conservation and Management of Straddling Fish Stocks and Highly Migratory Fish Stocks,* opened for signature 4 August 1995, 2167 UNTS 3 (entered into force 11 December 2001) ('UNFSA').

5 *Sustainable fisheries, including through the 1995 Agreement for the Implementation of the Provisions of the United Nations Convention on the Law of the Sea of 10 December 1982 relating to the Conservation and Management of Straddling Fish Stocks and Highly Migratory Fish Stocks, and related instruments,* GA Res 59/25, UN Doc A/Res/59/25 (17 January 2005, adopted 17 November 2004), para 73.

6 See, e.g. International Institute for Sustainable Development, 'Summary of the Resumed Fifth Session of the Intergovernmental Conference on an International Legally Binding Instrument under the UN Convention on the Law of the Sea on the Conservation and Sustainable Use of Marine Biodiversity of Areas Beyond National Jurisdiction: 20 February – 4 March 2023' (Report, 7 March 2023) 25(250) *Earth Negotiations Bulletin* 1–20 ('IISD, 5th Session').

7 *Agreement under the United Nations Convention on the Law of the Sea on the Conservation and Sustainable Use of Marine Biological Diversity of Areas Beyond National Jurisdiction,* opened for signature 20 September 2023, A/CONF.232/2023/4 (not yet in force) art 5(2) ('BBNJ').

8 See, e.g. International Institute for Sustainable Development, 'Summary of the Fourth Session of the Intergovernmental Conference on an Internationally Legally Binding Instrument under the UN Convention on the Law of the Sea on the Conservation and Sustainable Use of Marine Biodiversity of Areas Beyond National Jurisdiction' (Report, 21 March 2022) 25(225) *Earth Negotiations Bulletin* 1, 5 ('IISD, 4th Session').

9 BBNJ (n 7) art 10(2).

10 UNFSA (n 4).

11 See, e.g. Zoe Scanlon, "The art of 'not undermining': possibilities within existing architecture to improve environmental protections in areas beyond national jurisdiction' (2018) 75(1) *ICES Journal of Marine Science* 405; Ethan Beringen, Nengye Liu, and Michelle Lim,

documented inadequacies of existing international fisheries law,[12] makes the decision to avoid fisheries a missed opportunity. For example, the Food and Agriculture Organization (FAO) found that 33.3% of the tuna stocks analysed were fished at biologically unsustainable levels, despite the plethora of regional fisheries management organisations (RFMOs) tasked with regulating these stocks.[13]

This chapter explores whether the negotiating states' reluctance to address fisheries in the BBNJ instrument can be traced back to the regime-based narratives of international fisheries law and international biodiversity law. Regime interaction theory posits that international law is made up of a fragmented series of regimes, which can be defined as "sets of norms, decision-making procedures and organisations coalescing around functional issue-areas and dominated by particular modes of behaviour, assumptions and biases".[14] Hey focuses specifically on the idea of "particular modes of behaviour, assumptions and biases" and argues that regimes represent epistemic communities that are particularly guided by regime-based narratives.[15] These narratives themselves are built largely upon the foundational principles of the respective regimes, and interactions between the regimes are filtered through these narratives.[16] Hence, understanding these narratives allows a better understanding of how interactions between these regimes take place.

In this context, there are several potential "regimes" to consider. This chapter primarily analyses "international fisheries law" and "international biodiversity law", while acknowledging that both form a smaller part of the broader regime of the "law of the sea". Specifically, three foundational instruments are focused on in the analysis: UNCLOS and UNFSA for international fisheries law, and the Convention on Biological Diversity (CBD) for international biodiversity law.[17] It is important to analyse these foundational instruments given that governance principles formed at the beginning of a regime can be par-

'Australia and the pursuit of "not undermining" regional bodies at the biodiversity beyond national jurisdiction negotiations' (2022) 136 *Marine Policy* 104929.

12 See, e.g. Food and Agriculture Organization of the United Nations, *The State of World Fisheries and Aquaculture* (Report, 2022) ('FAO').

13 Ibid 52.

14 Margaret A Young, 'Introduction: The Productive Friction Between Regimes' in Margaret A Young (ed), *Regime Interaction in International Law: Facing Fragmentation* (Cambridge University Press, 2012) 11.

15 Ellen Hey, 'Regime Interaction and Common Interests in Regulating Human Activities in Areas Beyond National Jurisdiction' in Seline Trevisanut, Nikolaos Giannopoulos, and Rozemarijn Roland Holst (eds), *Regime Interaction in Ocean Governance: Problems, Theories and Methods* (Brill Nijhoff, 2020) 85.

16 Ibid 98–99.

17 *United Nations Convention on the Law of the Sea*, opened for signature 10 December 1982, 1833 UNTS 397 (entered into force 16 November 1994) ('UNCLOS'); UNFSA (n 4); *Convention on Biological Diversity*, opened for signature 5 June 1992, 1760 UNTS 79 (entered into force 29 December 1993) ('CBD').

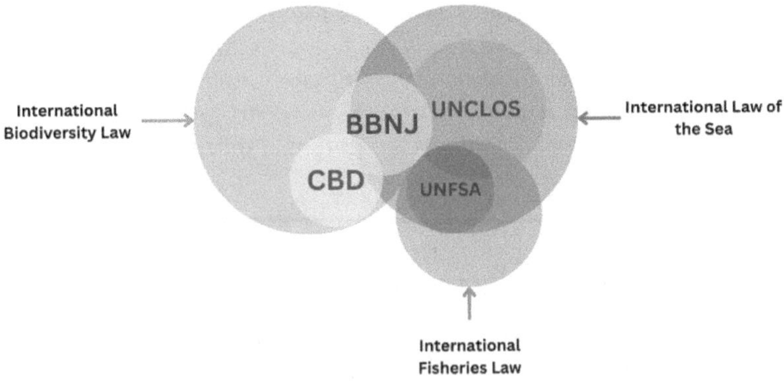

Figure 6.1 Visual representation of the regime complex to be analysed

ticularly influential in the future direction of its narrative.[18] The BBNJ instrument, being a part of both the law of the sea and international biodiversity law, can be seen as a site of interaction between these various regimes. Figure 6.1 offers a visual representation of this regime complex. As represented in Figure 6.1, international fisheries law operates within the framework of the law of the sea regime and interacts with international biodiversity law and the BBNJ without complete overlap (illustrated visually as the spheres touching). However, UNCLOS overlaps with both the BBNJ and UNFSA as they both act as implementing agreements for obligations found within UNCLOS.

As such, this chapter examines whether the differences in regime-based narratives between international fisheries law and international biodiversity law are responsible for the "whale in the room". Competing priorities between these separate regimes may have led to the artificial separation of this international biodiversity instrument from fisheries considerations, even though the two regimes share many common goals and subject matter.[19] Understanding these dynamics allows international environmental law to more readily adapt to cross-regime challenges, such as marine biodiversity loss, as the Earth system becomes increasingly unpredictable.

This chapter comprises three sections. The first defines and demonstrates the regime-based narratives that exist for international fisheries law and international biodiversity law through an analysis of UNCLOS, the UNFSA, and the CBD. This section explores the reasons for the divergence between these two regimes, despite their apparent similarities. The next section highlights the role of these regime-based narratives within the BBNJ negotiations and the final instrument, demonstrating the convergence of competing narratives and the ultimate effect that this process had on the treaty. Finally, the

18 Hey (n 15) 115.
19 See, e.g. UNFSA (n 4) art 2; CBD (n 17) art 1.

implications of these entrenched narratives for the emerging planetary crisis are discussed, with a particular focus on human-induced challenges for the management of high seas biodiversity. Ultimately, the chapter demonstrates how competing conceptions of marine biodiversity governance have been reflected in the BBNJ instrument, to the potential detriment of its coherence and effectiveness.

Defining the contrasting regime-based narratives of international fisheries law and international biodiversity law

When exploring regime interaction, it is crucial to define precisely what is included within the regimes to be analysed. In this case, "international fisheries law" and "international biodiversity law" are broad regime categories for analysis compared to the discussion of discrete instruments or institutions. That is why the analysis focuses on so-called foundational instruments within each regime: UNCLOS and the UNFSA for international fisheries law, and the CBD for international biodiversity law.[20] This helps to identify the foundational governance principles within the two regimes as well as the differing approaches they take to their mandates.

It is important to acknowledge that the international fisheries law regime in this context is much broader than simply UNCLOS and the UNFSA. They have been chosen as they form the regulatory framework for fishing activities on the high seas specifically. However, they are far from the only instruments and institutions that make up international fisheries law. For example, the role of the FAO is important as it has created a myriad of fisheries-related instruments under its purview.[21] These include the Compliance Agreement, the Port State Measures Agreement, and the Deep-Sea Fisheries Guidelines.[22] Additionally, regional bodies such as RFMOs play an important role in the regime beyond national jurisdiction, as they are indeed the focal point of much of the UNFSA.[23] It is beyond the scope of this chapter to review each of these instruments in detail, though they are referenced more generally as necessary

20 UNCLOS (n 17); UNFSA (n 4); CBD (n 17).

21 See, e.g. Food and Agriculture Organisation of the United Nations, 'Fisheries and Aquaculture' (Web Page, 2021) <https://www.fao.org/fishery/en/activities>.

22 *Agreement to Promote Compliance with International Conservation and Management Measures by Fishing Vessels on the High Seas*, opened for signature 24 November 1993, 2221 UNTS 91 (entered into force 24 April 2003); Food and Agriculture Organization of the United Nations, *Agreement on Port State Measures to Prevent, Deter and Eliminate Illegal, Unreported, and Unregulated Fishing*, opened for signature 22 November 2009, (entered into force 5 June 2016); Food and Agriculture Organization of the United Nations, *International Guidelines for the Management of Deep-Sea Fisheries in the High Seas* (Report, September 2008) ('DSF Guidelines').

23 See, e.g. Stefán Ásmundsson, 'Regional Fisheries Management Organisations (RFMOs): Who are they, what is their geographic coverage on the high seas and which ones should be considered as General RFMOs, Tuna RFMOs and Specialised RFMOs?' (2016); UNFSA (n 4).

to supplement the analysis of UNCLOS and the UNFSA in order to allow for the construction of a regime-based narrative for international fisheries law.

In respect of international biodiversity law, this chapter focuses chiefly on the CBD but it also acknowledges other instruments that are relevant to marine biodiversity and the high seas in particular. These include the Convention on International Trade in Endangered Species of Wild Fauna and Flora (CITES) and the Convention on the Conservation of Migratory Species of Wild Animals (CMS).[24] Additionally, several key soft law instruments can be consulted, including the Stockholm Declaration, the Rio Declaration, the Sustainable Development Goals, as well as the Aichi Biodiversity Targets and the Kunming–Montreal Global Biodiversity Framework (KMGBF).[25] These soft law instruments in particular are key resources for a number of governance principles under international biodiversity law. The BBNJ instrument itself fits more readily under this regime than international fisheries law. This chapter does not act as a comprehensive overview of every aspect of this extensive regime. Instead, it occasionally draws upon common threads between these instruments and institutions to reach a shared regime-based narrative for the purpose of analysis.

Additionally, it is necessary to briefly highlight the theoretical lens used to conduct the analysis. Hey provides a unique insight into the idea of regimes as "epistemic communities", not just a collection of norms and institutions.[26] She states that regimes form such communities "in which a certain way of knowing, also linked to expertise, including legal expertise, is foregrounded".[27] Hey argues that when regimes interact, there is competition between the respective regime-based narratives as to what to regulate, how it should be regulated, and who undertakes this regulation and receives the benefits and burdens.[28] Therefore, questions about what, how, and who are crucial in understanding the narratives of particular international regimes, such as international fisheries law and international biodiversity law.

Furthermore, in her analysis of the interactions between international regimes, some key insights emerge on the nature of these regime-based narratives. The first is that these narratives are based strongly upon the governing

24 *Convention on International Trade in Endangered Species of Wild Fauna and Flora*, opened for signature 3 March 1973, 993 UNTS 243 (entered into force 1 July 1975); *Convention on the Conservation of Migratory Species of Wild Animals*, opened for signature 23 June 1979, 1651 UNTS 333 (entered into force 1 November 1983).

25 Convention on Biological Diversity, 'Aichi Biodiversity Targets' (Web Page, 2020) <https://www.cbd.int/sp/targets/> ('CBD Aichi Targets'); Convention on Biological Diversity, 'COP 15: Final Text of the Kunming-Montreal Global Biodiversity Framework' (Web Page, 2022) <https://www.cbd.int/article/cop15-final-text-kunming-montreal-gbf-221222>.

26 Hey (n 15) 85.

27 Ibid.

28 Ibid.

principles within the regime, particularly if they are founding principles.[29] Hey argues that these principles, in particular, play a role in determining "how an activity is to be regulated and who matters in that regulatory context".[30] Secondly, Hey argues that institutional arrangements "co-determine who matters and which narrative prevails".[31] Both formal and informal institutional arrangements are said to contribute to this narrative.[32] Voting arrangements, for example, are argued to be a key way that formal decision-making processes can determine whose interests are represented by the regime-based narrative.[33] On the other hand, less formal arrangements, such as the composition of government representatives and stakeholders involved in this process, also determine this narrative.[34] Finally, Hey notes a "generational" conflict in the interaction between older regimes and their more recent counterparts,[35] and argues that regimes are highly "path dependent" in a way that is "engrained in law, which in turn is based on the political choices that were made at the time the regime was negotiated".[36] Hence, regime-based narratives are somewhat inflexible given that they emerge from the founding governing principles of the regime and are reinforced by its institutional relationships.[37] This is not to say that regimes cannot change and develop over time, but rather that such change is only possible within the constraints of the governing principles and institutional arrangements of the regime.

In this vein, the next section looks at the selected instruments from the regimes in order to define and contrast the regime-based narratives of international fisheries law and international biodiversity law. These regime-based narratives inform the subsequent analysis of the BBNJ instrument.

Regime-based narrative of international fisheries law: UNCLOS and UNFSA

Laws governing the distribution of fisheries have existed throughout history, though international fisheries law in its modern form was first outlined by UNCLOS in 1982.[38] This treaty puts in place the zonal approach, which dictates much of the form and function of international fisheries law today.[39] Article 87 of UNCLOS formally outlines the long-standing principle of the

29 Ibid 98–99.
30 Ibid.
31 Ibid 103.
32 Ibid 104.
33 Ibid 99–101.
34 Ibid 101–103.
35 Ibid 113–114.
36 Ibid 115.
37 Ibid.
38 UNCLOS (n 17).
39 Ibid arts 2–3, 55–57, 86.

freedom of the high seas, which allows states "freedom of fishing subject to the conditions laid down in section 2".[40] Section 2 further elaborates on this right, reaffirming in Article 116 that "All States have the right for their nationals to engage in fishing on the high seas", subject to certain provisions.[41] Article 117, for example, provides that states have a duty to take "such measures for their respective nationals as may be necessary for the conservation of the living resources of the high seas", while Article 118 calls for cooperation in these efforts.[42] Article 119 contains substantive provisions to this end, calling for the establishment of an "allowable catch" based on the "best scientific evidence available" to produce the "maximum sustainable yield".[43] It also requires states to "take into consideration" the effects on "associated or dependent" species to maintain or restore their populations above levels "at which their reproduction may become seriously threatened".[44]

It is also important to note that many stocks found within the high seas may move between the exclusive economic zone (EEZ) and areas beyond national jurisdiction (ABNJ). As such, Article 63 on so-called "straddling" fish stocks and Article 64 on highly migratory species are also especially relevant.[45] Article 63 calls upon the cooperation of the state in the management of such straddling stocks either "directly or through appropriate subregional or regional organizations".[46] Article 64 contains much the same obligations for highly migratory species, which are listed specifically in Annex I of UNCLOS, though with the goal of achieving "optimum utilization" as well as conservation.[47] Through their reference to regional and sub-regional bodies, these provisions provide room for the creation of further institutions in the realm of high seas governance, such as RFMOs. It is important to touch briefly upon the governance regime for the EEZ, as it reinforces similar governance principles for fisheries as in the provisions on the high seas. Specifically, Article 61 (conservation of the living resources) also discusses the determination of a total allowable catch, reliance on best scientific evidence, maximum sustainable yield (MSY), as well as associated and dependent species.[48] Meanwhile, Article 62 (utilisation of the living resources) calls for the promotion of "optimum utilization" and requires coastal states to allow other states to fish in their EEZ if they are not capable of harvesting the whole of their total allowable catch.[49]

40 Ibid art 87(e).
41 Ibid art 116.
42 Ibid arts 117–118.
43 Ibid art 119(1)(a).
44 Ibid art 119(1)(b).
45 Ibid arts 63, 64.
46 Ibid art 63(1).
47 Ibid art 64(1).
48 Ibid arts 61(2)–(3).
49 Ibid art 62.

Through this brief survey of the relevant provisions of UNCLOS, several key emerging governing principles are apparent in the initial stages of international fisheries law. The high seas are emphasised as an area of the ocean open to free fishing, tempered by some key principles. These begin with the determination of a total allowable catch (TAC) and the reliance on the best available scientific evidence to do so.[50] However, the parameters that govern the determination of the TAC are important for understanding the current international fisheries regime-based narrative. Namely, UNCLOS espouses the concept of maximum sustainable yield as a target for the TAC, while also requiring states to strive for optimum utilisation.[51] This means that states are required by UNCLOS to strike a delicate balance between avoiding the decline of specific fish stocks, as well as "associated and dependent" species, while simultaneously aiming to harvest as much as possible up to this point.[52] This is evidently a difficult objective for member states, particularly in relation to high seas fisheries with the range of possible actors and lack of scientific information. This also represents the starting point of the regime-based narrative for international fisheries.

While UNCLOS makes some concessions to conservation in the regulation of international fisheries, it is clear in the construction of these provisions that the purpose of this conservation is to allow for the continued exploitation of fish stocks. UNCLOS moves away from the historical imagination of the inexhaustibility of marine living resources, which had influenced other stages of the development of the law of the sea,[53] instead recognising that a certain amount of management would be required to allow states to continue exploiting fisheries resources. However, the balance struck in UNCLOS represents a largely impractical and unworkable approach to these fisheries. In striving for optimum utilisation and MSY, UNCLOS requires states to come right up to the point of unsustainable fishing, without tipping over it. Given the nature of common resource management in the case of the high seas, it is all but inevitable that states will exceed this tipping point, rather than stay within sustainable limits. While thinking surrounding MSY has since shifted to see it as a limit rather than a target,[54] the influence of this foundational principle on the regime-based narrative is significant.

Hence, in the emergence of international fisheries law, the regime-based narrative privileged exploitation over conservation, subordinating conservation goals in the name of achieving exploitation goals. If we consider the

50 Ibid art 119.

51 Ibid.

52 Ibid.

53 See, e.g. Vonintsoa Rafaly, 'The Concept of "Marine Living Resources": Navigating a Grey Zone in the Law of the Sea' (2021) 59 *Canadian Yearbook of International Law* 285, 286–288.

54 Abdullah Al Arif, 'Legal Status of Maximum Sustainable Yield Concept in International Fisheries Law and Its Adoption in the Marine Fisheries Regime of Bangladesh: A Critical Analysis' (2017) 32(3) *The International Journal of Marine and Coastal Law* 544, 551–552.

"what" of this narrative as the management of fishing activities on the high seas, the "how" was achieved through the application of principles such as the freedom of the high seas, TAC, MSY, and optimum utilisation.[55] This primarily served the economic interests of states and industries, although the costs of such measures were borne by marine biodiversity itself, representing the "who" in this narrative. While regimes can be very path dependent based upon their initial governing principles,[56] it is worth noting the inherent flexibility built into UNCLOS, which is sometimes called a "living instrument" due to drafting that allowed room for subsequent agreements and standards to clarify its provisions.[57] Especially central to this was the UNFSA, which was agreed upon to expand the issue of managing straddling and highly migratory species as set out in Articles 63 and 64.[58]

The UNFSA was an important instrument in shaping the face of modern international fisheries law. It was concluded in 1995 as an implementing agreement to UNCLOS and introduced a number of new principles, some of which originated in international environmental law, as well as creating a framework for the establishment and formalisation of regional bodies that would become central to the regime going forward.[59] Initially, the focus of the UNFSA seems to have been refined from UNCLOS with the statement of the objective of the instrument: "The objective of this Agreement is to ensure the long-term conservation and sustainable use of straddling fish stocks and highly migratory fish stocks through effective implementation of the relevant provisions of the Convention".[60]

Furthermore, Article 5 of the UNFSA in particular lays out some significant new principles for the development of the regime-based narrative.[61] These include the notion of "long-term sustainability", "precautionary approach", references to "ecosystem" thinking, considering the effects on "non-target species" as well as "associated or dependent species" and "endangered species", "protect[ing] biodiversity", and eliminating "over-fishing and excess fishing capacity".[62] However, while these seem to indicate the development of the initial narrative, it is also important to note that terms such as optimum utilisation and MSY still appear among these principles, indicating the continuation of the foundational UNCLOS principles.[63] Indeed, Hey has noted

55 UNCLOS (n 17) arts 87, 119.
56 Hey (n 15) 115.
57 See, e.g. Richard Alan Barnes, 'The Continuing Vitality of UNCLOS' in Jill Barrett and Richard Barnes (eds), *The United Nations Convention on the Law of the Sea: A Living Instrument* (BIICL, 2016) 459.
58 UNFSA (n 4).
59 UNFSA (n 4).
60 Ibid art 2.
61 Ibid art 5.
62 Ibid art 5.
63 Ibid arts 5(a)–(b).

the "resilient" nature of the concept, despite there being criticism even before the agreement of UNCLOS.[64] Meanwhile, Al Arif has described the effect of the UNFSA and subsequent developments as resulting in a "qualified" MSY, which must consider "relevant environmental and economic factors".[65]

In a further example of the development of the regime-based narrative, Article 6 is dedicated to expanding upon the precautionary approach.[66] It states that the precautionary approach should be applied generally to the "conservation, management and exploitation of straddling and highly migratory fish stocks".[67] The precautionary approach is defined in the text as follows:

"States shall be more cautious when information is uncertain, unreliable or inadequate. The absence of adequate scientific information shall not be used as a reason for postponing or failing to take conservation and management measures".[68] This closely resembles the use of the precautionary approach within international biodiversity law of the time.[69] However, the UNFSA not only contributed principles to international fisheries law but was also instrumental in providing an institutional architecture for the instrument.

The UNFSA operationalised states' duty to cooperate regarding straddling and highly migratory fish stocks found in Articles 63 and 64 of UNCLOS.[70] Article 8 of the UNFSA mandates that states targeting these kinds of fish stocks must either join a regional organisation or arrangement responsible for managing such a stock or establish one where one does not exist.[71] Subsequent articles within the UNFSA mandate how such RFMOs should be managed and established.[72] Currently, there is a range of RFMOs, covering most of the ocean, managing various migratory and straddling stocks.[73] As such, the UNFSA made a significant contribution to the institutions that operate within the international fisheries law regime. Indeed, the presence of RFMOs as key decision-making bodies has significant impacts on the narrative of this regime as they allow fishing states and other stakeholders to participate in the decision-making process, and influence particularly the "how" and "who" aspects of the narrative.

64 Ellen Hey, 'The Persistence of a Concept: Maximum Sustainable Yield' (2012) 27 *The International Journal of Marine and Coastal Law* 763, 771.

65 Abdullah Al Arif, *Sustainable Fisheries Management and International Law: Marine Fisheries in Bangladesh and the Bay of Bengal* (2022, Routledge) 37.

66 UNFSA (n 4) art 6.

67 Ibid art 6(1).

68 Ibid art 6(2).

69 See, e.g. United Nations, 'United Nations Conference on Environment and Development, Rio de Janeiro, Brazil, 3-14 June 1992' (Web Page) <https://www.un.org/en/conferences/environment/rio1992> ('Rio Declaration').

70 UNFSA (n 42) art 8.

71 Ibid arts 8(1)–(5).

72 Ibid arts 9–14.

73 See, e.g. Ásmundsson (n 23).

Having explored these central international instruments regarding international fisheries law, a narrative begins to emerge about the management of fisheries in ABNJ. Firstly, and most straightforwardly, the "what" of international fisheries law is the conservation and sustainable use of fisheries found in the high seas, as stated in the objective of the UNFSA.[74] It is on the points of "how" and "who" that a complete narrative begins to emerge. Initially, the narrative present in UNCLOS is analysed, followed by the ways that the UNFSA expanded on and changed this narrative.

Fisheries regulation in the high seas demonstrates a number of holdovers from the historic legal principle of "freedom of the high seas", most plainly evident in UNCLOS Article 87.[75] However, UNCLOS made clear that this was not without qualifications, which come in the form of subsequent articles requiring the "conservation" of the living resources of the high seas.[76] Likewise, states were expected to cooperate in the management of fish stocks that spent some portion of their life cycle in the high seas (straddling and highly migratory stocks).[77] It is in the governing principles established by UNCLOS as to how this would be achieved that the origins of the regime-based narrative can be observed. Indeed, UNCLOS's reliance on principles such as a TAC, determined with the aim to achieve MSY and optimum utilisation,[78] demonstrates an important foundational pillar of international fisheries law. That is, UNCLOS operationalised "conservation" in the high seas in service of the exploitation of fish stocks, often tellingly referred to within the instrument as "living resources".[79] From the construction of the provisions, it seems that this instrument was designed to allow states as much freedom on the high seas as possible, while also recognising that such resources were not inexhaustible and would need to occasionally be managed in order to continue fishing activities. Hence, the "how" of the regime-based narrative after UNCLOS reflects this balance of priorities and embeds some key principles which it will carry forward.

Finally, the "who" of the narrative is also reflected in this approach. The instrument places the burdens of these conservation measures on states which are required to ensure that "their nationals"[80] comply with the measures. However, the largely permissive system of high seas fisheries allows states, and by extension, their distant water fishers, to also be the major beneficiaries of the regime. It is also worth noting that, while hypothetically all states are granted these rights and obligations, given the nature of distant water fisheries, it is the states with significant distant water capacity and resources that

74 UNFSA (n 4) art 2.
75 UNCLOS (n 17) art 87.
76 Ibid arts 116–119.
77 Ibid art 118.
78 Ibid arts 63–64, 119.
79 See, e.g. ibid arts 117–119.
80 Ibid art 117.

most benefit from this system.[81] In other words, a small group of states with significant capacity to take advantage of this permissive regime benefit most from this approach to regulation.

However, while UNCLOS was a significant legal instrument, the UNFSA was specifically targeted at the regulation of fisheries that are found within the high seas and, as such, plays an important role in modifying the regime-based narrative. In particular, the UNFSA goes some length towards developing a more robust set of conservation principles, including referencing a number of environmental law concepts, such as the "precautionary approach" and "ecosystems", which are also prominent in international biodiversity law.[82] Furthermore, the UNFSA highlighted that its goal was for the "conservation and sustainable use" of fish stocks, a construction that was also emerging in international biodiversity law and which is not referred to within UNCLOS.[83] However, while the UNFSA introduced a number of principles to expand upon the "conservation" obligations within UNCLOS, it did not remove and indeed reinforced references to MSY and optimum utilisation.[84] This highlights that the UNFSA does not significantly rebalance the fundamental approach of UNCLOS to these stocks but rather clarifies and qualifies the content of the obligation to conserve the environment. This is, of course, what the UNFSA was designed to do as an implementing agreement to UNCLOS. So, while the question of "how" the regulation of international fisheries is to be achieved changes somewhat, it does not evolve significantly from the foundational governance principles of UNCLOS.

However, the UNFSA does make a significant contribution in terms of the "who" question through the establishment and endorsement of RFMOs as the key institutions for the management of high seas fisheries.[85] The formalisation of these regional arrangements as key bodies within the international regime determines both who makes the decisions and who may benefit from them. Having these bodies comprised of states with a vested interest in the stock largely guarantees that these states reap the benefits of regulation, albeit with a significant share of the regulatory responsibilities. This system assumes that states' particular interest in the stock will ensure that they remain motivated to maintain sustainable catch limits, which has not necessarily been the case in the past.

Through an analysis of the two central instruments within the international fisheries law regime, it can be argued then that a particular regime-based narrative has emerged. That is, one that aims to regulate fisheries activities on the

81 See, e.g. Douglas J. McCauley et al., 'Wealthy countries dominate industrial fishing' (2018) 4 *Science Advances* 2161 .

82 UNFSA (n 4) arts 5–6.

83 Ibid art 2.

84 Ibid arts 5(a)–(b).

85 Ibid art 8.

high seas in order to achieve "conservation and sustainable use".[86] In order to achieve this, several key governance principles are adhered to which attempt to address these two related concerns of conservation and sustainable use. What truly sets apart this regime-based narrative from that of international biodiversity law are the principles of MSY and optimum utilisation,[87] which frame the management of the "living resources" to be for the purposes of maintaining human exploitation. In this way, the regime-based narrative positions the notion of conservation as serving sustainable use directly. Indeed, it is argued that the concept of "sustainable use" within the narrative of international fisheries law draws upon the MSY concept rather than "sustainable development" as is more prominent in the foundations of international biodiversity law.[88] In this way, international fisheries law understands the goal of conservation and sustainable use in a way in which conservation is in service of sustainable use, which conversely means the maximum and optimum use of fisheries resources.

This narrative is of particular benefit to states with developed distant water fishing capabilities and the capacity to participate in RFMOs, which exert significant control over the regime and receive the benefit of harvesting the vast majority of the catch.[89] Smaller states with less capacity miss out on a share of this common resource. The narrative of international biodiversity law differs in a number of ways and is addressed next.

Regime-based narrative of international biodiversity law: the CBD

International biodiversity law differs from international fisheries law and the law of the sea more broadly as it is not structured based on a foundational instrument like UNCLOS. Instead, it has been described as a series of concentric circles containing all of the international legal instruments related to biodiversity, with those closer to the centre acting as the core of the loosely connected regime.[90] One of these central instruments is the 1992 CBD, which also has broad applicability, including to marine biodiversity.[91] This analysis focuses largely on the CBD and its contribution to the broader regime-based

86 Ibid art 2.

87 Ibid arts 5(a)–(b).

88 See, e.g. CBD (n 17) Preamble, art 8(e); Rio Declaration (n 69) Principles 1, 4, 5, 7–9, 12, 20–22, 24, 27; United Nations Sustainable Development, 'United Nations Conference on Environment and Development Rio de Janeiro, Brazil, 3 to 14 June 1992 AGENDA 21' (1992) ('United Nations Sustainable Development'); Werner Scholtz, '"Ethical and humane use', intrinsic value and the Convention on Biological Diversity: Towards the reconfiguration of sustainable development and use' (2021) 30 *Review of European, Comparative and International Environmental Law* 73, 77.

89 See, e.g. McCauley et al. (n 81).

90 José Juste Ruiz, 'Gaps in International Biodiversity Law and Possible Ways Forward' in Mar Campins Eritja and Teresa Fajardo del Castillo (eds), *Biological Diversity and International Law: Challenges for the Post 2020 Scenario* (SpringerLink, Switzerland, 2021) 35, 37.

91 Ibid; CBD (n 17).

narrative, while also drawing upon relevant soft law within the biodiversity regime.

Firstly, it is important to note the similarities between the two regimes, which are reflected particularly in the language used within the UNFSA, which was adopted three years after the CBD.[92] Immediately, the objectives of the CBD reflect similar language to that of the UNFSA:

> The objectives of this Convention, to be pursued in accordance with its relevant provisions, are the *conservation of biological diversity, the sustainable use* of its components and the fair and equitable sharing of the benefits arising out of the utilization of genetic resources.[93]
>
> (emphasis added)

This is strikingly similar to the UNFSA objective, though it also includes the sharing of benefits from genetic resources, something that will be addressed particularly in the high seas context by the BBNJ instrument.[94] It also sets the tone as a guiding aim of the international biodiversity law regime and hence the accompanying regime-based narrative.

Turning to the regime-based narrative, the "what" of international biodiversity law encompasses all human activities that may have an impact on biological diversity or biodiversity. Biological diversity is defined in the CBD as "the variability among living organisms from all sources including, inter alia, terrestrial, marine and other aquatic ecosystems and the ecological complexes of which they are part: this includes diversity within species, between species and of ecosystems".[95]

This is evidently much broader than the approach of international fisheries law, though it is also far less prescriptive as the instrument acts only to require states to adopt "national strategies, plans or programs" in line with the provisions of the instrument.[96] Furthermore, it reiterates that states have "the sovereign right to exploit their own resources pursuant to their own environmental policies" as long as this does not cause damage to the territory of other states or in ABNJ.[97] Regarding ABNJ, the instrument is also careful to limit its scope to areas within the territory of states as well as "processes and activities, regardless of where their effects occur, carried out under its jurisdiction or control" including in ABNJ.[98] Ultimately then, this instrument is relevant to international fisheries as flag state jurisdiction ensures that high seas vessels

92 UNFSA (n 4).
93 CBD (n 17) 1.
94 BBNJ (n 7) Part II.
95 CBD (n 17) art 2.
96 Ibid art 6(a).
97 Ibid art 3.
98 Ibid art 4.

are subject to the jurisdiction of the state in which they are registered.[99] It also highlights the broad concern of the regime-based narrative of international biodiversity law, which aims to achieve the "conservation and sustainable use" of a range of biodiversity including, but not limited to, fisheries.[100]

It is worth noting that the CBD directly addresses its relationship with the law of the sea regime as a whole, albeit in uncertain terms. Article 22 of the agreement outlines the "Relationship with Other International Conventions" and states: "Contracting Parties shall implement this Convention with respect to the marine environment consistently with the rights and obligations of States under the law of the sea".[101]

This article does not directly mention UNCLOS. It was contentious, though, during the negotiations of the CBD, that the relationship between the two conventions was relatively vague.[102] Taken at face value, it appears simply to acknowledge the existence of the law of the sea and the need for states to align their efforts under the CBD consistently with their obligations under UNCLOS and associated regimes. However, this provision has significant potential implications, which are examined in greater depth in the subsequent section.

There is evident overlap between the two regimes and the three key instruments examined, as UNCLOS and the UNFSA both dedicate substantial attention to regulating activities that affect life in the ocean or "living resources", while the CBD professes to cover activities affecting biodiversity as a whole, including marine biodiversity.[103] Additionally, both international fisheries law, as articulated in the UNFSA, and international biodiversity law, as outlined in the CBD, share a common objective of the "conservation and sustainable use" of marine resources.[104] However, the two regimes differ in how they attempt to achieve this goal and who may benefit, as well as bear the costs, of this pursuit.

The approach of the CBD to how the conservation and sustainable use of biodiversity are to be attained is through some specific measures to be pursued "as far as possible and appropriate"[105] and the "mainstreaming" of biodiversity concerns within states' national legal systems more generally.[106] Examples of these specific tools include mandating the creation of protected areas, rehabilitating damaged ecosystems, preventing alien or invasive species from being

99 UNCLOS (n 17) art 94.
100 CBD (n 17) art 1.
101 CBD (n 17) art 22(2).
102 Richard Caddell, "Only connect'? Regime interaction and global biodiversity conservation' in *Research Handbook on Biodiversity and Law* (Edward Elgar Publishing, 2016) 444–445.
103 UNCLOS (n 17) arts 117–119; UNFSA (n 4); CBD (n 17) arts 1–2.
104 UNFSA (n 4) art 2; CBD (n 17) art 1.
105 See, e.g. CBD (n 17) art 6(b).
106 See, e.g. K Friedman, S M Garcia, and J Rice, 'Mainstreaming biodiversity in fisheries' (2018) 95 *Marine Policy* 209.

introduced into the ecosystem, and listing threatened species.[107] Meanwhile, states are to "integrate consideration of the conservation and sustainable use of biological resources into national decision-making"[108] and

> Introduce appropriate procedures requiring environmental impact assessment of its proposed projects that are likely to have significant adverse effects on biological diversity with a view to avoiding or minimizing such effects and, where appropriate, allow for public participation in such procedures.[109]

These provisions highlight the "mainstreaming" approach of the CBD in attempting to integrate biodiversity concerns into all levels and areas of decision-making.[110] The convention also deals extensively with access to and the sharing of benefits from genetic resources.[111] This is less relevant for the issue of fisheries but has played a key role in the BBNJ negotiations.[112]

Overall, the character of the obligations in the CBD is flexible and permissive, deferring biodiversity action to national governments. Indeed, it has been described as "a treaty of uneasy compromises and delicately balanced interests".[113] This has been attributed to the divide between developing states, which required the conservation of biodiversity to not interfere with the development that they were undertaking, and developed states that were in a position to emphasise the need for conservation more strongly.[114] Indeed, much of the foundational impetus for the instrument was the push for "sustainable development", which aimed to balance these two interests in an integrated concept.[115] Sustainable development has been subject to much international discussion and can be broadly defined in line with the much-cited Brundtland Report as "development that meets the needs of the present generation without compromising the ability of future generations to meet their own needs".[116] As such, the term "sustainable use" within the CBD has been argued to be the operationalisation of "sustainable development".[117]

107 CBD (n 17) art 8.
108 Ibid art 10(a).
109 Ibid art 14(1)(a).
110 See, e.g. Friedman, Garcia, Rice (n 106).
111 CBD (n 17) arts 15–19.
112 See, e.g. IISD, 5th Session (n 6) and IISD, 4th Session (n 8).
113 Susan H Bragdon, 'The Evolution and Future of the Law of Sustainable Development: Lessons from the Convention on Biological Diversity' (1996) 8(3) *Georgetown International Environmental Law Review* 423, 434.
114 Rosie Cooney, 'CITES and the CBD: Tensions and Synergies' (2001) 10(3) *Review of European, Comparative & International Environmental Law* 259, 261–262.
115 Ibid.
116 World Commission on Environment and Development, *Our Common Future* (Oxford University Press, 1987) para 49 ('The Brundtland Report').
117 See, e.g. Scholtz (n 88).

The CBD has proven particularly influential through its codification of international biodiversity law and through the subsequent soft law actions taken by its Conference of the Parties (COP).[118] The most influential of these include the Aichi Biodiversity Targets and the new Kunming–Montreal Global Biodiversity Framework.[119] These initiatives have allowed the CBD COP to set target's on priority areas for biodiversity conservation and sustainable use.[120] For example, the Aichi target of 10% of ocean areas covered by marine protected areas (MPAs) by 2020 has been shown to drive an increase in marine protected areas, though concerns remain as to their efficacy.[121] This target has subsequently been updated in the KMGBF to 30% of ocean coverage by 2030.[122]

As such, the CBD and international biodiversity law more broadly differ in their approach to *how* to achieve the conservation and sustainable use of marine biodiversity compared to the approach of the UNFSA and the international fisheries law regime. It focuses on the general principles of international biodiversity law, highlights preferred legal tools, emphasises national-level action, and is broad in scope. Indeed, in drawing upon a notion of "sustainable use" that is intrinsically tied to "sustainable development", the CBD positions conservation and sustainable use as two necessary components needed to achieve "sustainable development" in relation to biodiversity.

The conservation of biodiversity in and of itself is a greater focus in this regime, compared to the observable narrative in the international fisheries law regime, which positions conservation as a means to the end of continued exploitation due to the influence of MSY on the concept of "sustainable use".[123] This is not to say that international biodiversity law moves away from an anthropocentric approach to its goal; rather, the regime-based narrative attempts to strike a balance between the two priorities in order to achieve a regime that furthers sustainable development. This is reflected in assessments of the CBD as a compromise between the interests of development and conservation held by developing and developed states,[124] as well as reflecting the broader themes of the 1992 United Nations Conference on Environment and Development at which the instrument was concluded.[125] Meanwhile, all states within the international fisheries regime with an interest in fisheries desire the

118 The Convention on Biological Diversity, 'Conference of the Parties (COP)' (WebPage) <https://www.cbd.int/cop/>.
119 CBD Aichi Targets (n 25).
120 Ibid.
121 Ibid Target 11.
122 Ibid Target 3.
123 See, e.g. UNFSA (n 4) art 5(b).
124 See, e.g. Cooney (n 114).
125 See, e.g. Rio Declaration (n 69); United Nations Sustainable Development (n 88); The Brundtland Report (n 116).

continuation of commercial fishing and recognise that conservation is a necessary part of managing these efforts.

Finally, it is important to address the actors within international biodiversity law and how they contribute to the determination of who benefits and undertakes burdens within the regime. The CBD itself is an instrument with a near-universal membership, including 196 state parties.[126] This is far more than the UNFSA, which has only 93 parties,[127] or even UNCLOS with 169 parties.[128] However, membership in other international biodiversity law instruments varies more greatly as well.[129] The CBD COP also plays a significant role in the continued proliferation of international biodiversity law and hence, has a central position in the regime as a whole. Due to this wide participation, the CBD COP can be said to be more representative than the majority of other existing international instruments. This is also in contrast to international fisheries law, which relies on regional bodies made up of states with a specific interest in fishing and particular fish stocks.[130] It is worth noting that the traditional power dynamics between larger and wealthier states evidently play into the CBD COP forum regardless, but it can be said that the competing interests between developed and developing states regarding conservation and sustainable use have contributed to a more balanced regime-based narrative.[131] Furthermore, delegates and other attendees at the CBD and other biodiversity-related meetings are likely drawn from the environment departments of member states and conservation non-governmental organisations (NGOs).[132] This again contrasts with international fisheries law, in which participants can include industry stakeholders and those bodies with a focus on the use of fisheries resources.[133]

Ultimately then, when examining the CBD and international biodiversity law more broadly, a pronounced difference in the approach to the "conservation and sustainable use" of marine biodiversity is observable. This is apparent

126 Convention on Biological Diversity, 'List of Parties' (Web Page) <https://www.cbd.int/information/parties.shtml> ('Convention on Biological Diversity List of Parties').

127 Oceans and the Law of the Sea United Nations, 'Chronological lists of ratifications of, accessions and successions to the Convention and the related Agreements' (Web Page, 2023) <https://www.un.org/Depts/los/reference_files/chronological_lists_of_ratifications.htm#Agreement%20for%20the%20implementation%20of%20the%20provisions%20of%20the%20Convention%20relating%20to%20the%20conservation%20and%20management%20of%20straddling%20fish%20stocks%20and%20highly%20migratory%20fish%20stocks> ('Oceans and the Law of the Sea United Nations').

128 Ibid.

129 See, e.g. CITES, 'List of Parties to the Convention' (Web Page) <https://cites.org/eng/disc/parties/index.php>; Convention on the Conservation of Migratory Species of Wild Animals, 'Parties and Range States' (Web Page) <https://www.cms.int/en/parties-range-states>.

130 See, e.g. Ásmundsson (n 23).

131 See, e.g. Cooney (n 114).

132 See, e.g. Hey (n 15) 101–103.

133 See, e.g. Matilda Tove Petersson et al., 'Patterns and trends in non-state actor participation in regional fisheries management organisations' (2019) 104 *Marine Policy* 146, 149–151.

in the differing scopes of the regimes, with overlap regarding commercial fish species, different approaches to achieving these goals, as well as different membership resulting in differing approaches to organisation and decision-making.

Having examined the narratives for each regime, this chapter now turns to how these regimes intersect within the BBNJ context. In particular, it focuses on the exclusion of fisheries considerations from the final biodiversity law instrument.

A site for regime interaction or regime separation? Fisheries at the BBNJ

The BBNJ instrument, concluded in a marathon 36-hour negotiating session in March 2023 at the United Nations Headquarters in New York,[134] is a significant achievement in international law-making. The negotiations faced strongly entrenched state interests and dealt with a wide array of contentious topics, including the sharing of benefits derived from marine genetic resources.[135] The delegates also managed to agree on an instrument that advances action on the conservation and sustainable use of marine biodiversity through the four package elements of MGR, area-based management tools (ABMTs) including marine protected areas, environmental impact assessments (EIAs), and capacity building and the transfer of marine technology (CBTT).[136] While many details surrounding the implementation of the new agreement have been left to the first session of the conference of the parties,[137] the framework is largely in place for a treaty that will regulate human activity in 67% of the world's oceans and 95% of the world's biodiversity habitat.[138] However, despite the understandable optimism, the instrument, as with many international agreements, is not as ambitious as may be required to achieve its mandate. Of particular concern is the lack of discussion about fisheries within the negotiations and the lack of references to fisheries in the final text, despite the fact that they represent the biggest cause of biodiversity loss in the high seas.[139] This section examines the role that the regime-based narratives of international fisheries law and international biodiversity law played in this result. Specifically, it is argued that the focus of the BBNJ, as a piece of international biodiversity law, made

134 IISD, 5th Session (n 6).
135 Ibid 5–7.
136 Ibid.
137 Ibid.
138 United Nations, *The Conservation and Sustainable Use of Marine Biological Diversity of Areas Beyond National Jurisdiction: A Technical Abstract of the First Global Integrated Marine Assessment* (Report, 2017) 1.
139 See, e.g. Pierre Cloutier de Repentigny, 'To the Anthropocene and beyond: the responsibility of law in decimating and protecting marine life' (2020) 11(1–2) *Transnational Legal Theory* 180, 182.

states reluctant to include international fisheries considerations directly due to differing regime-based narratives.

Inclusion of fisheries in the BBNJ instrument

Before examining the reasons for this omission, it is first important to highlight how exactly international fisheries are addressed within the final instrument. The only time that fish or fisheries are mentioned explicitly within the instrument is in Article 10 within Part II on MGRs and benefit sharing.[140] This part is designed to set up a system by which states that harvest MGRs from the high seas must share the benefits derived from these activities, both monetary and non-monetary.[141] MGRs are valued for their potential to lead to scientific breakthroughs and the commercialisation of such breakthroughs, and were not addressed in UNCLOS due to the recency of their discovery.[142] As such, Article 10(2) states:

The provisions of this Part shall not apply to:

(a) Fishing regulated under relevant international law and fishing-related activities; or
(b) Fish or other living marine resources known to have been taken in fishing and fishing-related activities from areas beyond national jurisdiction, except where such fish or other living marine resources are regulated as utilization under this Part.[143]

Hence, the only reference to fish and fisheries in the BBNJ instrument serves to exclude them from the MGR regulations. Article 10(2)(a) clearly highlights that the matter of regulating high seas fishing is considered settled by other "relevant international law".[144] Meanwhile, Article 10(2)(b) highlights that fish and other forms of "living marine resources" are not included under this part of the agreement when taken during "fishing and fishing-related activities", unless they are "regulated as utilization under this Part".[145] While the drafting here may be somewhat unclear, the definition of the "utilization of marine genetic resources" clarifies this issue, highlighting that "utilization" means "to conduct research and development on the genetic and/or

140 BBNJ (n 7) art 10(2).
141 Ibid art 14.
142 Lyle Glowka, 'Genetic Resources, Marine Scientific Research and the International Seabed Area' (1999) 8(1) *Review of European Comparative & International Environmental Law* 56, 56.
143 BBNJ (n 7) art 10(2).
144 Ibid art 10(2)(a).
145 Ibid art 10(2)(b).

biochemical composition of marine genetic resources, including through the application of biotechnology".[146]

As such, fish and other living creatures taken in the process of fishing are exempt from Part II on MGRs unless they are subsequently the object of scientific study as laid out in the above definition.[147] This article, containing the only direct reference to fish within the instrument, highlights the thoroughness with which fisheries were avoided within the instrument, as MGR rules were never intended to apply to fishing, although negotiators still felt the need to indicate this explicitly. In relation to package elements such as ABMTs and EIAs that are more relevant to fisheries activities, the instrument instead avoids mentioning fisheries specifically, defaulting to the concept of "not undermining" existing bodies and frameworks.[148]

While the establishment of high seas ABMTs may have an effect on fisheries if they are designed to restrict high seas fishing, there is no direct reference to fisheries within Part III on ABMTs.[149] Indeed, it allows for states to make ABMT proposals to the BBNJ COP, and a period of stakeholder consultation to be engaged in, which includes consulting the "Bodies of relevant legal instruments and frameworks and relevant global, regional, subregional and sectoral bodies".[150] This would include consultations with RFMOs, though they are not mentioned by name.[151] Meanwhile, decisions on ABMTs are to be made by the COP, which also has the power to put in place measures that are "compatible" with other relevant bodies as well as to make recommendations to the member states to adopt proposed measures through these bodies.[152] This means that ABMTs may be established in the absence of RFMOs, to complement RFMOs' existing measures, or through the processes of an RFMO if it falls under its area of competence.[153] This provision is accompanied by an obligation for the COP to "respect the competences of, and not undermine, relevant legal instruments and frameworks and relevant global, regional, subregional and sectoral bodies".[154]

What exactly is meant by "respect the competences of and, not undermine" is not entirely clear. However, from the structure of the ABMT decision-making provisions, it seems that the BBNJ COP may not take measures that interfere with the control that RFMOs have over high seas fisheries. However, the COP may make recommendations to states to implement particular measures. It is worth noting that states may object to any agreed-upon ABMT on

146 Ibid art 1(14).
147 Ibid art 10(2)(b).
148 See, e.g. ibid art 5(2).
149 Ibid Part III.
150 Ibid art 21(2)(b).
151 Ibid.
152 Ibid art 22(1).
153 Ibid.
154 Ibid art 22(2).

a number of grounds, including if it is "inconsistent with this Agreement or the rights and duties of the objecting Party in accordance with the Convention [UNCLOS]".[155] While this objection procedure is subject to a number of procedural checks, it still leaves reasonable scope for states with particular fisheries interests to object to measures taken under this provision.[156] Hence, the ABMT part of the BBNJ agreement takes some positive steps but also appears to leave open the potential for states to avoid taking action that may interfere with high seas fisheries. This is done by deferring an amount of decision-making control to RFMOs, using the potentially unclear stipulation of obliging states to "respect the competences of and, not undermine" these bodies, and allowing for objections by individual states.[157]

EIAs are also potentially relevant to fisheries. Indeed, Barnes highlights that the duty to conduct EIAs found within UNCLOS sees inconsistent application to fishing activities, with only some RFMOs requiring it in particular circumstances.[158] The new BBNJ instrument does little to clarify this point directly, instead framing the obligation to conduct EIAs in terms of the relationship between the agreement and relevant bodies.[159] Firstly, it requires EIAs to be conducted:

> When a Party with jurisdiction or control over a planned activity that is to be conducted in marine areas within national jurisdiction determines that the activity may cause substantial pollution of or significant and harmful changes to the marine environment in areas beyond national jurisdiction.[160]

It then further stipulates that parties to the BBNJ agreement are to

> promote the use of environmental impact assessments and the adoption and implementation of the standards and/or guidelines developed under article 38 in relevant legal instruments and frameworks and relevant global, regional, subregional and sectoral bodies of which they are members.[161]

The agreement goes on to detail how this is to be achieved, including outlining cooperation with the Scientific and Technical Body that is established under

155 Ibid arts 23(4)–(5).
156 Ibid arts 23(4)–(9).
157 Ibid art 22(2).
158 Richard Barnes, 'The Proposed LOSC Implementation Agreement on Areas Beyond National Jurisdiction and Its Impact on International Fisheries Law' (2016) 31, 583, 610–615.
159 BBNJ (n 7) Part III.
160 Ibid art 28(2).
161 Ibid art 29(1).

the instrument.[162] It also details the content of EIAs and notification requirements.[163] Ultimately, though, the instrument allows for the party "under whose jurisdiction or control the planned activity falls" to make the final decision on whether the activity will go ahead.[164] Hence, it does not clarify the uncertainty surrounding EIAs and fishing, seeming to simply require states to promote the adoption of the outlined EIA procedures within RFMOs.[165] What is yet to be seen is if high seas fishing could be said to "have more than a minor or transitory effect on the marine environment or [that] the effects of the activity are unknown or poorly understood",[166] thus meeting the threshold for a screening to determine if the fishing activity "may cause substantial pollution of or significant and harmful changes to the marine environment" and trigger an EIA.[167] Without directly addressing the requirement for EIAs to be conducted regarding fisheries, it is difficult to know if this part will have any impact on the conservation and sustainable use of marine biodiversity beyond national jurisdiction.

Across the BBNJ instrument, it becomes clear that any direct changes to international fisheries regulation were topics that were deliberately avoided either explicitly, such as in the case of MGR provisions, or indirectly, such as through the use of the concept of "not undermining".[168] When looking at positions throughout the negotiations, states have continually expressed their opposition to considering fisheries within the BBNJ instrument.[169] Indeed, this was a motivating factor for states initially opposed to any form of treaty, who argued that the status quo of high seas fisheries was acceptable.[170] It becomes clear then that the tiptoeing around the issue of fisheries in the final instrument is deliberate, given that fisheries issues are central to the conservation and sustainable use of marine biodiversity. The next section addresses how this separation between the new international biodiversity instrument and international fisheries law played out from a regime interaction perspective.

Regime separation in the BBNJ instrument

The reluctance of the negotiating states to deal directly with fisheries within the BBNJ can be attributed to several possible justifications. For example,

162 Ibid art 29.
163 Ibid arts 30–32.
164 Ibid art 34(1).
165 Ibid arts 29(1)–(3).
166 Ibid art 30(1).
167 Ibid art 28(2).
168 Ibid arts 5(2), 22(2).
169 See, e.g. IISD, 5th Session (n 6) and IISD, 4th Session (n 8).
170 Glen Wright et al., 'The Long and Winding Road: Negotiating a Treaty for the Conservation and Sustainable Use of Marine Biodiversity in Areas Beyond National Jurisdiction' (2018) 8 *Institut du développement durable et des relations internationales* 1, 52–54.

some have argued that fisheries are already adequately addressed by existing international fisheries law.[171] Indeed, it is this argument that likely led to the requirement to "not undermine" other relevant bodies, with states concerned that the new instrument may interfere with their established rights under international fisheries law.[172] Others have put forward that it is simply a pragmatic decision to avoid addressing an area with significant vested interests, particularly when the negotiations were so contentious on other issue areas, such as the sharing of benefits from MGRs.[173] However, while these arguments are both key practical reasons why fisheries were largely avoided at the negotiations, this chapter argues that a more fundamental divide can explain this phenomenon.

The BBNJ instrument is a site of multiple regime interactions. Hey, for example, frames the BBNJ negotiations as the convergence of three narratives: "the principles of the freedom of the high seas, the common heritage of mankind and the framing of the conservation of biodiversity as a common concern of humankind".[174]

Oral instead describes the BBNJ process as the convergence of a range of institutions that are responsible for governing the high seas and a process of determining how these institutions will interact with the new instrument.[175] She highlights that the new instrument has to relate to a plethora of bodies from RFMOs to the World Heritage Convention.[176]

This chapter analyses the BBNJ instrument in the context of its position within broader international regimes, as a new instrument straddling the area of overlap between international biodiversity law and the law of the sea (see Figure 6.1). However, it is argued that despite common subject matter and common goals, such direct overlap between international biodiversity law and international fisheries law has never been realised. Instead, they are two regimes that have developed "in parallel".[177] In order to understand why fisheries are barely addressed by the new BBNJ agreement, an analysis has been undertaken of the foundational instruments in both regimes. By going back to the foundation of the regime-based narratives of both regimes, the disconnect between

171 Ibid.

172 See, e.g. Scanlon (n 11); Beringen et al. (n 11).

173 See, e.g. Elizabeth Mendenhall et al., 'A Soft Treaty, Hard to Reach: The Second Inter-Governmental Conference for Biodiversity beyond National Jurisdiction' (2019) 108 *Marine Policy* 103664, 2.

174 Hey (n 15) 106.

175 Nilüfer Oral, 'The Institutional Schizophrenia of Ocean Governance through the Lens of the Conservation of Biological Diversity in Areas Beyond National Jurisdiction' in Seline Trevisanut, Nikolaos Giannopoulos, and Rozemarijn Roland Holst (eds), *Regime Interaction in Ocean Governance: Problems, Theories and Methods* (Brill Nijhoff, 2020) 52.

176 Ibid.

177 Alex G Oude Elferink, 'Environmental Impact Assessment in Areas Beyond National Jurisdiction' (2012) 27 *The International Journal of Marine and Coastal Law* 449, 469.

the two can be better understood.[178] This, in turn, explains why the BBNJ agreement, which is nominally a biodiversity law instrument, avoids directly addressing international fisheries, much as other biodiversity law instruments have in the past. To highlight the points of divergence between the regime-based narratives of international fisheries law and international biodiversity law, the following discussion addresses the interactions occurring regarding the "what", "how", and "who" questions for each.[179]

Firstly, on the issue of what is to be regulated, international fisheries law and international biodiversity law contain some overlap, yet are also conscious of delimiting which single regime or the other should regulate actions in relation to particular species. For example, as addressed above, both regimes have some competence over marine biodiversity.[180] International fisheries law is most concerned with regulating targeted commercial species as well as those that are classified as dependent, associated, or non-target to some extent.[181] Meanwhile, international biodiversity law in theory is applicable to all forms of life within the marine environment.[182] Nonetheless, rather than embracing the overlap as having the potential to allow meaningful collaborations between these regimes, the regime-based narratives reveal a reluctance to tread on the toes of the other regime, particularly regarding international biodiversity law. An example of this reluctance comes from the CBD, which in Article 22 reinforces the need for respecting the "rights and obligations of states under the law of the sea when implementing [the] agreement".[183] This statement, given the context of the two regimes, seems a clear reference to rights and obligations regarding marine living resources specifically, indicating that the CBD does not aim to interfere with such rights. The fact that this article specifically references the law of the sea, alongside a generic statement applying to rights and obligations from "any existing international agreement", indicates that fisheries, in particular, are likely to be an area of concern between the two regimes.[184] Indeed, in the International Union for the Conservation of Nature's Guide to the CBD, the authors state that this paragraph deliberately subordinates international biodiversity law to the law of the sea regime, including international fisheries law, stating that if there is a conflict between the two, the law of the sea regime "prevails".[185] It is, perhaps, not unreasonable to suggest then that this article is a precursor to the "not undermining"

178 See, e.g. Hey (n 15) 98–99.
179 Ibid 86.
180 UNFSA (n 4) art 3; CBD (n 17) arts 1–2.
181 See, e.g. UNFSA (n 4) art 5(d).
182 See, e.g. CBD (n 17) art 4.
183 Ibid art 22(2).
184 Ibid art 22(1).
185 L Glowka et al., 'A Guide to the Convention on Biological Diversity' (1994) 30 *Environmental Law and Policy Paper* No. 30, 109.

concept, highlighting the early tendency to try to delineate the roles of the respective regimes where possible.

Furthermore, tensions between biodiversity conservation interests and fisheries interests have been well documented in the literature.[186] It is important to note that regime-based narratives emerge among "epistemic communities" that are involved in the creation and administration of the regimes. In characterising the broad tensions between the two communities, Garcia et al. note that the following dichotomies impair efforts at integration between the two regimes:

> (1) conservation and development; (2) different administrations…; (3) short-term sectoral economic interests and long-term societal interests; (4) the rural producing sector and the urban consuming sector; and (5) developing countries (major exporters) and developed countries (major importers).[187]

Furthermore, Friedman et al. demonstrate a relationship between these conservation interests and fisheries interests that was combative, stating the reasons for this are as follows: "in fisheries circles driven by a perception that preservationist interests lacking expertise in fisheries were entering the functional and spatial responsibility of established fishery authorities, while environmental interests believed profits would be prioritised by the fisheries sector.[188]

However, Friedman et al. do highlight that despite much early action on threatened species being driven only by fisheries interests, there has been some increased cooperation between institutions from both regimes, such as CITES, CMS, and the FAO, though improvements could still be made.[189] It is these dynamics, then, that appear to lead to the desire to keep the regimes legally distinct, with international biodiversity law designed in a way that avoids the perception of significant interference in fisheries interests. However, this reluctance leads to gaps in coverage, particularly on the high seas.

When it comes to the high seas, the governance of fisheries and marine biodiversity in general is largely left to RFMOs.[190] However, RFMOs have limited mandates as well as limited capacity to manage the marine environment more broadly.[191] Crespo et al. highlight that 95% of high seas species are not

186 See, e.g. Serge M Garcia, Jake Rice and Anthony Charles, 'Governance of marine fisheries and biodiversity conservation: A history' in Serge M Garcia, Jake Rice and Anthony Charles (eds), *Governance of Marine Fisheries and Biodiversity Conservation: Interaction and Co-evolution* (Wiley-Blackwell, 2014) 3.

187 Ibid 10.

188 Friedman et al. (n 106) 216.

189 Ibid.

190 See, e.g. Guillermo Ortuño Crespo et al., 'High-seas fish biodiversity is slipping through the governance net' (2019) 3 *Nature Ecology & Evolution* 1273.

191 Ibid.

monitored by RFMOs.[192] Furthermore, the UNFSA only applies to "straddling and highly migratory stocks" or stocks that move between the high seas and the EEZ at some time in their life cycle.[193] Species that spend their entire life cycle in the high seas then are not directly included. The FAO Deep Sea Fisheries Guidelines are designed to address this but are non-binding.[194] The reluctance of a new BBNJ instrument to address fisheries and its reliance on the "not undermining" construction to justify this choice demonstrate clearly the deliberate divide between the regimes. Indeed, despite overlapping mandates, international biodiversity law, including the BBNJ, largely leaves high seas fisheries to international fisheries law.

The fundamental goal of both regimes, stated in the UNFSA and the CBD, respectively, demonstrates how the regimes approach the regulation of high seas fishing. That is, both regimes aim for the conservation and sustainable use of marine biodiversity, with the scope of the biodiversity to be protected varying between regimes.[195] Under the UNFSA and UNCLOS, international fisheries law is largely concerned with regulating activities in relation to directly targeted fish stocks and those that are "associated or dependent" stocks.[196] Meanwhile, international biodiversity law, such as the CBD, is nominally concerned with all forms of biodiversity, including those in the marine environment.[197] While the scope of the shared goal may differ, it is key differences in the conceptual root of the goal within both regimes that are most important to note. In particular, both regimes, though arriving at the same wording for their objective, reflect the political choices made at the time of their formation regarding their founding principles.[198]

In the case of the CBD, "conservation and sustainable use" are rooted in the popularisation of the principle of "sustainable development".[199] This means "conservation and sustainable use" under international biodiversity law can be seen as a means to address the developmental needs of current generations without affecting future generations' abilities to meet their needs.[200] Each element of the goal is therefore aimed at achieving this and is given relatively equal weight, taking into account both economic, such as monetary or food security benefits, and intangible cultural and aesthetic values, such as the

192 Ibid 1274.
193 UNFSA (n 4) art 3(1).
194 DSF Guidelines (n 22).
195 See, e.g. UNFSA (n 4) art 3; CBD (n 17) art 4.
196 UNFSA (n 4) arts 5(d)–(f).
197 CBD (n 17) art 4.
198 See, e.g. Hey (n 15) 115.
199 See, e.g. Scholtz (n 88); Rio Declaration (n 69); United Nations Sustainable Development (n 88); The Brundtland Report (n 116).
200 See, e.g. The Brundtland Report (n 116).

preservation of charismatic or culturally significant species and environments for future generations.[201]

On the other hand, international fisheries law, while aiming for the same goal, finds its conceptual foundations instead within the initial principles laid down by UNCLOS regarding the optimum utilisation and maximum sustainable yield of fish stocks.[202] While using the same language as international biodiversity law, international fisheries law is informed by these narratives when interpreting and applying the goal of "conservation and sustainable use".[203] Indeed, the concept of MSY is inherently focused on exploitation but does not carry with it concerns over future generations or other inherent conservation values. Instead, it is purely an economic policy or a "policy disguised as science"[204] that is concerned with maximum exploitation that can be sustained presumably indefinitely. This framing results in a different regime-based narrative surrounding "conservation and sustainable use" within international fisheries law. In this case, "conservation" is seen as a means to achieving the goal of "sustainable use", which in turn is conceived as maximum sustained use. This distinction means that there is a different balance of priorities and, hence, a different approach to how states aim to achieve this goal in international fisheries law.

Finally, it is important to examine the divergences surrounding who is driving the direction of these regime-based narratives. Both international legal regimes are largely centred around state actors that are responsible for making decisions regarding the law and implementing and enforcing these decisions.[205] Indeed, both regimes have a significant overlap in membership across their key instruments. UNCLOS has 169 parties, and the UNFSA has 93, while the CBD has 196 parties.[206] While the UNFSA agreement may stand out as having a relatively low number of parties, three of the top five high seas fishers are members – Japan, the Republic of Korea, and Spain.[207] Furthermore, the system of RFMOs ensures that most states with interests in high seas fisheries join regional bodies that largely adhere to the provisions of the UNFSA.[208] Given the near-universal participation in UNCLOS and the CBD, many of the same state actors are involved in the decision-making that occurs within

201 See, e.g. Garcia et al. (n 185) 10–14.
202 UNCLOS (n 17) art 119.
203 UNFSA (n 4) art 2.
204 Carmel Finley and Naomi Oreskes, 'Maximum sustained yield: A policy disguised as science' (2013) 70(2) *ICES Journal of Marine Science* 245.
205 UNCLOS (n 17); UNFSA (n 4); CBD (n 17).
206 Oceans and the Law of the Sea United Nations (n 127); Convention on Biological Diversity List of Parties (n 126).
207 McCauley et al. (n 81); ibid.
208 UNFSA (n 4) arts 9–14.

both regimes.[209] This means that decisions regarding the interaction, or lack thereof, between the instruments are made by states reflecting their particular cross-regime interests.

Some of the lack of a common narrative between the regimes can be due to differing representation at these meetings, such as delegations from different internal government departments being present.[210] Indeed, within the international fisheries regime, delegates are likely to be from national fisheries departments, whereas in international biodiversity law, interests from environment departments may be present instead.[211] The participation of non-state actors may also diverge, with the fisheries industry over-represented within international and regional fisheries bodies, while conservation and development NGOs may participate more often in the international biodiversity law regime.[212] However, despite these differences, state delegations are still beholden to official foreign policy and hence will prioritise national interests across all forums. Indeed, states shape these narratives within distinct regimes in a way that allows them to arrive at a regime that best serves their interests. It is likely then that the drive to maintain an effective separation between the regimes comes from states with particularly strong interests in fisheries, as well as fisheries industry representatives.

This phenomenon can be observed throughout the BBNJ negotiations in which states with a prominent fisheries industry were key advocates for the separation of fisheries from the instrument.[213] Additionally, the FAO was found to be the body issuing the most statements emphasising areas in which the BBNJ may be at risk of "undermining" existing fisheries frameworks in relation to MPAs and ABMTs.[214] These influential states and bodies that make up the international fisheries law regime were able to demonstrate that the political costs of including fisheries concerns within the agreement would be too high for other states to consider their inclusion. These costs centre on the threat of even more difficult negotiations or the failure to reach a widely agreed-upon final text. It is interesting to observe that despite some of this strident opposition to acknowledging the interaction between international fisheries law and international biodiversity law, the number of states that actively have fisheries interests in the high seas is relatively low.[215] Indeed, McCauley et al. demon-

209 Oceans and the Law of the Sea United Nations (n 127); Convention on Biological Diversity List of Parties (n 126).

210 See, e.g. Hey (n 15) 101.

211 Ibid.

212 See, e.g. Petersson et al. (n 133); Stuart R Harrop and Diana J Pritchard, 'A hard instrument goes soft: The implications of the Convention on Biological Diversity's current trajectory' (2011) 21(2) *Global Environmental Change* 474, 4.

213 See, e.g. IISD, 5th Session (n 6); Wright et al. (n 170).

214 Arne Langlet and Alice B M Vadrot, 'Not 'undermining' who? Unpacking the emerging BBNJ regime complex' (2023) 147 *Marine Policy* 105372, 7.

215 McCauley et al. (n 81).

strate that 97% of large-scale high seas fishing from 2015 to 2016 was conducted by boats registered in "high-income" states.[216] In addition, only five were responsible for 86% of the high seas catch: China, Taiwan, Japan, South Korea, and Spain.[217] Furthermore, only two states in the top 20, Vanuatu and Ukraine, were not classified as "high income"; they were instead described as "lower-middle income" countries.[218] This does not take into account illegal, unregulated, and unreported (IUU) fishing, which may be as high as 18% again of the total catch.[219]

As such, it becomes clear that states with high seas fisheries interests are particularly vocal in separating the current regime of international fisheries law from potential constraints that may be imposed upon them as a result of international biodiversity law. These high-income countries also have the ability to engage across both regimes to ensure this separation and the influence to push for these outcomes. It is likely, then, that the influence of those who make decisions directly affects the interaction between the regimes, as well as determining who benefits and who may bear the costs within each regime.

The BBNJ: a product of regime separation

Taking the above argument into account, several takeaways become evident about the role of regime-based narratives in the creation of the BBNJ instrument. Of the two regimes, the BBNJ fits most clearly into international biodiversity law but has relevance to the international fisheries law regime as they are both part of the broader law of the sea regime (see Figure 6.1). When examining the lack of direct consideration or acknowledgement of fisheries in this context, the question is, how do the interactions between international fisheries law and international biodiversity law lead to the exclusion of fisheries from a marine biodiversity instrument? Throughout the analysis, it has become clear that divergences in the respective regime-based narratives over questions of "what" "how", and "who" have led to this deliberate omission.

There is an observable split between the two regimes over what each shall cover. Indeed, there seems to be a particular reluctance within the regime-based narrative of international biodiversity law to interfere with the regulation of commercial fish species under the purview of international fisheries law. This is despite the fact that each regime includes high seas fish species within the scope of their respective regulations. Additionally, while key instruments within the respective regimes of the UNFSA and the CBD share a common goal of "conservation and sustainable use" of marine biodiversity,[220] they differ

216 Ibid.
217 Ibid 4.
218 Ibid.
219 Ibid 5.
220 UNFSA (n 4) art 2; CBD (n 17) art 1.

in how this goal is interpreted and achieved. Finally, the actors in each regime have a significant influence over who takes on the benefits and the burdens of the regime. It has been highlighted that due to the shared membership of the two regimes, but differing representation within delegations, priorities between the regimes may differ.[221]

It is clear that the BBNJ agreement, as a key part of the international biodiversity regime, has been both consciously and unconsciously kept separate from international fisheries law, despite clear reasons for connection and collaboration. The role of entrenched narratives stemming from the foundational instruments of these regimes cannot be discounted in understanding why the final form of the BBNJ instrument does not substantially address fisheries. These divergent regime-based narratives also have broader consequences for the future of ocean governance, as discussed below.

Conclusion: regime separation in the BBNJ and the planetary crisis

In many ways, the new BBNJ instrument offers hope for multilateral law-making as a way of addressing the shared challenges that will arise in an increasingly uncertain ocean environment. Indeed, as of September 2024, the agreement has already been signed by 91 states, including global great powers, the United States and China.[222] While some prominent high seas fishing nations, such as Japan, have yet to sign the agreement,[223] it had already received widespread support in the few weeks after it opened for signature on the 20 September 2023.[224] The agreement is also wide ranging and offers a potentially flexible legal framework for addressing threats to high seas biodiversity. However, as outlined throughout this chapter, it has also failed to substantively address commercial fishing, which is the biggest source of biodiversity loss in the high seas.

This omission is concerning in the broader context of a range of challenges faced by marine biodiversity. The world's oceans are increasingly burdened with the impacts of human activity. Climate change is expected to create warmer, more acidic oceans and drastically alter the coastlines of some states due to sea level rise.[225] A compounding threat to marine biodiversity is the impact of

221 Hey (n 15) 101.

222 High Seas Alliance, "Ratification Map" (Web Page, 2024) <https://highseasalliance.org/treaty-ratification/map/>.

223 Ibid.

224 United Nations Intergovernmental Conference on Marine Biodiversity of Areas Beyond National Jurisdiction, "Intergovernmental Conference on an international legally binding instrument under the United Nations Convention on the Law of the Sea on the conservation and sustainable use of marine biological diversity of areas beyond national jurisdiction (General Assembly resolution 72/249)" (Web Page) <https://www.un.org/bbnj/content/sign-agreement>.

225 See, e.g. Lijing Cheng et al., 'Improved Estimates of Ocean Heat Content from 1960 to 2015' (2017) 3 *Science Advances* e1601545; Shuyang Ma et al., 'Climate risks to fishing species and

overfishing, including illegal, unreported, and unregulated fishing.[226] Shipping is another ubiquitous use of the ocean, which causes a range of impacts from pollution to the spread of invasive species.[227] Additionally, pollution more broadly, particularly plastic pollution, is another cause for concern over the ongoing health of the marine environment.[228] Indeed, the cumulative impacts of climate change, biodiversity loss, and pollution represent a planetary crisis for the Earth's oceans.

This crisis is likely to result in an ocean environment that differs significantly from what states have come to expect and what international law assumes.[229] A stable and predictable ocean environment can no longer be taken for granted.[230] Some have gone as far as to say that humans are now the primary driver of change in the Earth system.[231] It follows that if the old assumptions on which the law is premised can no longer be relied upon, then neither can the regime-based narratives built around these assumptions. The concept of MSY, for example, assumes that it is possible to determine an allowable catch that will permit the continued exploitation of targeted stocks.[232] However, when it becomes difficult to monitor stocks, due to shifts in distribution or sudden losses of abundance,[233] this narrative and the law it informs become less effective. Indeed, regime-based narratives that perpetuate an "extractive imagi-

---

fisheries in the China Seas' (2023) 857 *Science of the Total Environment* 159325, 2; William W L Cheung et al., 'Projecting global marine biodiversity impacts under climate change scenarios' (2009) 10 *Fish and Fisheries* 235, 243; Dan Laffoley et al., 'Ocean acidification: scientific understanding and challenges' in David L VanderZwaag, Nilüfer Oral and Tim Stephens (eds), *Research Handbook on Ocean Acidification Law and Policy* (Edward Elgar, 2021) 11; Malin L Pinsky and Rebecca L Selden, 'Climate Variability, Climate Change, and Conservation in a Dynamic Ocean' in Phillip S Levin and Melissa R Poe (eds), *Conservation for the Anthropocene Ocean: Interdisciplinary Science in Support of Nature and People* (Elsevier Inc, 2017) 23, 26; Nilüfer Oral, 'UNCLOS and sea level rise' (2023) 149 *Marine Policy* 105454, 2.

226 See, e.g. Steven J Cooke et al., 'Searching for responsible and sustainable recreational fisheries in the Anthropocene' (2019) 94 *Journal of Fish Biology* 845, 846; Robert S Steneck and Daniel Pauly, 'Fishing through the Anthropocene' (2022) 29 *Current Biology* R942.

227 See, e.g. James Kraska and Daniel Rittschof, 'Toward a Global Regime of Vessel Anti-Fouling' (2015) 26(1) *Duke Environmental Law & Policy Forum* 53, 54; C Hewitt and Marnie L Campbell, 'The relative contribution of vectors to the introduction and translocation of invasive marine species' (2010) *The National System for the Prevention and Management of Marine Pest Incursions* 1.

228 See, e.g. Judith S Weis, *Marine Pollution: What Everyone Needs to Know* (Oxford University Press, 2015); Kathryn A Willis et al., 'Cleaner seas: reducing marine pollution' (2022) 32 *Reviews in Fish Biology and Fisheries* 145, 145; Jenna R Jambeck et al., 'Plastic waste inputs from land into the ocean' (2015) 347(6223) *Science* 768, 768.

229 See, e.g. Davor Vidas et al., 'International law for the Anthropocene? Shifting perspectives in regulation of the oceans, environment and genetic resources' (2015) 9 *Anthropocene* 1, 4.

230 Ibid.

231 Yadvinder Malhi, 'The Concept of the Anthropocene' (2017) 42 *Annual Review of Environment and Resources* 77.

232 UNCLOS (n 17) art 119.

233 See, e.g. Ma et al. (n 225); Pinsky and Selden (n 225).

nary"[234] that sees the ocean as a vast pool of resources to be divided up for the benefit of private interests, will become increasingly untenable and ineffective as prevailing ocean conditions continue to become uncertain and unstable.

Hence, the law that is tasked with the "conservation and sustainable use" of the biodiversity of the oceans,[235] which includes both international biodiversity law and international fisheries law, will have to be better informed, more coordinated, flexible, and representative to adapt to human-induced changes in the ocean environment. As a part of this, existing regime-based narratives, as well as their interaction in practice, will need to be reconsidered.

This chapter has sought to better understand some of the potential obstacles to effective legal adaptation to uncertain ocean conditions by examining the regime-based narratives that determine how international legal regimes may interact with one another in the process of international law-making. In the case of the BBNJ, it became clear that it was not capable of completely addressing the challenge of the conservation and sustainable use of high seas biodiversity due to a range of entrenched factors in the make-up of the broader regime complex. If future international law-making, such as through the BBNJ COP, can consider these underlying regime-based narrative factors, it may be possible to address these tensions more directly and secure more complete outcomes for marine biodiversity.

The dynamic interaction between competing regime-based narratives has resulted in a BBNJ agreement that, while transformative in many ways, stoically avoids directly addressing the "whale in the room". The management of high seas fisheries is a key part of conserving and sustainably utilising biodiversity, but because of the regime-based narratives of international fisheries law and international biodiversity law, which focus on differing approaches to "what", "how", and "who" questions, it has been largely avoided within the final text. Avoiding hard decisions about the single biggest cause of marine biodiversity loss is not a viable solution to the management of a vast and complex ocean area in uncertain futures. The first step to dealing with the "whale in the room" is understanding why nobody wants to talk about it. This chapter takes a regime interaction approach in attempting to understand how the relationship between international fisheries law and international biodiversity law has influenced the outcomes for the BBNJ. It is hoped that it may shed some light on the role these underlying narratives play in shaping international law, as well as demonstrating that points of commonality and overlap between regimes should be acknowledged and clarified, rather than precluded as an inconvenience.

234 See, e.g. Surabhi Ranganathan, 'Ocean Floor Grab: International Law and the Making of an Extractive Imaginary' (2019) 30(2) *The European Journal of International Law* 573.

235 UNFSA (n 4) art 2; CBD (n 17) art 1.

7 The principle of common heritage of humankind as a bridge between deep seabed mining and biodiversity conservation

Carina Costa de Oliveira, Harvey Mpoto Bombaka, and Ana Flávia Barros-Platiau[1]

Introduction

As the worldwide demand for critical minerals increases, deep seabed mining becomes an option for the near future. However, current economic viability and technological challenges still prevent the mining industry from investing in one of the planet's final frontiers.[2] In fact, the interest in deep seabed minerals has a triple feature: it is very recent, science driven, and shaped by the principle of the common heritage of mankind (CHM). Under the auspices of the International Seabed Authority (ISA), the first exploration contract dates to 2001 for polymetallic nodules, 2011 for polymetallic sulphides, and 2014 for cobalt-rich ferromanganese crusts.[3] A growing number of contractors are carrying out research, and it is just a matter of time until they develop the necessary competences to start mining. The deep seabed and the subsoil are considered to constitute the common heritage of mankind, and the exploitation phase of deep seabed mining will be regulated by the Regulations on Exploitation of Mineral Resources in the Area.[4] That is the reason why the

1 The attendance at the workshop where this chapter was presented was supported by CNPq (314444/2021-1; 404153/2021-6); Capes (23038.019523/2022-11) and FAP-DF: 00193.00001489/2021-13. The authors would like to acknowledge the revision of the text made by Nitish Monebhurrun.

2 See Virginie Tassin Campanella (ed), *Routledge Handbook of Seabed Mining and the Law of the Sea* (Routledge Handbooks, 1st ed, 2024); Ana Flávia Barros-Platiau and Sandrine Maljean-Dubois, 'La gouvernance globale de la biodiversité en haute mer. Enjeux juridiques de fragmentation et défragmentation' in Daniel Compagnon and Estienne Rodary (eds), *Les Politiques de biodiversité* (Presses de Sciences Po, 1st ed, 2017), 47–64.

3 To date, the ISA has approved 31 contracts for exploration, involving 22 different countries (at least 12 of which are from developing states) and covering more than 1.3 million square kilometres of the seabed. See International Seabed Authority, *Exploration Contracts* (Web Page, 27 April 2024) <https://www.isa.org.jm/exploration-contracts/> ('Exploration Contracts').

4 International Seabed Authority, *Draft Regulations on Exploitation of Mineral Resources in the Area*, UN Doc ISBA/24/LTC/WP.1, 9 July 2018 ('*Draft Regulations on Exploitation of Mineral Resources in the Area*'); *Draft regulations on exploitation of Mineral resources in the*

DOI: 10.4324/9781003518570-7

negotiation of the Mining Code started in 2014, under the International Seabed Authority, at the demand of Nauru.[5]

It is noteworthy that research on the economic potential of marine mineral resources is far more developed than research on the negative externalities of mining activities for marine biodiversity and ocean health.[6] Therefore, as we move closer to the exploitation of deep seabed minerals, there is an urgent need for a clearer promotion of the CHM principle. Considering the services that the ocean provides for humanity, such as the regulation of the planet's temperature, the production of half of the oxygen in the atmosphere, the biodiversity richness, and the sequestration of carbon dioxide, it is necessary to envisage the ocean as a "life support system".[7] In the context of the triple crisis explored in this book, the exposure of marine biodiversity to new risks created by deep seabed mining[8] must be thoroughly discussed.[9]

Initially, the CHM – recently updated to the common heritage of humankind (CHH) – had the objective of transforming an ideal of fairness into a legal reality in the law of the sea. The CHM concept "must be understood as part of the effort by the growing number of newly independent States in the 1960s and 1970s to reshape international law to reflect developing country concerns and priorities".[10] However, the unfolding of negotiations and the subsequent legal formulations of the concept deviated from its original meaning. Consequently, we contend that the CHM principle has had its ups and

Area – Consolidated President's text, UN Doc ISBA/29/C/CRP.1, 16 February 2024 ('*Draft regulations on exploitation of Mineral resources in the Area – Consolidated President's text*').

5 See Campanella (n 2); Carina Costa de Oliveira, Gabriela Garcia Batista Lima Moraes, and Harvey Mpoto Bombaka, 'Projeto de código de explotação dos fundos marinhos: avanços na definição de proteção ao patrimônio comum da humanidade e da diligência devida no direito do mar' in Tarin Cristino Frota Mont'alverne et al. (eds), *Meio ambiente marinho, Sustentabilidade e Direito* (Lumen Juris, Rio de Janeiro, 2019).

6 See Michelle Allsopp et al., *Review Of The Current State Of Development And The Potential For Environmental Impacts Of Seabed Mining Operations: Greenpeace Research Laboratories Technical Report (Review)* (Report, March 2013); Charles Schmidt, 'Going deep: cautious steps towards seabed mining' (2015) 123(9) *Environmental Health Perspectives*, 234–241. See also Antje Boetius and Matthias Haeckel, 'Mind the seafloor' (2018) 359(6371) *Science*, 34–36; Cindy Lee Van Dover et al., 'Biodiversity loss from deep-sea mining' (2017) 10(7, 2, 17) *Nature Geoscience*, 464–465.

7 Rachel Tiller et al., 'Shake it Off: Negotiations suspended, but hope simmering, after a lack of consensus at the fifth intergovernmental conference on biodiversity beyond national jurisdiction' (2023) 148 *Marine Policy;* Marta Fava, 'Why is Ocean Conservation so important?' *UNESCO* (Web Page, 25 April 2024) <https://oceanliteracy.unesco.org/ocean-conservation/>.

8 *Draft Regulations on Exploitation of Mineral Resources in the Area* (n 5).

9 See Allsopp et al. (n 7); Schmidt (n 7) 234–241.

10 Jutta Brunnée, 'Common Areas, Common Heritage and Common Concern' in Daniel Bodansky, Jutta Brunnée and Ellen Hey (eds), *The Oxford Handbook of International Environmental Law* (OXUP, 2007), 562.

downs since its inception in 1967.[11] While its highest point may be considered the United Nations Convention on the Law of the Sea (UNCLOS) in 1982, it lost part of its legal significance with the Implementation Agreement in 1994. As the 2023 Biological Diversity of Areas beyond National Jurisdiction (BBNJ) Agreement established the CHH principle in Article 7, there are strong expectations that the CHH principle will be included in the final text of the ISA Regulations on Exploitation of Mineral Resources in the Area. The principle can be seen as a governance mechanism to achieve sustainable development, although its legal significance has been challenged.[12] In this sense, the principle of the CHH makes it possible to bring nuance to the interpretation of texts by considering the capacity as well as the national realities of states. The preamble of the president's text for the Regulations on Exploitation of Mineral Resources in the Area states that

> The Area and its resources are the common heritage of humankind, and the Exploitation of the resources of the Area shall be carried out for the benefit of humankind as a whole, on whose behalf the Authority acts. The objective of these Regulations is therefore to regulate the Exploitation of the resources of the Area consistent with the Convention, including the duty to ensure effective Protection for the Marine Environment from harmful effects caused by those activities.[13]

The evolution and legal relevance of principles do change with time. In this sense, they "start with political slogans reflecting fears about environmental hazards" before they are "embodied in enforceable laws".[14] Working on the principles of the polluter pays, prevention, and precaution, De Sadeleer argued that these principles of environmental law emerge from a combination of at least four factors: fears associated with the risks caused by industrial society,

11 Taylor Prue, 'The Common Heritage of Mankind: Expanding the Oceanic Circle' in Dirk Werle et al. (eds), *The Future of Ocean Governance and Capacity Development: Essays in of Elisabeth Mann Borgese (1918-2002)* (Brill Nijhoff, Leiden, 2019), 142–150; Marie Claude Smouts, 'Du Patrimoine Commun de l'Humanité aux Bien Publics Globaux' in Marie Christine Cormier-Salem et al. (eds) *Patrimoines naturels au Sud : territoires, identités et stratégies locales* (IRD Éditions, Paris, 2005), 53–70.

12 According to Tiller et al., "the CHM was mentioned 82 times during the BBNJ Intergovernmental (IGC-5) and 41 times in IGC-1; 56 times in IGC-2, 18 times in IGC-3, and 8 times in IGC-4". See Tiller et al. (n 8) 4; Rüdiger Wolfrum, 'The Principle of the Common Heritage of Mankind' (1983) 43 *Zeitschrift fur Auslandisches Offentliches Recht und Volkerrecht*, 312–337; Victor Ventura and Cavalcanti de Mello Filho, 'The Common Heritage of Mankind' in Sergey Sayapin et al. (eds), *International Conflict and Security Law* (T.M.C. Asser Press, The Hague, 2022).

13 *Draft regulations on exploitation of Mineral resources in the Area – Consolidated President's text* (n 5) preamble.

14 See Nicolas de Sadeleer, *Environmental Principles: from Political Slogans to Legal Rules* (Oxford University Press, 2020).

scientific alerts, ethical considerations, and established legal practice. In this vein, the CHM principle seems to follow the same pathway. We raise the question of whether the CHM can help achieve sustainable development on the deep seabed. That is, to delicately balance commercial interest in mining and biodiversity conservation on one of the planet's final frontiers,[15] the deep seabed. Before analysing the practical difficulties facing the CHM, as well as its reinvigoration due to negotiations of the Regulations on Exploitation of Mineral Resources in the Area and the BBNJ Agreement, a brief presentation of the construction of the legal significance of the CHM principle is presented.

The construction of the legal significance of the CHM principle: a roller-coaster movement

The concept of the common heritage of mankind[16] was first raised by Ambassador Arvid Pardo of Malta[17] before the UN General Assembly in August 1967.[18] He pointed out the necessity of governing the seabed and

15 "But I am speaking of exploring an unknown world at our doorstep. It is really our last frontier here on earth. I am speaking of mountain chains that are yet to be discovered, of natural resources that are yet to be tapped, of a vast wilderness that is yet to be charted. This is the sea around us." See Gerhard Peters, John Woolley, 'US President Johnson's remarks at the Commissioning of Oceanographer', *The American Presidency Project* (Web Page, 5 May 2024) <https://www.presidency.ucsb.edu/documents/remarks-the-commissioning-the-research-ship-oceanographer>.

16 Pierre-François Mercure, 'L'échec des modeles de gestion des ressources naturelles selon les caracteristiques du concept de patrimoine commun de l'humanité' (1996) 28(1) *Revue De Droit D'ottawa*, 4; François-Guy Trebulle, 'La propriété à l'épreuve du patrimoine commun: Le renouveau du domaine universel' in *Etudes offertes au professeur malinvaud* (Lexis Nexis, 2007); Erik Franckx, 'The International Seabed Authority and the Common Heritage of Mankind, the Need for States to Establish the Outer Limits of their Continental Shelf' (2010) 25(543) *The International Journal of Marine and Coastal Law*, 567; Michael Lodge, 'The Common Heritage Of Mankind' (2012) 27(733) *The International Journal of Marine and Coastal Law*, 742; John Noyes, 'The Common Heritage of Mankind, Past, Present, and Future' (2012) 40 *Denver Journal of International Law & Policy* 447; Kemal Baslar, *The Concept of the Common Heritage of Mankind in International Law* (Nijhoff Publishers, 1998); Scott Shackelford, 'The tragedy of the common heritage of mankind' (2008) 27 *Stanford Environmental Law Journal* 101; Christopher Joyner, 'Legal Implications of the Concept Of The Common Heritage Of Mankind' (1986) 35 *The International and Comparative Law Quarterly* 190; Alexandre-Charles Kiss, La notion de patrimoine commun de l'humanité (1983) 175 Académie de droit international, 103 e s; Daniel Bardonnet, 'Le projet de convention de 1912 sur le Spitsberg et le concept de patrimoine commun de l'humanité' in *Humanité et droit international, Mélanges René-Jean Dupuy* (Pedone, Paris, 1991), 13.

17 Arvid Pardo was a diplomat and a Maltese and Swedish university professor. He is known as the "Father of the Law of the Sea Conference". See Surabhi Ranganathan, 'What If Arvid Pardo Had Not Made his Famous Speech? (False) Contingency in the Making of the Law of the Sea' in Ingo Venzke and Kevin Jon Heller (eds), *Contingency in International Law: On the Possibility of Different Legal Histories* (Oxford, 2021, online ed, Oxford Academic, 23 September 2021) 1.

18 See UNGA, *Resolution 2749 (XXV) on Declaration of Principles Governing the Sea-bed and the Ocean Floor, and the Subsoil thereof, beyond the Limits of National Jurisdiction*, UN Doc A/RES/2749(XXV), 16th December 1970 ('*Resolution 2749*'). See also Kiss (n 17) 103.

the ocean floor, and the subsoil thereof beyond the limits of national jurisdiction for exclusively peaceful purposes and the exploitation of their resources in the interest of mankind.[19] In 1970, Resolution 2749 was approved by the General Assembly, declaring that "The sea-bed and ocean floor, and the subsoil thereof, beyond the limits of national jurisdiction (hereinafter referred to as the Area), as well as the resources of the Area, are the common heritage of mankind."[20] Later, the text of the United Nations Convention on the Law of the Sea incorporated this formulation by further clarifying its legal contours. Article 136 states that "The Area and its resources are the common heritage of mankind". Article 137.1 points out that "No State may claim or exercise sovereignty or sovereign rights over any part of the Area or its resources; nor shall any State or natural or juridical person appropriate any part thereof." Moreover, the concept of CHM is closely linked to five essential obligations: non-appropriation, peaceful use, rational exploitation of resources, international management, and equitable distribution of benefits.[21]

UNCLOS was complemented in 1994 by an Implementation Agreement[22] which established the International Seabed Authority responsible for the management of the Area. The concept of CHM "would provide the basis for specific principles concerning the Area; accordingly, all the rules and principles for activities in the seabed should be based on that notion".[23] For example, in his statement in 1967, Pardo argued before the United Nations General Assembly that the transfer of technology should be an intrinsic part of the common heritage of mankind.[24] The idea was also defended by many delegates, particularly those of developing countries, during the negotiations of the Third United Nations Conference on the Law of the Sea[25] and was consolidated in Part XI of UNCLOS (Article 144) as well as in Article 5 of Annex III of the convention.

The Seabed Chamber of the International Tribunal for the Law of the Sea (ITLOS) reiterated the importance of the existing connection between the CHM and some obligations referred to in UNCLOS. ITLOS stated that

19 See Alain Piquemal, 'Le fond des mers: patrimoine commun de l'humanité' (1973) 2 *Centre national pour l'exploitation des océans – série rapport économique et juridique*, 269.

20 This resolution granted the first solemn consecration of the concept of Common Heritage of Humanity. See *Resolution 2749* (n 19).

21 See the consistency of articles 136 and 137 of the *Convention on the Law of the Sea* (n 2).

22 *Agreement Relating to the Implementation of Part XI of the United Nations Convention on the Law of the Sea of 10 December 1982*, opened for signature 28 July 1994, UN Doc A/RES/48/263 (entered into force 16 November 1994) ('*1994 Agreement*').

23 *Committee on the Peaceful Uses of the Seabed and the Ocean Floor beyond the Limits of National Jurisdiction*, UN GAOR, 24th sess, Supplement No. 22 (A/7622) (1969), 14 [20].

24 A. See Piquemal (n 20) 3.

25 Came into force on 16 November 1994, after the sixtieth instrument of ratification. The list was composed of 58 developing countries, including Iceland and Yugoslavia. See also Jean-François Brault, 'Le transfert des techniques marines et la position américaine à l'égard de la Convention sur le droit de la mer' (1988) 4 *Revue québécoise de droit international*, 389.

> The role of the sponsoring State, as set out in the Convention, contributes to the realization of the common interest of all States in the proper application of the principle of the common heritage of mankind which requires faithful compliance with the obligations set out in Part XI. The common interest role of the sponsoring State is further confirmed by its obligation, set out in article 153, paragraph 4, of the Convention, to "assist" the Authority, which, as stated in article 137, paragraph 2, of the Convention, acts on behalf of mankind.[26]

However, with the legal approach adopted by the United Nations Agreement relating to the implementation of Part XI of UNCLOS (1994), the legal content of the common heritage of mankind was significantly modified.[27] According to the Montego Bay Convention (Article 155.2/311.6), the principle was emptied of its essential legal consistency[28] due to divergences arising between developed and developing states. During the negotiations at the Third United Nations Conference on the Law of the Sea, two main criteria inherent in the concept of CHM were the sticking points between developed and developing countries.[29] The first criterion referred to the conditions for restricting production and access to mineral markets. The aim of this criterion was to protect land-based mineral producers.[30] The second criterion referred to the constraints on states and companies possessing the technologies to transfer them to the Enterprise and to the states that needed them. The reservations expressed by the developed countries regarding these two criteria caused an insurmountable blockage to the adoption of UNCLOS. The adoption of the United Nations Agreement relating to the implementation of Part XI of UNCLOS made it possible to resolve the crisis.[31] However, the adoption of the 1994 Agreement had a regressive effect on the obligations mentioned above.

First, the 1994 Agreement removed differential treatment between land and marine mining states. For example, Section 6(d) of the 1994 Agreement states that

26 International Tribunal for The Law Of The Sea, *The responsibilities and obligations of States sponsoring persons and entities with respect to activities in the Area (Advisory Opinion)* (Report, 2011) [76] ('*The responsibilities and obligations of States sponsoring persons and entities with respect to activities in the Area*').

27 Hang Zhou and Jieyi Xie, 'Revisiting heritage in the ocean: common heritage of [Hu]mankind, maritime heritage and beyond?' (2024) 30(6) *International Journal of Heritage Studies*, 687–702; Surabhi Ranganathan, 'The Law of the Sea and Natural Resources' in Eyal Benvenisti and Georg Nolte (eds), *Community Interests Across International Law* (Oxford Academic, 19 July 2018).

28 Harvey Mpoto Bombaka, 'Em direção ao abandono do patrimônio comum da humanidade em direito do mar' in Carina Costa de Oliveira et al. (eds), *A função do direito na gestão sustentável dos recursos minerais marinhos* (Editora Processo, Rio de Janeiro, 2021), 167–189.

29 Ibid 175.

30 Ibid 175–176.

31 Ibid 176.

> There shall be no discrimination between minerals derived from the Area and from other sources. There shall be no preferential access to markets for such minerals or for imports of commodities produced from such minerals, in particular: (i) By the use of tariff or non-tariff barriers; and (ii) Given by States Parties to such minerals or commodities produced by their State enterprises or by natural or juridical persons which possess their nationality or are controlled by them or their nationals.

While providing more economic guarantees to companies in developed countries that were involved in deep seabed mining, these provisions were detrimental to developing countries whose economies were based on land-based mining of the same natural resources. This undermined the operation of the CHM principle.[32] Secondly, the 1994 Agreement regressed the obligations relating to technology transfer. By way of illustration, while Article 144, paragraph 1 of UNCLOS gives sufficient power to the authority to impose the transfer of technology to the Enterprise and to the states that need it ("the Authority shall take measures"),[33] point 1 (b) of Annex 5 to the 1994 Agreement states that "[i]f the Enterprise or developing States are unable to obtain seabed mining technology, the Authority may request the contractors and the sponsoring State or States to cooperate". This subtle phraseological nuance sufficiently dilutes the scope of Article 144 to the point of reducing the authority's power. Furthermore, Article 5 of Annex III to UNCLOS sets out the conditions that the authority imposes on companies in the following terms:

> When submitting a plan of work, any applicant shall make available to the Authority a general description of the equipment and methods to be used in carrying out activities in the Area and other relevant information which is not industrial property and which relates to the characteristics of the proposed techniques, as well as information indicating where such techniques are available.

The 1994 Agreement, via point 2 of Section 5 of its Annex, sets aside the above article in the following terms: "The provisions of art. 5 of Annex III to the Convention shall not apply." These provisions clearly demonstrate the approach, if not the clear intention, of blocking the obligation to transfer technology in any form whatsoever.

32 See Oliveira, Moraes, and Bombaka (n 6) 15–33. See also Ventura and Cavalcanti (n 13).

33 Regarding the meaning of the term as explained by the Virginia commentary, the word shall have the meaning of an obligation; this means that the authority must take measures. However, Article 1(b) of Section 5 of the *1994 Agreement* (n 23) departs significantly from this meaning. Cf. Myron Nordquis (ed), *United Nations Convention on the Law of the Sea 1982: A Commentary Volume 2* (cover Martinus Nijhoff Publishers, August 1993).

In addition, regarding technology transfer, Regulation 2 states that "(iv) Participation in revenues by the Authority and the transfer of technology to the Enterprise and developing States as provided for in the Convention and the Agreement" is a fundamental policy and principle of the exploitation of mineral resources in the Area. In addition to this, Articles 144 and 148 of UNCLOS provide the legal basis for technology transfer.[34] Regulation 63 of Part VII regarding the financial terms of an exploitation contract also reinforces the differentiated treatment for developing states in these terms:

> Furthermore, the Council may provide incentives, including financial incentives, to those Contractors entering into joint arrangements with the Enterprise under article 11 of annex III to the Convention, and developing States or their nationals, to stimulate the transfer of technology thereto and to train the personnel of the Authority and of developing States.[35]

The limit of this text is the use of "may provide incentives" in Regulation 63. It would be stronger to use expressions such as "shall" in this article. The CHM is intricately linked to the equitable sharing of resources (Article 140.2 of the convention) and to the protection and conservation of the marine environment, including the "natural resources of the Area and the prevention of damage to the flora and fauna of the marine environment".[36] Part XI serves as a complementary framework to the overarching obligation outlined in Article 192 of the convention, affirming that: "States have the obligation to protect and preserve the marine environment." While the explicit conservation of marine biodiversity was not literally presented in Part XII of UNCLOS, the interpretative lens[37] applied to Article 192, aligned with environmental treaties such as the Convention on Biological Diversity (CBD), can furnish a legal foundation for the integration of marine biodiversity conservation within the broader scope of the obligation delineated in Article 192. The inclusive definition of biological diversity, encapsulating the marine environment and its characterisation as a common concern of humankind, indisputably intertwines

34 "The effective participation of developing States in activities in the Area shall be promoted as specifically provided for in this Part, having due regard to their special interests and needs, and in particular to the special need of the land-locked and geographically disadvantaged among them to overcome obstacles arising from their disadvantaged location, including remoteness from the Area and difficulty of access to and from it". See *Convention on the Law of the Sea* (n 2) 148.

35 See *the Draft Regulations on Exploitation of Mineral Resources in the Area* (n 5).

36 Ibid 145(b).

37 The interpretation mentioned in this paragraph is based on Articles 31.1, 31.2, and 31.3 of the *Vienna Convention on the Law of Treaties*, opened for signature 23 May 1969, 1155 UNTS 331 (entered into force 27 January 1980).

biodiversity conservation as an imperative linked to the protection and preservation of the marine environment. This obligation was explicitly codified within the BBNJ, an implementing agreement of the convention.

The CHM principle has been strengthened in the framework of the conservation and the sustainable use of marine biodiversity in areas beyond national jurisdiction (BBNJ). After 20 years of BBNJ negotiations, the CHM was included as a principle in the 2023 final text of the BBNJ Agreement. It is noteworthy that the title of the principle changed to a more modern one, which is "Common Heritage of Humankind".[38] This treaty will certainly influence the content of the principle.[39] Moreover, with the adoption of the BBNJ treaty, the connection between the CHH and the sustainable development principle is stronger than ever. The sustainable development principle, which was consolidated in 1992 during the Earth Summit in Rio,[40] can be highlighted by the following substantive and procedural elements: integration of environmental protection and economic development; the right to development; sustainable conservation and utilisation of natural resources; inter-generational equity; intra-generational equity; and the polluter pays principle.[41] In this sense, the CHH and the sustainable development objective are comprehensive in terms of scope and complementarity and are mutually supportive.[42]

Although sustainable development can be considered a principle of environmental law,[43] this is arguable since its legal application and relevance are much broader and thus remain controversial. However, there is no doubt that it is an objective that all international actors must implement. In this sense, the CHH is a "governance" principle that would contribute to the implementation of sustainable development goals,[44] notably those of the UN 2030 Agenda, as

38 *1994 Agreement* (n 23) art 7(b). CHH is utilised instead of CHM in this chapter, taking into account the political and prospective legal revision of the nomenclature of the principle.

39 Samantha Robb, Aline Jaeckel, and Catherine Blanchard, 'How could the BBNJ Agreement affect the International Seabed Authority's Mining Code?', *EJIL: Talk!* (Web Page, 15 November 2023) <ejiltalk.org/how-could-the-bbnj-agreement-affect-the-international-seabed-authoritys-mining-code/>.

40 *Rio Declaration On Environment And Development*, GA CONF.151/26, UN Doc A/CONF.151/26 (12 August 1992), principle 27 ('*Rio Declaration On Environment And Development*').

41 Günther Handl, Patricia Birnie, and Alan Boyle, *International Law and the Environment* (Oxford University Press, 2nd ed, 2002); (2002) 13(1) *Yearbook of International Environmental Law*, 867–869.

42 See Ventura and Cavalcanti (n 13) 1.

43 Louis Kotzé et al., 'Courts, Climate litigation and the evolution of earth system law' (2023), 15 *Global Policy*, 1–18.

44 "The principle of CHM can provide theoretical basis for marine management approaches and lay the foundation for the law of the sea". Chuanliang Wang and Yen-Chiang Chang, 'A new interpretation of the common heritage of mankind in the context of the international law of the sea' (2020) 191 *Ocean & Coastal Management.*

well as to other frameworks such as the Global Biodiversity framework.[45] In a nutshell, the CHH is a principle that should govern all the instruments related to seabed mining and BBNJ obligations jointly.

Even though the latest draft of the Regulations on Exploitation of Mineral Resources in the Area and the BBNJ Agreement tend to restore and strengthen the CHH content, it is still too early to foresee the real impact of the principle on the sustainable development of states. In this sense, it is relevant to analyse the practical difficulties facing the CHH regarding the challenges linked to the sustainable development of states before highlighting the reinvigoration of the CHH due to the negotiation of the Regulations on Exploitation of Mineral Resources in the Area and the BBNJ Agreement.

The practical difficulties facing the CHH regarding the challenges linked to the sustainable development of states

The practical difficulties facing the CHH regarding the challenges linked to the sustainable development of states can be synthesised into two main arguments: the paralysis of the Enterprise and the process of the appropriation of marine mineral resources by companies.

The paralysis of the Enterprise

High-quality technology remains essential for all entities engaged in exploration and exploitation activities on the seabed. This necessity extends beyond mere economic feasibility, encompassing the provision of reliable information crucial for ensuring the uniform protection of the marine environment and for facilitating scientific research. UNCLOS established the Enterprise as an innovative tool to be the operational arm of the authority, so that states could enjoy the sharing of potential benefits from deep seabed mining.[46] However, the substantial amendments made by the 1994 Agreement have changed the legal scope of the Enterprise. At the same time, it limits the possibility of the Enterprise playing an important role in the governance of the oceans: granting the land-locked and developing states a technical and legal framework adapted to their national realities for exploiting the seabed, while avoiding what the Seabed Disputes Chamber of ITLOS considers to be "sponsorship by convenience".[47] This section discusses the practical difficulties hindering

45 *Kunming–Montreal Global Biodiversity Framework*, UNEP, UN Doc CBD/COP/DEC/14/5 (19 December 2022).

46 *Convention on the Law of the Sea* (n 2) Annex 5 art 1; Hao Shen, 'A critical assessment of the International Seabed Authority's implementation of the Common Heritage of Mankind principle from the perspective of benefit-sharing regime' (2023) 23(3) *International Environmental Agreements*, 355–371.

47 See *The responsibilities and obligations of States sponsoring persons and entities with respect to activities in the Area* (n 27) [159]. See also Harvey Mpoto Bombaka, 'Le traitement différen-

the operationalisation of the Enterprise, considering the normative evolution of the law of the sea.

The Enterprise has the function to explore and exploit the CHH for the benefit of all humankind, especially for land-locked and developing states.[48] In this logic, the Enterprise appeared as a counterweight in the exploration and exploitation of the seabed, breaking the monopoly that private companies from developed countries could hold over countries deprived of the capacity to exploit the seabed. These counterweights can also play an important role in containing the practice of "sponsoring by convenience", an issue that could be prejudicial to the uniform protection of the marine environment.[49] In other words, the Enterprise was conceived as a mechanism of international cooperation for the interest and action of humankind.[50]

However, the current configuration of the law of the sea demonstrates that the Enterprise is in a state of functional paralysis.[51] Indeed, although UNCLOS grants the Enterprise functional autonomy, the 1994 Agreement substantially changed the legal scope of this body. Even though the 1994 Agreement brought a little more pragmatism to the implementation of Part XI, it reduced the Enterprise's autonomy.[52] This is evidenced by the temporary modification of the general operating regime of the Enterprise: mandatory financing was eliminated, the procedure for carrying out mining activities was modified, and the mandatory technology transfer regime was removed.[53]

---

cié en droit international de la mer' (PhD Thesis, University of Brasília joint supervision with Aix Marseille University, 2022), 206–207.

48 *Convention on the Law of the Sea* (n 2) Annex III(a).

49 This issue will be developed in detail *infra*. See *The responsibilities and obligations of States sponsoring persons and entities with respect to activities in the Area* (n 27) [159].

50 According to Egede and Charles: "13 members of the Group of Latin American and Caribbean Countries (GRULAC) proposed the idea and the rationale of the Enterprise in a 1971 working paper: 'In keeping with the principle of common heritage, the co-sponsors of the working paper envisage the establishment of a system in which mankind, in the capacity of owner, would participate directly in the administration and management of the Area and the exploitation of its resources'". See Edwin Egede and Charles Eden, 'Common heritage of mankind and the deep seabed area beyond national jurisdiction: past, current, and future prospects' (2021) 55(6) *Marine Technology Society Journal*, 18–19.

51 See Nitish Monebhurrun, 'A paralisia funcional da Empresa' in Carina Costa de Oliveira et al. (n 29) 253–281.

52 *Convention on the Law of the Sea* (n 2) Annex IV art 125.1, 140, 148, 155.2.

53 International Seabed Authority, *Secretary-General's Informal Consultations on Outstanding Issues relating to the Deep Seabed Mining Provisions of the United Nations Convention on the Law of the Sea: Collected Documents* (2002). See also Myron Nordquist, Satya Nandan, and Rosenne Shabtai (eds), 6 *United Nations Convention on the Law of the Sea 1982: A Commentary* (Martinus Nijhoff Publishers, 2002), 521. See also Ferrara, 'Article 170: The Enterprise' in Alexander Proelß et al., 1 *The United Nations Convention on the Law of the Sea: A Commentary* (Bloomsbury Publishing, 2017), 1214.

An in-depth analysis of Section 2 of the 1994 Agreement reveals that the Enterprise was "downgraded".[54] The first observation is the transfer of the functions of the Enterprise to the secretariat of the International Seabed Authority without specifying a duration.[55] Nevertheless, Section 2, Item 1 of the 1994 Agreement states that "The Secretariat of the Authority shall perform the functions of the Enterprise until it begins to operate independently of the Secretariat." Although the transfer of these functions deprives the Enterprise of a good part of its competences under UNCLOS, it is important to emphasise that it was necessary to fill the legal gap that could arise from the Enterprise's inactivity.[56]

In fact, during the first part of the 28th Annual Session of the International Seabed Authority, which ended on 31 March 2023, the issue of the Enterprise repeatedly came up for negotiation.[57] With the support of several states such as those comprising the African group, Brazil, Trinidad and Tobago, and others, the council adopted a decision to establish the position of an interim director general of the Enterprise.[58] While the absence of a set deadline for the transfer of power to the Enterprise remains an unresolved issue, the essence of the matter remains intact. Reinitiating discussions on this matter will pave the way for progress, offering an opportunity to elucidate the intricacies surrounding the operationalisation of the Enterprise. However, the 1994 Agreement has eviscerated the Enterprise, making it difficult to envision how it will operate even with a director.

The Enterprise faces a significant hurdle in the form of financial constraints, compounded by the withdrawal of funding obligations initially outlined in UNCLOS.[59] Section 2, Item 3 of the 1994 Agreement states that

> The obligation of States Parties to fund one mine site of the Enterprise as provided for in Annex IV, article 11, paragraph 3, of the Convention shall not apply and States Parties shall be under no obligation to finance any of the operations in any mine site of the Enterprise or under its joint-venture arrangements.[60]

54 Egede and Eden (n 51) 19, 40–52. See also Ferrara (n 55) 1210.

55 See *Convention on the Law of the Sea* (n 2) art 170 [2].

56 *Convention on the Law of the Sea* (n 2) Section 4, Subsection E: 'The Entreprise', Article 170(1).

57 See International Seabed Authority, *The Decision of the Council of the International Seabed Authority relating to the establishment of the position of an interim director general of the Enterprise*, UN Doc ISBA/28/C/23 (21 July 2023).

58 International Institute for Sustainable Development, 'Summary of the Twenty-eighth Annual Session of the International Seabed Authority (First Part): 16–31 March 2023' (Report, 4 April 2023) 25(251) *Earth Negotiations Bulletin* ISA-28 1st Part Final, 1 ('Summary of the Twenty-eighth Annual Session of the International Seabed Authority').

59 Bombaka (n 49) 107.

60 International Seabed Authority, *Report of the Special Representative of the Secretary-General of the International Seabed Authority for the Enterprise,* UN Doc ISBA/28/C/2 (13 February 2023).

More recently, during the first part of the 25th Session of the International Seabed Authority, the council requested the secretary general to establish a "voluntary fund" to provide the authority with the resources necessary to finance the activities of the special representative of the secretary general for Enterprise.[61] The fund was established on 1 March 2019.[62] On 31 May 2023, the fund had a balance of $3,528.[63] The numbers shown may reflect the way things are configured. The same difficulty arises regarding the rules applicable to the procedure for the transfer of technology to the Enterprise since they have been substantially modified.

Originally, through Articles 144, 273, 274, and Annex III, Article 5, UNCLOS proposed a mandatory technology transfer to the Enterprise. This was removed by Section 2, point 6 of the 1994 Agreement. This provision states that: "Article 170, paragraph 4, Annex IV and other provisions of the Convention relating to the Enterprise shall be interpreted and applied in accordance with this section." This introduces the notion of the precedence of the 1994 Agreement over UNCLOS, potentially resulting in the erosion of the privileges accorded to the Enterprise within UNCLOS. During the first part of the 28th Annual Session of the International Seabed Authority, regional groups underscored that the ISA "may or may not" provide incentives, suggesting amending the draft regulation to attest that the council may provide incentives to contractors to further the engagement of the Enterprise.[64] Recent developments look promising: in the consolidated version of the draft, provisions have been identified to this effect. These include Regulations 63(1) and 63(2)[65] and Regulation 3(f)(vi)[66] which indicate the possibility for the council to provide financial incentives to contractors entering into joint agreements with the Enterprise. This is a positive step forward in the negotiation of the Regulations on Exploitation of Mineral Resources in the Area. Let us hope that such provisions will be maintained in the final version.

Nevertheless, it should be remembered that the progression of the new negotiations towards the restoration of the Enterprise had already been identified in the non-consolidated version. Some states are tending to restore legal force to the Enterprise.[67] In its policy and fundamental principles, the Draft

61 International Seabed Authority, *Decision of the Council of the International Seabed Authority relating to the Special Representative of the Secretary-General of the International Seabed Authority for the Enterprise*, UN Doc ISBA/25/C/16 (1 March 2019).

62 Ibid.

63 International Seabed Authority, *Report of the Secretary-General of the International Seabed Authority under article 166, paragraph 4, of the United Nations Convention on the Law of the Sea*, UN Doc ISBA/28/A/2 (31 May 2023) [23].

64 *1st Part of the 28th Annual Session of the International Seabed Authority: Summary report* (n 60) 7.

65 See *Draft regulations on exploitation of Mineral resources in the Area – Consolidated President's text* (n 5) Regulation 63 [1] and [2].

66 Ibid Regulation 3 [f] (vi).

67 See *Draft Regulations on Exploitation of Mineral Resources in the Area* (n 5) s 2.

Regulations for the Exploitation of Mineral Resources in the Area include the application of the CHM in compliance with Part XI of the convention. The draft also uses an approach allowing the Enterprise access to technology, on fairer terms. In the same vein, the consolidated version of the draft reinforces the role of the Enterprise. The consolidated version includes other interesting principles such as inter-generational equity, open access to non-confidential data, and information.[68]

Despite this significant progress of the texts to the advantage of the Enterprise, it remains uncertain whether it is possible to see a conciliatory approach between UNCLOS and related texts such as the 1994 Agreement in the context of the operationalisation of the Enterprise. Even if this could theoretically be possible in the future, stakeholder practice (including the states involved in seabed activities) is getting ahead of theory. For example, the pressure exerted by companies to initiate the process of appropriation through seabed mining contributes to this uncertainty.

The process of appropriation of marine mineral resources by companies

The way in which the practices of sponsored companies and sponsoring states are taking shape may give rise to a kind of appropriation of the seabed by a small group of actors operating in the sector.[69] On the one hand, many developing countries are not able to engage in mining activities in the Area or to propose a joint venture to the Enterprise; on the other hand, they know that they are entitled to enjoy the potential resources of the seabed.[70] These two points appear to be inherently contradictory: states have contributed to the stagnation of the Enterprise, while simultaneously acknowledging that its functionality is compromised. Within the institutional framework of the authority, the representation of their interests has evolved to become uncertain and ambiguous, leading to the marginalisation of developing countries within the CHM framework.[71] Proposing that the Enterprise can successfully negotiate a contract that comprehensively addresses its requirements for funding, technology, and scientific expertise is both unrealistic and excessively ambitious.[72]

68 See *Draft regulations on exploitation of Mineral resources in the Area – Consolidated President's text* (n 5) Regulation 2 [4].

69 See Nitish Monebhurrun, 'The functional paralysis of the Enterprise' (2023) 1 (1) *Ottawa Journal of International and Public Affairs*, 31–60.

70 Monebhurrun (n 52) 267.

71 Edwin Egede, Mati Pal, and Charles Eden (eds), *A Study Related to the Issues on the Operationalization of the Enterprise: Legal, Technical and Financial Implications for the International Seabed Authority and for States Parties to the United Nations Convention on the Law of the Sea* (Technical Report, June 2019).

72 Ibid 29 [101].

Strategically, developing countries would obviously not wait to consider alternative mechanisms to participate in the activities in the Area.[73] It is known that under UNCLOS and the ISA[74] states can sponsor public or private companies to carry out exploration or exploitation activities in the Area. According to UNCLOS, exploration or exploitation activities in the Area are organised and controlled by the authority on behalf of humankind and may be conducted or carried out not only by the Enterprise, but also

> in association with the Authority by States Parties, or state enterprises or natural or juridical persons which possess the nationality of States Parties or are effectively controlled by them or their nationals, when sponsored by such States, or any group of the foregoing which meets the requirements provided in this Part and in Annex III.[75]

Based on this possibility, and not always having the necessary resources, technology, and ***know-how*** to operate a seabed exploration or exploitation activity *proprio motu*, developing countries can alternatively opt for exploration contracts signed directly with private operators.[76]

For a company to start activities in the Area, it is mandatory to be sponsored by a state. The "sponsorship" mechanism is a very important element of the system for the exploration and exploitation of the resources of the Area established in UNCLOS.[77] The sponsorship provided by states parties for the exploration and exploitation of resources within the Area is designed to guarantee that contractors adhere to the obligations delineated in UNCLOS and other relevant international treaties. Given that contractors are entities subject to domestic law, and international treaties hold binding authority exclusively for states parties, establishing a mechanism for enforcing obligations on con-

73 This expression is defined in Article 1, paragraph 1(3), of the convention as "all activities of exploration for, and exploitation of, the resources of the Area". See *Convention on the Law of the Sea* (n 2).

74 International Seabed Authority, *Decision of the Council of the International Seabed Authority relating to amendments to the Regulations on Prospecting and Exploration for Polymetallic Nodules in the Area and related* matters, UN Doc ISBA/19/C/17 (22 July 2013), art 9 ('*Regulations on Prospecting and Exploration for Polymetallic Nodules in the Area and related matters*'); International Seabed Authority, *Decision of the Assembly of the International Seabed Authority relating to the regulations on prospecting and exploration for polymetallic sulphides in the Area*, UN Doc ISBA/16/A/12/Rev.1 (15 November 2010), art 9 ('*Regulations on prospecting and exploration for polymetallic sulphides in the Area*'); International Seabed Authority, *Decision of the Assembly of the International Seabed Authority relating to the Regulations on Prospecting and Exploration for Cobalt-rich Ferromanganese Crusts in the Area*, UN Doc ISBA/18/A/11 (22 October 2012), art 9.

75 *Convention on the Law of the Sea* (n 2) 153, point 2 (a) and (b).

76 Monebhurrun (n 52) 267.

77 *The responsibilities and obligations of States sponsoring persons and entities with respect to activities in the Area* (n 27) [74].

tractors becomes crucial, thereby underscoring the significance of sponsorship.[78] The role of the sponsoring state is to contribute "to the realization of the common interest of all States in the proper application of the principle of the common heritage of mankind which requires faithful compliance with the obligations set out in Part XI".[79]

As noted earlier, most developing countries do not have national companies with the technological and financial capacity to undertake seabed exploration and mining on their own account.[80] As a result, these states generally choose to sponsor private sector entities to participate in the Area's activities.[81] Thus, there are scenarios in which – as we highlighted in the first part of this section – a private company from a developed country prefers to establish a "subsidiary" in a developing country, such as small Pacific Island States, because they have less stringent application of the obligations relating to marine exploitation activities. Consequently, companies can take advantage of differentiated legal obligations – *de facto* less stringent through the sponsorship of some developing states.[82]

As an example, Nauru is a small Pacific island developing state with vast and rich marine areas under its jurisdiction, having the right to engage in exploitation activities in the Area like any other state. However, Nauru does not have the technological and financial capacity either to operate on its own[83] or to monitor the operations of any company under its jurisdiction. Nauru is one of the states that has developed the most advanced legal instruments for seabed mining, considering recent developments in the law of the sea. At first sight, this can be explained by the importance of its maritime space. However, on closer inspection, it is noted that NORI, a Nauru-sponsored company,[84] has as its principal shareholders two of the world's largest mining companies, namely: Teck Cominco Limited and Anglo American Limited. These companies are listed on the Toronto Stock Exchange and the Alternative Investment Market, a sub-market of the London Stock Exchange. These are companies whose parent companies are based in developed states but which set up subsidiaries in small island developing states. This can be explained by the intention of these companies to benefit from flexibilities and differential treatment to the advantage of small island developing states.[85] Thus, this places developing

78 Ibid para 75.
79 Ibid para 76.
80 See Harvey Mpoto Bombaka, 'Os desafios da implementação da obrigação de due diligence no contexto da exploração do mar: aspectos nacionais e internacionais' (Master's Thesis, University of Brasília, 2017), 115.
81 Ibid.
82 Bombaka (n 49) 208.
83 Bombaka (n 81) 115.
84 While Nauru Ocean Resources Inc (NORI) is now wholly owned by two Nauruan foundations, whose purpose is education, training, health, and environmental rehabilitation in Nauru, apparently, "there remains significant foreign interest at Nauru Ocean Resources Inc". See Tim Poisel, 'Deep Seabed Mining: Implications of Seabed Disputes Chamber's Advisory Opinion', (2012) 19 *Australian International Law Journal*, 213–233.
85 See Bombaka (n 49).

states in an interesting situation in which they have the possibility to exploit the seabed without going through the Enterprise.

Certainly, with sponsorship in place, developing states are relieved of the necessity to bypass the Enterprise for seabed exploitation, allowing them to directly access benefits. So far, more than one-third of the exploration contracts signed between the authority and contracting companies are sponsored by developing countries.[86] Although these kinds of activities may provide economic development for the developing countries that sponsor the companies, the question of how exploration by a state-sponsored company can benefit humankind remains open. In fact, in the absence of the operationalisation of the Enterprise, the resources of the Area may benefit only a few actors. "Designed to prevent the activities in the Area from having only a capitalist purpose, the Enterprise would theoretically act as a corrective to pure market logic by socializing the benefits derived from the exploited resources."[87]

In this sense, there is ongoing appropriation of resources by private operators without respecting the principle of equitable redistribution. In the case of Nauru Ocean Resources Inc., the shareholders are from Canada, which means that a significant part of the benefits will ultimately go to Canadian recipients. In their applications, Nauru Ocean Resources Inc. and Tonga Offshore Mining Ltd have indicated that they intend to develop their activities in the Area for the benefit of their sponsor countries and the international community,[88] but it is unclear how this goal will be materialised.

This is a real issue and worrying enough for the Legal and Technical Commission of the International Seabed Authority to dedicate one of its sessions to the theme of the "Monopolization of Activities in the Area".[89] Moreover, the situation remains delicate insofar as most of the developing states, which sponsor the exploration and exploitation of the seabed, do not have the capacity to control the activities carried out by sponsored companies. They may lack the capacity to impose the application of environmental obligations, such as the precautionary principle or other obligations relating to monitoring activities in the Area, such as the application of best environmental practices, the use of the ecosystem-based management approach, the use of the integrated approach to ocean management, the use of the best available scientific information, the adoption of emergency measures to protect the marine environment, or the

86 See 'Exploration Contracts' (n 4). See also Bombaka (n 84) 199.

87 Monebhurrun (n 52) 269.

Ibid.

88 International Seabed Authority, Legal and Technical Commission, *Nauru Ocean Resources Inc.: Application for Approval of a Plan of Work for Exploration*, UN Doc ISBA/14/LTC/L.2 (21 April 2008) [28]; Tonga Offshore Mining Ltd, *Application for Approval of a Plan of Work for Exploration*, International Seabed Authority, UN Doc ISBA/14/LTC/L.3 (21 April 2008) [28].

89 International Seabed Authority, *Monopolization of activities in the Area*, UN Doc ISBA/20/LTC/11 (6 June 2014).

assessment of the environmental impact.[90] In the opinion of the ITLOS Seabed Disputes Chamber, compliance with or enforcement of these obligations may also be considered a relevant factor in the sponsoring state's fulfilment of its "due diligence" obligation.[91] As a result, this has the potential to compromise the achievement of a "uniform protection" for the marine environment,[92] which was raised by the ITLOS Seabed Disputes Chamber.[93]

The apprehension articulated by the Seabed Disputes Chamber underscores a fundamental concern – particularly in the context of developing states. It is not merely the inadequacy or incompleteness of legislation that poses the greatest challenge; rather, it is the deficiency in the capacity to rigorously monitor and ensure compliance with these laws that emerges as a significant issue.[94] These deficiencies can manifest in various facets, including judicial or fiscal. Indeed, the reality is that certain companies wield greater wealth and technological sophistication than many developing states. Therefore, considering that the majority of companies engaging in seabed activities possess highly advanced capabilities, it stands to reason that reinforcing their due diligence obligations, which apply to all actors in the production chain (including the company, engineers, etc.), should promote better environmental protection.[95] This can be achieved through the application of the mechanism contained in the principles of good governance, "Good industry practice":

> Good industry practice means the exercise of that degree of skill, diligence, prudence and foresight which would reasonably and ordinarily be expected to be applied by a skilled and experienced person engaged in the marine mining industry and other related extractive industries worldwide, including best environmental practice, the performance and process requirements under the rules, regulations and procedures of the Authority and applicable standards that may be adopted by the Authority from time to time.[96]

That means acting in "a manner that is technically competent and at a level of diligence and prudence reasonably and ordinarily exercised by experienced

90 *The responsibilities and obligations of States sponsoring persons and entities with respect to activities in the Area* (n 27) [121]–[150]. See also *Draft regulations on exploitation of Mineral resources in the Area – Consolidated President's text* (n 5) Regulation 2.

91 *The responsibilities and obligations of States sponsoring persons and entities with respect to activities in the Area* (n 27) [242].

92 See Bombaka (n 49) 209.

93 *The responsibilities and obligations of States sponsoring persons and entities with respect to activities in the Area* (n 27) [159].

94 See Bombaka (n 49) 209.

95 Ibid.

96 International Seabed Authority, *Key terms: distinguishing between good industry practice and best practices under the draft regulations on exploitation of mineral resources in the Area*, UN Doc ISBA/25/C/11 (15 January 2019), 2 [7].

operators engaged in a similar activity and under similar circumstances".[97] Therefore, it is a matter of each stakeholder in the production chain going "beyond the legal minimum and finding new ways of managing opportunities and risks, on the basis of new knowledge and experience".[98]

Furthermore, although in the authority's view, good industry practice "does not replace clear and unambiguous obligations established under the regulations and in an approved plan of work",[99] and the legal obligations arising from it are still vague, it still serves as a point of reference to be improved and better delineated in the future for good governance of the oceans.

Notwithstanding the practical challenges encountered by the CHH in addressing issues associated with the sustainable development of states – articulated through two prominent challenges, namely the stagnation of the Enterprise and the corporate appropriation of marine mineral resources – the CHH has experienced a revitalisation during the negotiations on the Exploitation Code and the BBNJ Agreement.

The reinvigoration of CHH due to negotiations of the Regulations on Exploitation of Mineral Resources in the Area and the BBNJ Agreement

Amid the escalating threats posed by mining and drilling practices that have cast doubt upon the pertinence of the CHH principle, various initiatives from ISA member states and other stakeholders have emerged,[100] seeking to reaffirm the CHH in recent negotiations. The paramount impact of the CHH principle on achieving sustainable development of states during these negotiation processes lies in its capacity to fortify the protection of the marine environment, balancing the interests of commercial mining and biodiversity conservation in the deep seabed. The draft of the Regulations on Exploitation of Mineral Resources in the Area has principles, policies, and instruments that can contribute to achieving sustainable development as well as the BBNJ Agreement.

The revitalisation of the CHJ reinforced within the Regulations on Exploitation of Mineral Resources in the Area negotiations

There are many challenges in operationalising best environmental practices in deep seabed mining regulation.[101] Moreover, there are numerous restrictions

97 Ibid 3 [9].

98 Ibid 5 [23].

99 Ibid 3–4 [13].

100 See 'Momentum for a Moratorium', *Deep Sea Conservation Coalition* (Web Page, 25 November 2023) <https://deep-sea-conservation.org/solutions/no-deep-sea-mining/> ('Momentum for a Moratorium').

101 Leonardus Gerber and Renée Groga, 'Challenges of operationalizing good industry practice and best environmental practice in deep seabed mining regulation' (2020) 114 *Marine Policy*.

on the authority's powers to unilaterally suspend and terminate contracts.[102] The two-year deadline to complete the ISA Regulations on Exploitation of Mineral Resources in the Area, based on a submission made by Nauru in June 2021, resulted in strong pressure for its approval before July 2023.[103] Nevertheless, the ISA was unable to conclude the negotiation process by November 2023. In this sense, preventative and precautionary measures were considered key to protecting the marine environment. Based on a sustainable development perspective, the environmental instruments are the environmental impact assessments (EIAs), the environmental impact statement (EIS), the environmental management and monitoring plan, and the regional environmental management plans (REMPs). Another approach to addressing negotiations regarding mining exploitation is through a prohibition perspective, which entails implementing a moratorium or precautionary pause on mining activities. It is important to present those principles and instruments connected to the environmental protection of the marine environment. Over time, the cleavage between states in favour and those against mining grew stronger after the emergence of a true coalition supporting a moratorium or pause based on the scientific community's demand.[104]

The draft ISA Regulations on Exploitation of Mineral Resources in the Area mention the CHM in the preamble and in Regulation 2 on principles, approaches, and policies.[105] Previous versions of the draft mentioned the principle only in the preamble and in an annex.[106] The 2019 version connects the principle to other economic policies such as "healthy development of the world economy and the balanced growth of international trade, and to promote international cooperation for the overall development of all countries, especially developing States".[107] Moreover, the principle also refers to a social perspective such as: "d) Provide for the protection of human life and safety".

102 Alberto Pecoraro, 'The Regulatory Powers of the International Seabed Authority: Security of Tenure and Its Limits' (2022) 53 (4) *Ocean Development & International Law*, 377–402.

103 *1994 Agreement* (n 23) Annex s 1, 15, (b). See Pradeep Singh, 'The two-year deadline to complete the International Seabed Authority's Mining Code: Key outstanding matters that still need to be resolved' (2021) 134(3) 104804 *Marine Policy*; Catherine Blanchard et al., 'The current status of deep-sea mining governance at the International Seabed Authority' (2023) 147 *Marine Policy*, 147.

104 'Twenty-four States have adopted stances opposing deep-sea mining in international waters, each grounding their positions on distinct perspectives', *Deep Sea Conservation Coalition* (Web Page, 25 November 2023) <https://savethehighseas.org/voices-calling-for-a-moratorium-governments-and-parliamentarians/> .

105 See International Seabed Authority, *Draft Regulations on Exploitation of Mineral Resources in the Area* (Consolidated text), ISBA/29/C/CRP.1 (16 February 2024), Regulation 2. 2.

106 See International Seabed Authority, *the 2017 version of the Draft Regulations on Exploitation of Mineral Resources in the Area*, UN Doc ISBA/23/LTC/CRP.3* (8 August 2017), Preamble and annex X s 3 [3.3] k.

107 See International Seabed Authority, *Draft Regulations on Exploitation of Mineral Resources in the Area* (Prepared by the Legal and Technical Commission), ISBA/25/C/WP. 1 (22 March 2019), Regulation 2.

Regarding the environmental perspective, Regulation 2, e) mentions different principles and approaches such as ecological integrity, ecosystem approach and precautionary approach. Among the principles, Regulation 2, e) (h) states that: "(h) Ensure the effective management and regulation of the Area and its resources in a way that promotes the development of the common heritage for the benefit of mankind as a whole". In this sense, there is a strong connection between sustainable development and the CHM.

Regarding the environmental content of the principle, the precautionary approach is the key. Based on Principle 15 of the Rio Declaration,[108] the precautionary approach is pointed out in Regulation 2, e) ii. Even if the terminology of the principle remains to be seen by some countries as an approach,[109] ITLOS has already stated that "The provisions of the aforementioned Regulations (The Nodules Regulations and the Sulphides Regulations) transform this non-binding statement of the precautionary approach in the Rio Declaration into a binding obligation".[110] The Draft Regulations on Exploitation of Mineral Resources in the Area express this mandatory obligation nature of the approach in Part IV on the protection and preservation of the marine environment. Regulation 44, Section 1 regarding the obligations relating to the marine environment states that states and contractors shall: "a) Apply the precautionary approach, as reflected in principle 15 of the Rio Declaration on Environment and Development, to the assessment and management of risk of harm to the Marine Environment from Exploitation in the Area".

In addition to this obligation, other important obligations are also mentioned in Regulation 44:

> (b) Apply the Best Available Techniques and Best Environmental Practices in carrying out such measures; (c) Integrate Best Available Scientific Evidence in environmental decision- making, including all risk assessments and management undertaken in connection with environmental assessments; (d) Promote accountability and transparency in the assessment evaluation and management of Environmental Effects from Exploitation in the Area, including through the timely release of and access to relevant environmental data and information and opportunities for stakeholder participation.

108 "In order to protect the environment, the precautionary approach shall be widely applied by States according to their capabilities. Where there are threats of serious or irreversible damage, lack of full scientific certainty shall not be used as a reason for postponing cost-effective measures to prevent environmental degradation." *Rio Declaration On Environment And Development* (n 41) Principle 15.

109 *Regulations on prospecting and exploration for polymetallic sulphides in the Area* (n 76) art 33 [2].

110 *The responsibilities and obligations of States sponsoring persons and entities with respect to activities in the Area* (n 27) [127].

The application of the best available techniques and practices requires the technological and financial capacities of states and contractors, which vary depending on the state. Regarding the precautionary principle, ITLOS stated that the precautionary approach must be implemented based on each state's capacity.[111] However, regarding the application of the best available techniques and practices, it is unclear whether or not there is different treatment between states.

The procedural requirements for the assessment of environmental impacts arising from the different stages of deep seabed mining are drafted in the regulations and have been included in the future Regulations on Exploitation of Mineral Resources in the Area.[112] It has also been complemented by standards and guidelines that were published in January 2022.[113] These binding and non-binding requirements provide for the sustainable management of the resources. However, there are still concerns regarding these standards and guidelines (Regulations 45, 94, and 95). During the 28th Session of the Council Meeting, a regional group pointed out that: "all standards and guidelines to be developed should be SMART (specific, measurable, achievable, relevant, and time-bound) and FAIR (findable, accessible, interoperable, and reusable) so that contractors can comply, and regulators assess compliance". Some delegates suggested the adoption of a provision that the ISA shall not approve any exploitation activities unless environmental standards have been

111 Ibid 129.

112 *Draft Regulations on Exploitation of Mineral Resources in the Area* (n 5). See Maila Guilhon et al., 'Revisiting procedural requirements for the assessment of environmental impacts arising from the different stages of deep seabed mining: Current practices at the International Seabed Authority and recommendations for improvement' (2022) 96 *Environmental Impact Assessment Review*, 1–14; Jonathan Moses and Anne Margrethe Brigham, 'Whose benefit? A comparative perspective for the ISA' (2021) 131 *Marine Policy*.

113 International Seabed Authority, *Draft standard and guidelines for the environmental impact assessment process*, UN Doc ISBA/27/C/4 (2022) (31 January 2022); International Seabed Authority, *Draft guidelines for the preparation of environmental impact statements*, UN Doc ISBA/27/C/5 (31 January 2022); International Seabed Authority, *Draft guidelines for the preparation of Environmental Management and Monitoring Plans*, UN Doc ISBA/27/C/6 (31 January 2022); International Seabed Authority, *Draft standard and guidelines on the development and application of environmental management systems*, UN Doc ISBA/27/C/7 (31 January 2022); International Seabed Authority, *Draft guidelines on the tools and techniques for hazard identification and risk assessments*, UN Doc ISBA/27/C/8 (31 January 2022); International Seabed Authority, *Draft standard and guidelines for the safe management and operation of mining vessels and installations*, UN Doc ISBA/27/C/9 (31 January 2022); International Seabed Authority, *Draft standard and guidelines on the form and calculation of an Environmental Performance Guarantee*, UN Doc ISBA/27/C/10 (31 January 2022); International Seabed Authority, *Draft guidelines for the establishment of baseline environmental data*, UN Doc ISBA/27/C/11 (31 January 2022); International Seabed Authority, *Draft standard and guidelines for the preparation and implementation of emergency response and contingency plans*, UN Doc ISBA/27/C/12 (31 January 2022).

adopted. A delegate stressed the need for indicators and quantitative thresholds to assess the fulfilment of environmental objectives.[114]

The obligation to make an EIA is well established in international law,[115] specifically in the law of the sea.[116] However, the other mentioned instruments still need to be developed and implemented to be seen as a common practice in international law. The CHM is an overarching governance principle that provides for a framework encompassing all the instruments that will be implemented in seabed mining.

States and non-governmental organisations (NGOs) have been advocating for a moratorium or a precautionary pause on seabed mining.[117] In the 28th Session of the Council, which took place in March 2023, many concerns were raised regarding the need to protect the ocean, which is already facing pollution, biodiversity loss, and climate change effects. The concerns highlighted the importance of further study of deep seabed ecosystems prior to authorising mining activities. A precautionary pause was defended by countries such as Chile, Germany, Canada, and Brazil "to allow for fully considering the precautionary principle and for filling existing knowledge gaps".[118] Portugal stated that "in line with the precautionary principle, deep sea mineral exploitation activities should not take place before appropriate regulations are in place".[119] States such as the UK, Switzerland, and the Russian Federation also made similar statements. Argentina, Norway, Costa Rica, and Jamaica used the CHH to argue that a robust environmental framework be established prior to exploitation activities. In addition, they highlighted the need to conclude the payment mechanism for benefit-sharing, which was also highlighted by Brazil.[120]

The Federated States of Micronesia, together with Vanuatu, as members of the alliance of countries calling for a deep seabed mining moratorium, stressed the need to respect the ecosystem approach, the polluter pays principle, and the precautionary principle, calling for rigorous environmental impact assessments

114 International Seabed Authority, *Regional Environmental Management Plans Part IV*, UN Doc ISBA/28/C/IWG/ENV/CRP.1 (2 March 2023), Section 1, Regulation 45.

115 *The responsibilities and obligations of States sponsoring persons and entities with respect to activities in the Area* (n 27) [141]; *1994 Agreement* (n 23) s 1 [7].

116 *1994 Agreement* (n 23) s 1 [7]; *Regulations on Prospecting and Exploration for Polymetallic Nodules in the Area and related matters* (n 75) art 31 [6]; *Regulations on prospecting and exploration for polymetallic sulphides in the Area* (n 75) 33 [6].

117 See 'Momentum for a Moratorium' (n 101).

118 Summary of the Twenty-eighth Annual Session of the International Seabed Authority (n 59) 4.

119 Ibid.

120 International Seabed Authority, *28th Session, Part I - Open session for general statements, March 27. Statement from Brazil, delivered by Ambassador Elza Moreira Marcelino de Castro* (Web Page, 20 November 2023) <https://www.isa.org.jm/wp-content/uploads/2023/03/Brazil-statement.pdf>.

and public participation in decision-making.[121] France, which is also in favour of a moratorium, stated that a robust inspection mechanism must be developed. It stated the impossibility of adequately assessing the potential effects of mining on the marine environment due to the lack of scientific evidence and baselines.

Ghana, speaking for the African Group, and Togo advocated for the interest of developing countries and called for the operationalisation of the Enterprise.[122] China gave a more nuanced speech:

> It underscored the need to make exploitation reasonable, orderly, and sustainable, adding that deep sea activities are instrumental to generating scientific data, enhancing our understanding of the ocean. It highlighted that the development of the exploitation regulations remains 'our utmost task at present,' adding that if they cannot be concluded in a timely manner, clear arrangements are needed to be able to advance in good faith.[123]

Another important policy included in the Draft Regulations on Exploitation of Mineral Resources in the Area is the regional environmental management plans. During the 28th Session of the Council, delegates discussed a revised, streamlined draft regulation, noting that the Legal and Technical Commission (LTC) shall only consider an application for a plan of work if a REMP has been adopted by the council for the area concerned.[124]

One important challenge is the development of the necessary structure for implementing the above-mentioned instruments. The ISA has limited powers to issue orders and limited capacity to analyse complex instruments such as EIAs.[125] In addition to this, developing states have less capacity to implement and monitor them. ITLOS stated that as per the application of the precautionary approach:

> by stating that the precautionary approach shall be applied by States 'according to their capabilities', the first sentence of Principle 15

121 International Seabed Authority, *Republic Of Vanuatu—National Statement—International Seabed Authority Council Meeting, 16-31 March 2023* (Web Page, 25 November 2023) <https://www.isa.org.jm/wp-content/uploads/2023/03/Statement_Vanuatu.pdf>.

122 International Seabed Authority, Opening Remarks Delivered On Behalf Of The African Group To The Council Of The International Seabed Authority At The First Part Of The Twenty-Eighth Session—16th March, 2023 (Web Page, 25 November 2023) <https://www.isa.org.jm/wp-content/uploads/2023/03/African-Group-Opening-Remarks.pdf>.

123 Summary of the Twenty-eighth Annual Session of the International Seabed Authority (n 59) 5.

124 International Seabed Authority, *Draft Regulations on Exploitation of Mineral Resources in the Area* (Consolidated text), ISBA/29/C/CRP.1 (16 February 2024), Regulation 44bis.

125 Guilhon et al. (n 113) 1–14; Moses and Brigham (n 113).

introduces the possibility of differences in application of the precautionary approach in light of the different capabilities of each State.[126]

This is an example of the differential treatment that is still unclear regarding environmental issues. As ITLOS has pointed out, there is always the danger that "[t]he spread of sponsoring States of convenience would jeopardize uniform application of the highest standards of protection of the marine environment, the safe development of activities in the Area and protection of the common heritage of mankind".[127]

Another limit is the synergy of the seabed mining regime with other regimes. During the 28th session, many delegations highlighted the importance of the draft regulation on pollution control (Regulation 49), with different views on whether explicit references to marine litter and underwater noise should be included. Further discussion will be needed on the restriction of mining discharges (Regulation 50), with some delegations requesting the reintroduction of reference to the London Convention and Protocol on the Prevention of Marine Pollution by Dumping Wastes and Other Matters.[128] This coherence and synergy must be strengthened by the future BBNJ institutional framework and the CBD regime.[129]

The CHM reinforced by the BBNJ Agreement

The Intergovernmental Conference on the International Legally Binding Instrument under UNCLOS on the Conservation and Sustainable Use of Marine Biological Diversity of Areas Beyond National Jurisdiction (BBNJ Agreement) was finalised by delegates in March 2023, and the text was adopted on 19 June 2023. The CHM principle was strengthened in several ways. First, it is important to point out how the CHM principle is presented in the BBNJ Agreement as well as how it may contribute to the sustainable development objective.

The BBNJ text included the common heritage of humankind as a general principle of the treaty after a long discussion that started at the beginning of the negotiations, more than two decades ago. Delegates decided to replace the term "mankind" with "humankind", which is in line with the evolution of the principle. Even though developed countries wanted to only mention the principle in the preamble, developing countries were able to maintain the concept as a general principle applicable to the whole treaty. Article 7 on general

126 *The responsibilities and obligations of States sponsoring persons and entities with respect to activities in the Area* (n 27) [129].

127 Ibid para 159.

128 *Draft Regulations on Exploitation of Mineral Resources in the Area* (n 5) Regulations 49–50.

129 Convention on Biological Diversity, *Fourth meeting of the Subsidiary Body on Implementation* (Web Page) <https://www.cbd.int/meetings/SBI-04>.

principles and approaches states as follows: "b) The principle of the common heritage of humankind which is set out in the Convention".

BBNJ negotiations have demonstrated that developed countries were very reluctant and sceptical about the use of the principle in the context of the conservation and sustainable use of marine biological diversity. Until the end of the negotiations, there was a division between developed and developing countries on this issue. The principle was only confirmed in the final text on the last day of the negotiations.

The future interpretation of the CHH principle as stated in the convention will be of paramount importance. The text states that the principle must be interpreted in conformity with UNCLOS. Since BBNJ is an implementing agreement of UNCLOS, it can be argued that the text must be interpreted in line with what is stated by the convention. Considering that the convention refers to the CHM only as a principle governing the Area (Article 136), there is space for further questioning of the content of the principle.

In addition to this principle, other principles are also part of this general article:

> c) the freedom of marine scientific research, together with other freedoms of the high seas; d) the principle of equity and the fair and equitable sharing of benefits; e) the precautionary principle or precautionary approach, as appropriate; f) an ecosystem approach; g) an integrated approach to ocean management.

The impacts of climate change on the marine environment were also pointed out in this article. One important social perspective also included in this article is the "j) use of relevant traditional knowledge of Indigenous Peoples and local communities, where available"; "k) the respect, promotion and consideration of their respective obligations, as applicable, relating to the rights of Indigenous Peoples or of, as appropriate, local communities when taking action to address the conservation and sustainable use of marine biological diversity of areas beyond national jurisdiction". Another important element of sustainable development is the differentiated treatment that must be given to states. This general article recognises the special circumstances of small island developing states, least-developed countries, and landlocked developing countries.

The BBNJ Agreement consolidates CHH as a fundamental principle underpinning the implementation of an institutional framework for the conservation and sustainable use of marine biological diversity. This is intertwined with the sustainable management of the ocean that has also been developed by the ISA's regime. The environmental content of the principle is reflected in other principles and approaches, such as the precautionary, the integrated, and the ecosystem approaches, as well as economic and social elements that are also well represented in the treaty.

The CHH principle also justifies the creation of a comprehensive institutional framework that will manage the conservation and the sustainable use of marine biodiversity beyond national jurisdiction. The agreement created a Conference of the Parties, a scientific and technical body, a secretariat, and a clearing-house mechanism. However, it is not yet possible to know what will be achieved by these institutional arrangements in terms of coherence and synergy with other institutional frameworks, such as the ISA. The agreement guarantees in Article 5 that it "shall be interpreted and applied in a manner that does not undermine relevant legal instruments and frameworks and relevant global, regional, subregional, and sectoral bodies and that promotes coherence and coordination with those instruments, frameworks, and bodies". The CHH principle could be used in the future as an argument to connect biological and mineral resources governance.

In this sense, the BBNJ Agreement provides a detailed regime to govern the conservation and sustainable use of marine biodiversity in areas beyond national jurisdiction. The environmental instruments, such as the area-based management tools, including marine protected areas (Part III of the agreement), and the environmental impact assessment (Part IV), will have to be implemented in line with similar instruments managed by other international organisations such as the ISA. The BBNJ Agreement also provides for strategic environmental assessments, which sets a higher standard for environmental prevention than ISA instruments, such as regional environmental management plans.[130] It is worth noting that the BBNJ Agreement has higher standards for EIAs than the EIA established by ISA regulations. It will be necessary to establish linkages between both frameworks to strengthen coherence between the procedures.[131]

BBNJ is also more innovative regarding the engagement of Indigenous Peoples and local communities and their traditional knowledge. The ISA's legal framework for mineral exploration does not include this cultural and social perspective. The draft of the Regulations on Exploitation of Mineral Resources in the Area contains some references to this issue in bracketed text. The BBNJ negotiations have exerted influence on ISA debates as was seen at the 28th Session of the Council.

Another important contribution of the BBNJ Agreement is the transfer of marine technology. The language of the agreement is mandatory and provides for specific obligations regarding the transfer of marine technologies. This is key in the context of the fast development of technologies applicable to environmental protection. The agreement is in conformity with the Montego Bay Convention (Article 40).

To summarise, the principle was strengthened by the final two important negotiations: the Regulations on Exploitation of Mineral Resources in the

130 Robb, Jaeckel, and Blanchard (n 40) 2.
131 Ibid.

Area under the ISA and the BBNJ Agreement under DOALOS. However, the real impact of the principle will be to give more coherence to the governance of the marine environment. This contribution will be clearer once the BBNJ institutional framework is set up and following the implementation of the instruments provided for the Regulations on Exploitation of Mineral Resources in the Area. Another clear contribution of the principle is to strengthen the sustainable development of the states. In this sense, the CHH principle can contribute to the balance between the interests of commercial mining and biodiversity conservation in the deep seabed, particularly within the context of the triple planetary crisis. These negotiations took a step further towards possible future recognition of the CHH as a general principle of international law, considering that it has been accepted in the context of BBNJ negotiations by most of the states parties and fully supported by different actors, such as international NGOs.

Conclusion

The key conclusions of the chapter refer to the legal evolution of the CHH principle as well as its function regarding the sustainable development of states and the balance between mining interests and biodiversity conservation in the deep seabed. There are increasing expectations that the CHH principle can contribute to the robustness of the law of the sea to deal with global challenges and planetary crises. Although the principle can be a basis for coherence and for synergy in ocean governance, it was unthinkable before the last sessions of negotiations of BBNJ and the Regulations on Exploitation of Mineral Resources in the Area that the principle would regain such preeminence in 2023 multilateral negotiations.

This chapter undertook a critical evaluation of the legal standing of the CHH principle in the current context of the law of the sea. It has had its ups and downs since its inception in 1967. While its highest point may be considered UNCLOS in 1982, it lost part of its legal significance with the implementation agreement in 1994. Because the 2023 BBNJ treaty incorporated the CHH principle in Article 7, it increases the likelihood that the CHH principle will be included in the final text of the ISA Regulations on Exploitation of Mineral Resources in the Area. The legal impact of the principle at the interface between deep seabed mining and biodiversity conservation is the central question of this chapter.

Furthermore, one important impact of the CHH principle is in regard to the sustainable development of states. The principle contributes to the balance between interests of commercial mining and biodiversity conservation in the deep seabed mining. However, there are some economic limits to this objective, such as the Enterprise's paralysis and the restricted participation of developing states in deep seabed mining activities. The CHH principle can be a governance mechanism to support the sustainable development of states because it offers a comprehensive framework encompassing different obligations and instruments capable of guaranteeing biodiversity conservation in the context of seabed mining.

Addressing challenges regarding sustainable development is imperative for revitalising global governance endeavours. The sharing of benefits regarding mining and biodiversity exploitation is one way to increase inter-generational and intra-generational equity. The transfer of marine technology is another way. The implementation of environmental instruments such as EIAs, REMPs, strategic environmental assessments, and ABMTs constitutes other options. With the Kunming–Montreal Global Biodiversity Framework and the long-term strategic approach to mainstreaming biodiversity, the biodiversity regime is reaching out to other regimes, such as the BBNJ and ISA cases.

However, given the North–South divide and the empowerment of companies, the four elements of the CHH principle are hard to reconcile: joint management, non-appropriation, benefit-sharing from mineral exploitation, and the peaceful use of resources. In this sense, the CHH is a "governance" principle that would contribute to the conservation of marine biodiversity in the context of seabed mining. The implementation of sustainable development agenda,[132] notably those of the UN 2030 Agenda, as well as to other frameworks such as the Global Biodiversity framework, is key to more coherence within ocean governance.

The next steps regarding the impact of the principle relate to other regimes, such as climate. Maybe climate stability should be considered a CHH. Also, the Moon Treaty needs a more specific regime so that the application of the CHH principle becomes clearer. Finally, outer space remains poorly regulated despite the accelerated and unsustainable use of satellites, as well as the weaponisation of space. Subsequently, the principle should be recognised as a general principle of international law rather than being specific to each individual international regime.

132 "The principle of CHM can provide theoretical basis for marine management approaches and lay the foundation for the law of the sea." Chuanliang Wang and Yen-Chiang Chang, 'A new interpretation of the common heritage of mankind in the context of the international law of the sea' (2020) 191(1) *Ocean & Coastal Management.*

8 Is international law fit for purpose for the green shipping transition?

Ethan Beringen and Nengye Liu

Introduction

International shipping contributes to each of planetary crises, specifically within the marine environment. This chapter addresses the intersection between vessel-source pollution and climate change and examines how international shipping law is increasingly recognising the need to address these challenges.

The shipping industry carries more than 80% of global trade products, providing an essential service to the world's economy.[1] In the course of these shipping activities, vessel-source pollution, either accidental or operational, is responsible for approximately 11% of marine pollution.[2] Additionally, maritime transport contributes to nearly 3% of global greenhouse gas (GHG) emissions.[3] Historically, international shipping law has concentrated on traditional forms of pollution, such as oil spills and chemical discharges into the ocean. However, it is increasingly urgent to recognise airborne emissions, particularly GHG emissions from ships, as a critical aspect of vessel-source pollution.

The International Maritime Organization's (IMO) Fourth GHG Study, published in 2020, finds that shipping's share of global anthropogenic GHG emissions increased from 2.76% in 2012 to 2.89% in 2018.[4] Under a business-as-usual scenario, shipping emissions could increase by 90% to 130% of their 2008 levels by 2050.[5] Therefore, it is imperative that states begin to accelerate maritime decarbonisation to meet one of the main goals of the 2015 Paris Agreement – to "hold the increase in the global average temperature to well below 2°C above pre-industrial levels".[6]

1 United Nations Conference on Trade and Development, *Review of Maritime Transport* (Report, 2021).
2 Ozan Bayazit and Mehmet Kaptan, 'Evaluation of the risk of pollution caused by ship operations through bow-tie-based fuzzy Bayesian network' (2023) 382 *Journal of Cleaner Production* 135386, 1.
3 International Maritime Organization, *Fourth Greenhouse Gas Study 2020* (Report, 2020) 1.
4 Ibid.
5 Ibid 3.
6 *Paris Agreement on Climate Change*, opened for signature (22 April 2016), [2016] ATS 24 (entered into force 4 November 2016) art 2(2).

DOI: 10.4324/9781003518570-8

Decarbonisation is a key part of addressing the impacts of shipping on anthropogenic climate change. The push to decarbonise has sometimes been called green shipping, which refers to "the use of resources and energy to transport people and goods by ship and specifically concerns the reduction in such resources and energy in order to preserve the global environment from GHGs and environmental pollutants generated by ships".[7] According to Clarksons, the term green shipping "encompasses a range of strategies and technologies in order to (1) reduce carbon emissions; (2) minimise air and water pollution; and (3) promote ecological balance".[8] Under international law, there is a comprehensive international legal framework established for the prevention, control, and reduction of vessel-source pollution. The United Nations Convention on the Law of the Sea (UNCLOS)[9] creates a jurisdictional regime by allocating state jurisdiction at sea among flag, coastal, and port states.[10] Meanwhile, the IMO is designated by UNCLOS as the "competent international organization" to tackle vessel-source pollution.[11] The IMO has adopted a series of conventions to address accidental and operational pollution from international shipping. These include the International Convention for the Prevention of Pollution from Ships 1973, as modified by the Protocol of 1978 (MARPOL),[12] the International Convention for the Safety of Life at Sea (SOLAS),[13] the International Convention on the Control of Harmful Anti-Fouling Systems on Ships (Anti-Fouling Convention),[14] and the International Convention for the Control and Management of Ships' Ballast Water and Sediments (BWM

7 Taehee Lee and Hyunjeong Nam, 'A Study on Green Shipping in Major Countries: In the View of Shipyards, Shipping Companies, Ports, and Policies' (2017) 33(4) *The Asian Journal of Shipping and Logistics* 253, 254; see also M Tadros, M Ventura and C Guides Soares, 'Review of current regulations, available technologies, and future trends in the green shipping industry' (2023) 280 *Ocean Engineering* 114670, 1.

8 Clarksons, *What is green shipping?* (Web Page, 2024) <https://www.clarksons.com/glossary/what-is-green-shipping/>.

9 *United Nations Convention on the Law of the Sea*, opened for signature 10 December 1982, 1833 UNTS 397 (entered into force 16 November 1994) ('*UNCLOS*').

10 See, e.g. Erik Japp Molenaar, *Coastal State Jurisdiction over Vessel-Source Pollution* (Kluwer Law International, 1998).

11 *UNCLOS* (n 10) art 211(1).

12 International Convention for the Prevention of Pollution from Ships, adopted 2 November 1973, amended by the *Protocol of 1978 Relating to the International Convention for the Prevention of Pollution from Ships, 1973*, opened for signature 17 February 1978, 1340–1341 UNTS 61 (entered into force 2 October 1983) ('*MARPOL*').

13 *International Convention for the Safety of Life at Sea*, opened for signature 1 November 1974, 1184–1185 UNTS 2 (entered into force 25 May 1980) ('*SOLAS*').

14 *International Convention on the Control of Harmful Anti-Fouling Systems on Ships*, opened for signature 5 October 2001, 3356 UNTC (entered into force 17 September 2008) ('*Anti-Fouling Convention*').

Convention).[15] These measures address a range of potential pollutants and are subsequently examined.

The adequacy of the current international shipping regime to deal with vessel-source pollution resulting in GHG emissions has come into sharp focus due to recent developments in the law of the sea. Specifically, in a historic Advisory Opinion on Climate Change and International Law published in 2024,[16] the International Tribunal for the Law of the Sea (ITLOS) made it clear that "Anthropogenic GHG emissions into the atmosphere constitute pollution of the marine environment within the meaning of Article 1, paragraph 1, subparagraph 4, of the Convention [UNCLOS]."[17] Further, the ITLOS stated that "According to Article 194 (1), State Parties to the Convention [UNCLOS] have the specific obligations to take all necessary measures to prevent, reduce and control marine pollution from anthropogenic GHG emissions and to endeavour to harmonize their policies."[18]

Given these developments, this chapter asks whether the current international legal framework on the prevention, reduction, and control of vessel-source pollution is sufficient to deal with GHG emissions from shipping and accelerate the green shipping transition. This is achieved through conducting a comprehensive review of the current international legal regime on the prevention of vessel-source pollution. The first section assesses the relationship between UNCLOS and the IMO as the foundation of the international shipping regime. Subsequently, the chapter addresses the latest developments within the international legal framework on vessel-source pollution through an analysis of relevant instruments under the IMO. The final section aims to examine possible future directions regarding the regulation of GHG emissions in the shipping sector, ultimately highlighting some of the challenges for international law in helping to facilitate the green shipping transition.

The existing vessel-source pollution regime: the international maritime organization and the United Nations Convention on the Law of the Sea

The International Martime Organization

The International Maritime Organization (IMO) is an international body that, according to Article 1(a) of its establishing convention, aims to provide a forum "to encourage and facilitate the general adoption of the highest

15 International Convention for the Control and Management of Ships' Ballast Water and Sediments, adopted 13 February 2004, 3282 UNTC (entered into force 8 September 2017) ('*BWM Convention*').

16 *Request for An Advisory Opinion submitted by the Commission of Small Island States on Climate Change and International Law* (Advisory Opinion) (International Tribunal for the Law of the Sea, No 31, 21 May 2024) ('*ITLOS Advisory Opinion*').

17 Ibid para 179.

18 Ibid para 243.

practicable standards in matters concerning maritime safety, efficiency of navigation and prevention and control of marine pollution from ships".[19] Issues of pollution prevention have been at the core of the IMO's mandate since its formation in 1958.[20] However, in its early years, the IMO was mostly focused on safety concerns with the conclusion of an update to the SOLAS Convention. The Torrey Canyon disaster in 1967 is widely considered to have provided the impetus for the IMO's renewed focus on marine pollution, culminating in the conclusion of the International Convention for the Prevention of Pollution from Ships in 1973, which was later modified by protocol in 1978.

The conclusion of UNCLOS in 1982 played a key role in crystallising the IMO as "*the* competent international organisation" (emphasis added) to address marine pollution from shipping, among other functions.[21] In service of this mandate, the IMO would go on to facilitate environmental conventions to accompany MARPOL and SOLAS, including the Anti-Fouling Convention and the BWM Convention. Each of these key IMO conventions is discussed in greater detail below.

It is important to touch briefly on the institutional structure of the IMO. It is made up of five key committees, as well as an assembly and a council.[22] The Marine Environment Protection Committee (MEPC) is the most relevant body for addressing vessel-source pollution, though the Marine Safety Committee (MSC) also plays a crucial role in preventing pollution-related accidents.[23] The Legal Committee, Technical Cooperation Committee, and Facilitation Committee round out the major organs of the IMO, with various sub-committees playing a supportive role.[24] These committees act as forums for negotiation and debate that allow states to come to an agreement on measures that usually need to be arrived at via consensus.[25] As an international body concerned with standard setting for the shipping industry, it is important that the IMO is able to adjust these standards in a timely manner. Therefore, the IMO relies on a system of tacit acceptance in which after the amendment of an annex by majority vote, states have a set time period to opt out of the amendment.[26] If states do not raise objections before the end of this set time,

19 Convention on the Intergovernmental Maritime Consultative Organization, adopted 6 March 1946, 289 UNTS 3 (entered into force 17 March 1958) art 1(a).

20 Ibid.

21 *UNCLOS* (n 10) art 211(1).

22 International Maritime Organization, *Structure of the IMO* (Web Page, 2019) <https://www.imo.org/en/About/Pages/Structure.aspx>.

23 Ibid.

24 Ibid.

25 Harilaos N Psaraftis and Christos A Kontovas, 'Influence and transparency at the IMO: the name of the game' (2020) 22 *Maritime Economics and Logistics* 151, 152.

26 See, e.g. Lei Shi, 'Successful Use of the Tacit Acceptance Procedure to Effectuate Progress in International Maritime Law' (1998–1999) 11 *University of San Francisco Maritime Law Journal*, 299.

then they will be taken to have accepted the amendment.[27] This procedure is a prominent part of the decision-making process under MARPOL and SOLAS.[28]

The United Nations Convention on the Law of the Sea

Famously described as a "constitution for the oceans",[29] UNCLOS is a significant achievement in international law as a foundational framework convention for a vast area of the planet. The treaty, which was concluded in 1982, entered into force in 1994. While UNCLOS covers a wide range of topics, Part XII on the "Protection and Preservation of the Marine Environment" is most relevant to the current discussion. However, Parts II and III, which address the "territorial sea and contiguous zone" and the "exclusive economic zone" (EEZ), are also important to note.[30] Part XII pays the most attention to addressing marine pollution. Specifically, Article 211 of UNCLOS provides the key legal obligation, which reads as follows:

> 1. States, acting through the competent international organization or general diplomatic conference, shall establish international rules and standards to prevent, reduce and control pollution of the marine environment from vessels and promote the adoption, in the same manner, wherever appropriate, of routeing systems designed to minimize the threat of accidents which might cause pollution of the marine environment, including the coastline, and pollution damage to the related interests of coastal States. Such rules and standards shall, in the same manner, be re-examined from time to time as necessary.[31]

It is worth noting first that the competent international organisation mentioned here, as well as elsewhere in UNCLOS, specifically refers to the IMO.[32] Secondly, this represents a clear obligation on states to take action to prevent vessel-source pollution through the creation of "international rules and standards".

It has long been debated whether these obligations to prevent pollution included GHG emissions, both those generated from land-based activities

27 Ibid 302.
28 Ibid.
29 See, e.g. Third United Nations Conference on the Law of the Sea, President, *Tommy T.B. Koh's Remarks at the Final Session of the Conference at Montego Bay "A Constitution for the Oceans"*, 6 and 11 December 1982.
30 *UNCLOS* (n 10) pts II, III, and XII.
31 Ibid.
32 See, e.g. ibid Annex VIII, art 2(2), which lists the IMO as the appropriate body for "navigation, including pollution from vessels and by dumping" in the context of dispute resolution.

and those from vessels.[33] For example, the issue of ocean acidification, the absorption of atmospheric carbon pollution by the world's oceans reducing their pH, represented a regulatory gap as it falls between UNCLOS on the one hand and the climate regime on the other.[34] That is why Part XII of UNCLOS was the focus of the request for an advisory opinion submitted by the Commission of Small Island States (COSIS) on Climate Change and International Law. The COSIS, which consisted of Antigua and Barbuda, Tuvalu, the Republic of Palau, Niue, the Republic of Vanuatu, and Saint Lucia, asked the ITLOS to advise on the specific obligations of state parties to the UNCLOS, including Part XII, to (1) prevent, reduce, and control pollution of the marine environment in relation to the deleterious effects from climate change; and (2) protect and preserve the marine environment in relation to climate change impacts.[35] The ITLOS interprets that anthropogenic GHG emissions fall within the definition of marine pollution under Article 1(1)(4) of UNCLOS.[36] This interpretation fills a regulatory gap by integrating GHG emissions into the existing pollution regime. It also demonstrates the nature of UNCLOS as a living convention that can evolve to deal with emerging challenges facing the world's oceans and the planet.[37] Hence, it has been confirmed by the ITLOS that GHG emissions are considered to be a pollutant under the UNCLOS definition. Consequently, the IMO, as the competent international organisation, and state parties to UNCLOS have an obligation to "prevent, reduce and control" this form of vessel-source pollution.[38]

Having already briefly examined the IMO and how it allows states to create the relevant international rules and standards, it is important to address how UNCLOS grants state jurisdiction to enforce the domestic laws that implement these standards. One of the primary functions of UNCLOS is to establish the fundamental jurisdictional rules that apply in the world's oceans. This is done primarily through the application of three kinds of jurisdiction: flag-state, coastal-state, and port-state jurisdiction. Each of these is examined in turn in the context of vessel-source pollution and GHG emissions.

33 See, e.g. Ellycia R Harrould-Kolieb, 'The UN Convention on the Law of the Sea: A governing framework for ocean acidification?' (2020) 29 *Review of European, Comparative and International Environmental Law* 257, 260–262.

34 Tim Stephens, 'Warming waters and souring seas: climate change and ocean acidification' in Donald Rothwell et al. (eds), *The Oxford Handbook of the Law of the Sea* (Oxford University Press 2015) 777–798.

35 *ITLOS Advisory Opinion* (n 17) para 3.

36 Ibid para 179.

37 See, e.g. Richard Alan Barnes, 'The Continuing Vitality of UNCLOS' in J Barrett and R Barnes (eds), *The United Nations Convention on the Law of the Sea: A Living Instrument* (BIICL, 2016) 459.

38 *UNCLOS* (n 10) art 211(1).

Flag state jurisdiction

Article 94(1) of UNCLOS lays out the basis for flag state jurisdiction, stating that each state shall "exercise its jurisdiction and control in administrative, technical and social matters over ships flying its flag".[39] States must also enact their own domestic legislation that "at least" has "the same effect as that of generally accepted international rules and standards", per Article 211.[40] The ITLOS Advisory Opinion therefore generates pressure for changes in domestic legislation regarding vessel-source GHG emissions. This is because flag states have an obligation to enact and enforce laws consistent with the generally accepted rules of the IMO conventions, specifically related to the prevention, reduction, and control of anthropogenic GHG emissions. The flag state also retains priority over the coastal state in these matters per Article 228 of UNCLOS, which states that if a flag state institutes proceedings against an offending vessel within six months of the proceedings being instituted by the coastal state, the coastal state action will be suspended.[41]

However, flag state jurisdiction has often proven unreliable in practice given the differences in domestic laws and enforcement capabilities between flag states.[42] The term "flag of convenience" has been coined to refer to the registration of vessels in states with open registry systems.[43] These open registries allow for vessels that are largely unrelated to the flag state to register for a fee in pursuit of more favourable regulatory conditions, such as lower taxes.[44] This has resulted in some states having a disproportionate number of vessels registered under their flag and lacking the capacity to enforce regulations, such as those on vessel-source pollution standards.[45] Aside from capacity, there is also a question of motivation when it comes to states offering flags of convenience, as they may become unappealing to certain ship owners if the registry state is stringent in enforcing environmental standards and thus miss out on registry revenue.[46] This does not apply to all states offering an open registry, but certain states such as those on the Paris Memorandum of Understanding on Port State Control (Paris MoU) blacklist are examples of this phenomenon.[47] These states include Vanuatu, Azerbaijan, Tanzania, Belize, Moldova, Comoros, Togo, Cameroon, and Vietnam. The topic of flags of convenience

39 *UNCLOS* (n 10) art 94(1).
40 Ibid art 211.
41 Ibid art 228.
42 Weipan Zhang et al., 'Governance of global vessel-source marine oil spills: Characteristics and refreshed strategies' (2021) 213 *Ocean and Coastal Management* 105974, 8.
43 Ibid.
44 Ibid.
45 Ibid.
46 Ibid.
47 Paris MoU on Port State Control, *White, Grey and Black List* (Web Page) <https://www.parismou.org/detentions-banning/white-grey-and-black-list>.

then is likely to continue to be an issue in the enforcement of standards to prevent vessel-source GHG emissions.

Given then that flag state jurisdiction cannot be completely relied upon for the regulation of vessel-source pollution, it is important that other sources of enforcement jurisdiction provided for by UNCLOS work in tandem with flag state jurisdiction to help enforce these regulations.

Coastal state jurisdiction

The extent of coastal state jurisdiction over vessel-source pollution depends on where in the ocean a vessel is located. The territorial sea of a state has the greatest legislative jurisdiction per Article 21(1)(f) of UNCLOS, which states that coastal states may make laws about "the preservation of the environment of the coastal State and the prevention, reduction and control of pollution thereof".[48] These laws may not interfere with the right to innocent passage set out in UNCLOS or relate to the "construction, design manning or equipment" of the vessel per Article 21(2).[49] Coastal states have less control within their exclusive economic zone, which only allows them to adopt laws that conform to "generally accepted international rules and standards established through the competent international organization or general diplomatic conference" per Article 211(5).[50]

When it comes to enforcing coastal state laws, Article 220 allows states various rights of enforcement against violations of their laws addressing pollution occurring in their own waters.[51] In the territorial sea, states may inspect, institute proceedings, and detain the vessel, provided there are "clear grounds for believing that a vessel... has... violated laws and regulations of that State... for the prevention, reduction and control of pollution from vessels" per Article 220(2).[52] In the EEZ, coastal states may only "require the vessel to give information regarding its identity and port of registry, its last and its next port of call and other relevant information required to establish whether a violation has occurred" per Article 220(3).[53] Furthermore, the coastal state has the right to

> undertake physical inspection of the vessel for matters relating to the violation if the vessel has refused to give information or if the information supplied by the vessel is manifestly at variance with the evident factual situation and if the circumstances of the case justify such inspection.

48 *UNCLOS* (n 10) art 21(1)(f).
49 Ibid art 21(2).
50 Ibid art 211(5).
51 Ibid art 220.
52 Ibid art 220(2).
53 Ibid art 220(3).

(Article 220[5])[54]Finally, Article 220(6) allows states to institute proceedings, including detention, against a vessel in its EEZ when there is

> clear objective evidence that a vessel… has… committed a violation… resulting in a discharge causing major damage or threat of major damage to the coastline or related interests of the coastal State, or to any resources of its territorial sea or exclusive economic zone.[55]

Coastal state jurisdiction in relation to pollution is primarily aimed at allowing states to legislate and enforce laws, in line with the international standards of the IMO, in order to protect their own marine environment from the actions of vessels within their own marine environment. Moreover, the ITLOS Advisory Opinion has raised the bar for "due diligence" in the case of transboundary harm caused by GHG emissions, which now goes beyond merely the "best efforts" of a coastal state.[56] Instead, "the obligation of due diligence requires a State to put in a place a national system, including legislation, administrative procedures and an enforcement mechanism necessary"[57] to regulate anthropogenic GHG emissions from their jurisdiction, including those from vessels, and "to exercise adequate vigilance to make such a system function efficiently".[58] It remains to be seen how coastal states will respond to the advisory opinion in exercising their jurisdiction.

Port state jurisdiction

Port state jurisdiction is based upon the notion that a state's port represents its sovereign territory as it is landward of the outermost points of the harbour from which the baseline is measured.[59] With that in mind, the state has jurisdiction to make and enforce its own domestic laws in relation to vessel-source pollution.[60] This has the potential to be straightforward and uncomplicated in the case of violations occurring while the vessel is docked at a port, and a somewhat unique application of jurisdiction for violations committed elsewhere.

The port state is seen by some as a "safety net" that allows environmentally sub-standard ships that would otherwise slip through coastal and flag state jurisdiction to be held to account.[61] It has been accepted in international customary law, via the International Court of Justice, that a coastal state may

54 Ibid art 220(5).
55 Ibid art 220(6).
56 *ITLOS Advisory Opinion* (n 17) para 240.
57 Ibid para 235.
58 Ibid.
59 *UNCLOS* (n 10) arts 11, 8(1).
60 Ibid art 2(1).
61 Z Oya Özçayir, 'The Use of Port State Control in Maritime Industry and Application of the Paris MOU' (2009) 14 *Ocean and Coastal Law Journal* 201, 202.

regulate its ports.[62] This ability is also implied within UNCLOS at Articles 25(2), 211(3), and 255.[63]

Furthermore, as mentioned above, port states are considered to have absolute legal control over a vessel within the port just as they would have over any foreign national within their territory. However, when it comes to imposing conditions on vessels that are entering the port, there is a question of extra-territorial jurisdiction.[64] In particular, the regulation of the construction, design, equipment, and manning (CDEM) of a visiting ship by a port state is regarded as slightly more complicated as it can be argued to be a case of imposing laws on foreign ships that are built outside the jurisdiction.[65] However, it has been more convincingly posited that this is not an issue of extra-territoriality as vessels ultimately have a choice as to whether to enter certain ports and the relevant laws regarding pollution need to be duly publicised as per Article 211(3) of UNCLOS.[66]

More difficult, perhaps, is the ability of port states to prosecute vessels entering their port for conduct outside of their territory that violates international pollution standards.[67] However, it appears that this conduct can also be prosecuted if it occurs within the port state's own territorial sea and EEZ, as outlined in the above section on coastal state jurisdiction.[68] In this case, it would simply be a matter of the enforcement taking place within the port, rather than at sea.[69] In the case of incidents occurring outside of the port state's waters, Article 218 of UNCLOS allows for a vessel "voluntarily" within a state's port to be investigated by the port state "where the evidence so warrants" and proceedings to be instituted "in respect of any discharge from that vessel outside the internal waters, territorial sea or exclusive economic zone of that State in violation of applicable international rules and standards".[70] Port states also have the ability to exercise some extra-territorial jurisdiction as granted by UNCLOS.

In terms of the measures that might be taken, there is a distinction between jurisdiction and control. In exercising jurisdiction, for example, the port state will enforce its laws, as has been discussed above. However, port state control

62 *Case concerning Military and Paramilitary Activities In and Against Nicaragua (Nicaragua v United States of America)* [1986] ICJ Rep 111, [123].

63 *UNCLOS* (n 10) arts 25(2), 211(3), 255.

64 See, e.g. Robin Churchill, 'Port State Jurisdiction Relating to the Safety of Shipping and Pollution from Ships—What Degree of Extra-territoriality?' (2016) 31 *The International Journal of Marine and Coastal Law* 442.

65 Ibid 445.

66 Ibid 454–458.

67 Ibid 458–459.

68 Ibid 458–461.

69 Ibid.

70 *UNCLOS* (n 10) art 218.

involves smaller mandates such as fines or ordering repairs.[71] Finally, it is worth noting the role of memoranda of understanding (MoUs). These agreements are regional; for example. the Paris MoU applies to the European Union (EU) and North America, while the Tokyo MoU applies to the Asia-Pacific.[72] These MoUs oblige member states to enforce port state control measures in order to improve the standard of vessels in line with IMO obligations.

Thus, port state jurisdiction plays an essential role in the prevention of vessel-source GHG pollution, particularly through the imposition of CDEM standards for visiting ships. For example, it could allow for the enforcement of the obligations related to the Energy Efficiency Design Index (EEDI) and the Ship Energy Efficiency Management Plan (SEEMP) under Annex VI of MARPOL, which are discussed in greater depth in subsequent sections.

Having now examined the foundational aspects of the international legal framework for the prevention, reduction, and control of vessel-source pollution, it is important to explore the specific sources of obligations regarding this issue. This includes a brief overview of the key IMO conventions that address vessel-source pollution and some key obligations they contain. This will serve to highlight the current regime for the prevention of vessel-source pollution, as well as demonstrate the relative lack of consideration of GHG emissions as a category of vessel-source pollution within existing instruments under the IMO.

The existing vessel-source pollution regime: IMO conventions

MARPOL

MARPOL is the most significant international treaty dealing with the problem of vessel-source marine pollution. It has been continually updated to fulfil this purpose, in line with the obligation of Article 211(1) of UNCLOS, which mandates the establishment of international rules and standards to prevent vessel-source pollution. MARPOL engages robustly in this manner of standard setting by regulating the construction, design, equipment, and manning of ships and establishing port state inspection systems to promote compliance. In this way, both flag state and port state jurisdictions are relied upon to some extent to implement and enforce the convention.

Article 2(3) of MARPOL highlights a specific focus on operational vessel-source pollution by defining a "discharge" as "any release from a ship" of "harmful substances", while expressly excluding "dumping" as per the

71 See, e.g. Ho-Sam Bang, 'Is Port State Control an Effective Means to Combat Vessel-Source Pollution? An Empirical Survey of the Practical Exercise by Port States of Their Powers of Control' (2008) 23 *International Journal of Marine and Coastal Law* 717.

72 Paris MoU on Port State Control, *Organisation* (Web Page, 2024) <https://www.parismou.org/about-us/organisation>; *Memorandum of Understanding on Port State Control in the Asia-Pacific Region*, adopted 1 December 1993, (entered into force 1 April 1994).

London Protocol as well as seabed mining operations and "legitimate scientific research into pollution abatement or control".[73] Meanwhile, Article 2(2) defines a "harmful substance" as "any substance which, if introduced into the sea, is liable to create hazards to human health, to harm living resources and marine life, to damage amenities or to interfere with other legitimate uses of the sea".[74] This is in line with the definition of pollution in UNCLOS, which implies that anthropogenic GHG emissions are included as well.[75]

Despite this specific focus, there is still a wide variety of activities and types of pollutants that this definition covers. They are largely dealt with individually through the use of annexes to the convention, which can be updated periodically as standards may change. There are six annexes to MARPOL, each dealing with a different type of pollution, and each is briefly examined in turn. The first two annexes are compulsory along with Annex VI, but Article 14 of MARPOL outlines that Annexes III, IV, and V are optional.[76]

Annex I is responsible for the "Prevention of pollution by oil and oily water" and first came into force in 1983.[77] It introduces a range of measures including discharge limits on oily or oily discharge from ships of more than 400 gt,[78] discharge equipment standards,[79] standards to limit the damage caused by oil spills from 600 tonnes and above (deadweight) tankers,[80] as well as regulations regarding the use of separate tanks required for oil and ballast water among other measures.[81] In 1992, Annex I was amended to make double hulls compulsory for tanker vessels over 5000 dwt constructed after 6 July 1996 unless an alternative was approved by the IMO.[82] Since 1995, tankers that reach 30 years of age or older are also required to be either converted to a double hull or retired.[83] As a result of lobbying by the European Union after a number of oil spill disasters,[84] the timelines for phasing out single hull tankers were brought forward in 2001 and again in 2003.

Annex II addressing the "Control of pollution by noxious liquid substances in bulk", came into force in 1983. It focuses on categorising and providing discharge regulations for chemical substances that may be transported in bulk.[85] It also addresses the standards required for the washing, piping, and

73 *MARPOL* (n 13) art 2(3).
74 Ibid art 2(2).
75 *UNCLOS* (n 10), art 1(1)(4).
76 *MARPOL* (n 13) art 14.
77 *MARPOL* (n 13) Annex I.
78 Ibid reg 15.
79 Ibid regs 13–14.
80 Ibid reg 19.
81 Ibid regs 16, 18.
82 Ibid reg 19.
83 Ibid reg 20.
84 See, e.g. Veronica Frank, 'Consequences of the Prestige sinking for European and international law' (2005) 20 *International Journal of Marine and Coastal Law* 18.
85 *MARPOL* (n 13) annex II reg 6.

pumping required aboard a vessel, depending on the substance.[86] No noxious substance may be discharged within 12 nm of the shore and must generally be discharged at an appropriate port reception facility.[87]

Annex III of the MARPOL Convention first entered into force in 1992 and addresses the "Prevention of pollution of harmful substances carried by sea in package form".[88] The "harmful substances" to be regulated in this case are those listed in the IMO International Maritime Dangerous Goods Code.[89] This annex then deals with goods that may cause pollution in case of accident or poor storage practices and attempts to limit the likelihood of this eventuality. To this end, it regulates issues such as packing, marking, labelling, documentation, stowage, quantity limitations, exceptions, and port state control over these measures.[90]

Annex IV, in force from 2003, addresses "Pollution by sewage from ships".[91] Sewage from ships consists largely of the water used on a ship for toilets, medical drainage, living spaces for animals, and other wastewater that is combined with these sources per the definitions in Regulation 1.[92] As such, the annex requires every ship to be fitted with either treatment facilities or storage facilities for this waste.[93] It also forbids the discharge of this sewage except under particular conditions, such as at a steady rate, at least 3 nm from land for treated sewage and 12 nm for untreated.[94]

Annex V deals with "Pollution by garbage from ships" and entered into force in 1988.[95] Importantly, it prohibits the disposal into the sea of "all plastics, including but not limited to synthetic ropes, synthetic fishing nets, plastic garbage bags and incinerator ashes from plastic products which may contain toxic or heavy metal residues".[96] It goes on to stipulate the particular conditions under which other kinds of garbage may be disposed of into the sea both within and outside of special areas.[97]

Annex VI is the most recent MARPOL annex, which entered into force in 2005.[98] Annex VI is concerned with the "Prevention of air pollution from ships".[99] This is particularly relevant for the discussion within this chapter as the

86 Ibid regs 11–12.
87 Ibid reg 13.
88 *MARPOL* (n 13) Annex III.
89 *The International Maritime Dangerous Goods Code*, IMO Res A 17/Res.716, adopted 6 November 1991, updated 1 January 2020 (entered into force 1 June 2022).
90 *MARPOL* (n 13) Annex III, regs 2–8.
91 *MARPOL* (n 13) Annex IV.
92 Ibid reg 1.
93 Ibid reg 9.
94 Ibid reg 11.
95 *MARPOL* (n 13) Annex V.
96 Ibid reg 3.
97 Ibid.
98 *MARPOL* (n 13) Annex VI.
99 Ibid.

shipping industry attempts to address the threat of climate change. However, this annex deals with a wide range of pollutants, including nitrous oxides (NOx), sulphur oxides (SOx), and particulate matter (PM).[100] Emissions control areas (ECAs) can also be used to regulate each of these different substances by applying more stringent standards in particular geographic regions.[101] Regarding the regulation of SOx, a resolution was introduced in 2020, reducing the allowable sulphur content in ship fuel to 0.5% m/m, down from the previous 3.5% m/m limit.[102] The limit was already much stricter in the special areas (0.1% m/m); however, this still represents a significant reduction.[103] States may choose to comply with this regulation by using low-sulphur fuels or through the use of exhaust cleaning systems or "scrubbers".

It was only in 2011 with the adoption of a Chapter 2 amendment that measures for combating GHG emissions were introduced to the annex, chiefly through energy efficiency measures such as the Energy Efficiency Design Index and the Ship Energy Efficiency Management Plan.[104] These measures have acted as a foundation that has been built upon for the transition to green shipping. They will be discussed next.

SOLAS

While the SOLAS Convention focuses on the safety of shipping operations, there is an evident link to the prevention of vessel-source pollution. Reducing instances of accidents and dangerous practices reduces the likelihood of damage caused to the marine environment from these practices, and substances that may be unsafe for human health are also likely unsafe for the broader marine environment.

Some of the chapters of SOLAS relevant to mitigating and preventing vessel-source pollution are briefly highlighted below. Firstly, Chapter II-1 lays out safety standards for construction to ensure that the vessel will be safe and stay afloat in the event of an accident.[105] Of particular interest are the "goal-based standards" for oil tankers and bulk carriers from 2010, which were designed to create standards for preventing pollution damage and danger to those on board in the event of an accident.[106]

Chapter V of SOLAS relates to the safety of navigation and provides some important measures such as the installation of voyage data recorders (VDRs)

100 Ibid regs 12–15.
101 Ibid reg 14, app III.
102 Ibid reg 14.
103 Ibid.
104 Ibid ch 2.
105 *SOLAS* (n 14) ch II–1.
106 *Adoption of the International Goal-Based Ship Construction Standards for Bulk Carriers and Oil Tankers*, IMO Res MSC.290(87), adopted 21 May 2010 (entered into force 1 January 2012).

and automatic ship identification systems (AIS).[107] These measures allow for reporting and routing measures to be implemented in service of preventing vessel-source pollution.[108]

Chapter VII of SOLAS deals with the carriage of dangerous goods, imposing standards for their safe package and transport.[109] This again is an important part of the prevention of pollution from shipping. This chapter is also linked to several IMO codes that are worth mentioning briefly: the International Code for the Construction and Equipment of Ships Carrying Dangerous Chemicals in Bulk,[110] the International Code for the Construction and Equipment of Ships Carrying Liquified Gases in Bulk,[111] the International Maritime Dangerous Goods Code, and the Code for the Safe Carriage of Irradiated Nuclear Fuel, Plutonium and High-Level Radioactive Wastes in Flasks on Board Ships.[112] Overall, SOLAS plays an important subsidiary role in the prevention of pollution from ships, though it is less directly relevant to GHG emissions.

Anti-Fouling Convention

Anti-fouling is the process of coating the hulls of vessels with particular chemicals in order to prevent biofouling, which is the accretion of various organisms on a ship.[113] Biofouling is an issue for the shipping industry as it can significantly slow a ship and increase fuel consumption. An IMO study found that just a 0.5 mm coverage of biofilm on 50% of the hull can increase emissions by 25%, with larger growths, such as barnacles, causing up to a 55% increase in GHG emissions.[114] Hence, efforts to address the challenge of biofouling will also play a role in efficiency standards for ships and reduce their GHG emissions. Aside from increased fuel consumption, biofouling also introduces invasive species into new ecosystems as the ship travels.[115] In fact, one Australian

107 *SOLAS* (n 14) ch V.
108 Ibid.
109 Ibid ch VII.
110 *2007 Amendments to the International Code for the Construction and Equipment of Ships Carrying Dangerous Chemicals in Bulk Resolution*, IMO Res MEPC 56/23/Add.1, adopted 13 July 2007 (entered into force 13 July 2007).
111 *Adoption of Amendments to the International Code for the Construction and Equipment of Ships Carrying Liquefied Gases in Bulk*, IMO Res MSC 82/24/Add.1, adopted 5 December 1996 (entered into force 8 December 2006).
112 *Adoption of the International Code for the Safe Carriage of Packaged Irradiated Nuclear Fuel, Plutonium and High-Level Radioactive Wastes on Board Ships*, IMO Res MSC.88(71), adopted 27 May 1999.
113 James Kraska and Daniel Rittschof, 'Toward a Global Regime of Vessel Anti-Fouling' (2015) 26(1) *Duke Environmental Law & Policy Forum* 53, 55.
114 GloFouling Partnership and the International Maritime Organization, *Preliminary results: Impact of Ships' Biofouling on Greenhouse Gas Emissions* (Web Page) <https://wwwcdn.imo.org/localresources/en/MediaCentre/Documents/Biofouling%20report.pdf>.
115 Melissa A Frey et al., 'Fouling Around: Vessel Sea-Chests as a Vector for the Introduction and Spread of Aquatic Invasive Species' (2014) 5(1) *Management Biological Invasions* 21, 27.

Government study estimated that 59.8% of non-native species found in the study area – selected Australian ports – were introduced via biofouling.[116] Biofouling is undesirable from both an industry and an environmental point of view.

However, solutions to this issue that have been adopted in the past have also proven destructive to the environment. Anti-fouling coatings on a ship's hull are designed to kill the organisms that may attach themselves to a vessel, but they have also been shown to leach into the ocean water, causing deleterious effects on the marine environment.[117] Arsenic and lime used to be a popular coating before the industry moved towards an organotin tributylin (TBT) coating in the 1960s.[118] This substance has since been shown to be extremely harmful to marine life, causing, for example, sex changes in snails and molluscs.[119] Furthermore, while concentrations of only 10 ng are shown to have these effects, in the 1990s, levels of TBT reached 50 ng per litre in global shipping lanes.[120]

The IMO noted these concerns in 1989 and adopted a resolution in 1990 to recommend the elimination of TBT coatings on non-aluminium-hulled vessels of less than 25 m in length and eliminate the use of anti-fouling paints with a leaching rate of more than 4 mg of TBT per day.[121] Later in 1999, an IMO resolution called for a global prohibition on the application or reapplication of organotin compounds that act as anti-fouling systems by 2003 and a complete prohibition by 2008.[122] It was decided that a new treaty instrument would be developed to help meet these goals and address anti-fouling systems more comprehensively.

The Anti-Fouling Convention was adopted in 2001 and entered into force in 2008. The delay between adoption and ratification was due to the need for at least 25 states to join the agreement to trigger its entry into force a year later. This number was reached when Panama joined the agreement in

116 Chad Hewitt and Marnie Campbell, 'The relative contribution of vectors to the introduction and translocation of invasive marine species' (2010) *The National System for the Prevention and Management of Marine Pest Incursions* 37.

117 International Maritime Organization, *Anti-fouling systems* (Web Page, 2019) <https://www.imo.org/en/OurWork/Environment/Pages/Anti-fouling.aspx>.

118 Ibid.

119 Jessica Straw and Dan Rittschof, 'Responses of Mud Snails From Low to High Imposex Sites to Sex Pheromones' (2004) 48(11–12) *Marine Pollution Bulletin* 1048.

120 Kraska and Ritschof (n 114) 56.

121 *Measures to Control Potential Adverse Impacts Associated with the Use of Tributyl Tin Compounds in Anti-Fouling Paints*, IMO Res MEPC.46(30), adopted 16 November 1990.

122 *Anti-Fouling Systems used on Ships*, IMO Res A 21/Res. 895, adopted 25 November 1999 (entered into force 4 February 2000).

2007.[123] The convention currently has 97 parties, representing 96.04% of the world's fleet.[124]

The Anti-Fouling Convention defines anti-fouling systems as "a coating, paint, surface treatment, surface, or device that is used on a ship to control or prevent attachment of unwanted organisms".[125] Article 4 contains the primary obligations for states "to prohibit and/or restrict... the application, re-application, installation, or use of harmful anti-fouling systems".[126] Harmful anti-fouling systems are outlined in Annex I of the convention as those that consist of organotin compounds and these prohibitions follow the same timelines as the 1999 resolution.[127] These measures apply to ships under the flag of member states as well as ships under their authority and ships entering their port, "shipyard or offshore terminal".[128] It is worth noting briefly that fixed and floating platforms, floating storage units, and floating production storage and off-loading units are exempt if constructed before 2003 and "have not been in dry-dock on or after 1 January 2003".[129]

The Anti-Fouling Convention also lays out the process for adding to the Annex I list of harmful prohibited anti-fouling systems through Article 6 and the formation of a technical committee.[130] This option was taken in 2017 to examine the chemical cubutryne by the Sub-Committee on Pollution Prevention, with early evidence suggesting that it is highly damaging to the marine environment.[131] The amendment was eventually adopted by the MEPC at its seventy-sixth session in June 2021 and entered into force on 1 January 2023.[132]

Finally, it is worth mentioning the 2023 IMO Guidelines for the control and management of ships' biofouling to minimise the transfer of invasive aquatic species.[133] These guidelines were originally adopted in 2011. They focus more closely on the prevention of the transfer of invasive species from biofouling than on the harmful effects of anti-fouling systems.[134] These guidelines apply to various stakeholders in the shipping industry, such as ship designers, shipbuilders, anti-fouling paint manufacturers and suppliers, states,

123 Kraska and Ristchof (n 114) 59.

124 International Maritime Organization, *Status of Treaties* (Web Page, 2024) <https://wwwcdn.imo.org/localresources/en/About/Conventions/StatusOfConventions/StatusOfTreaties.pdf>.

125 *Anti-Fouling Convention* (n 15) art 2.

126 Ibid art 4.

127 Ibid Annex I.

128 Ibid.

129 Ibid.

130 Ibid art 6.

131 International Maritime Organization, *Anti-Fouling Systems* (n 118).

132 Ibid.

133 *2023 Guidelines for the Control and Management of Ships' Biofouling to Minimize the Transfer of Invasive Aquatic Species*, IMO Res MEPC 80/17/Add.1, adopted 7 July 2023.

134 Ibid.

including environmental and regulatory agencies, classification societies, ship-owners, ship operators, charterers, shipmasters, port authorities, ship cleaning and maintenance operators, inspection organisations, ship repair, dry-docking and recycling facilities, and any other interested parties.[135] Furthermore, the guidelines lay out the requirements for a biofouling management plan[136] and a biofouling record book[137] as best practices in these areas. However, the guidelines are still non-binding, and despite calls to integrate them into the Anti-Fouling Convention or MARPOL via amendment,[138] nothing has been done to strengthen them. Hence, biofouling is a multifaceted problem for the prevention of vessel-source pollution as it can increase fuel consumption, leading to increased GHG emissions, as well as introduce invasive species; the anti-fouling substances can also act as a damaging pollutant. This highlights that in addressing the challenge of GHG emissions from ships, international lawmakers will need to be wary of problem shifting between environmental threats.

BWM Convention

As is the case with biofouling, ballast water is also a key driver in the introduction of invasive species into different marine ecosystems. It was responsible for an estimated 24% of introduced species discovered in one study (on top of the 59.8% from biofouling).[139] Article 196 of UNCLOS aims to prevent this, stating: "States shall take all measures necessary to prevent, reduce and control… the intentional or accidental introduction of species, alien or new, to a particular part of the marine environment, which may cause significant and harmful changes thereto."[140] A key obligation of states is to address technologies and activities that may cause the invasion of alien species. The obligation is further reflected in the Convention on Biological Diversity, which in Article 8(h) obligates states to "[p]revent the introduction of, control or eradicate those alien species which threaten ecosystems, habitats or species".[141]

Ballast water is seawater that is taken onto ships in order to ensure maneuverability and stability. However, this water and the organisms within it are often discharged far from where they were taken on board, resulting in their introduction into a foreign marine ecosystem.[142] It has been estimated that 10 billion tonnes of ballast water is transported each year, carrying with it some

135 Ibid reg 3.1.
136 Ibid reg 10.
137 Ibid reg 11.
138 See, e.g. Kraska and Ritshof (n 114) 65–69.
139 Hewitt and Campbell (n 117) 37.
140 *UNCLOS* (n 10) art 196.
141 Convention on Biological Diversity, adopted 5 June 1992, 1760 UNTS 79 (entered into force 29 December 1993).
142 See, e.g. D A Wright, 'Compliance assessment for the ballast water convention: time for a re-think? A U.K. case study' (2021) 20(4) *Journal of Marine Engineering and Technology* 254.

7000 species.[143] Given both the seriousness of this issue and the international legal obligations to prevent the introduction of alien species, ballast water management has been an ongoing subject at the IMO for a significant period.

In 1993, the IMO first published non-binding IMO Guidelines for Preventing the Introduction of Unwanted Organisms and Pathogens from Ships' Ballast Water and Sediment Discharges.[144] These guidelines were later revised in 1997 and set in place the procedure for the exchange of ballast water between ships in transit, thereby returning the ballast water to its original location.[145] This is in contrast to exploring options for ballast water treatment, which became more prominent in the BWM Convention. The BWM Convention was adopted in 2004 but only came into force in 2017. This is because it was not to come into force until ratified by at least 30 states that represented at least 35% of the gross tonnage of the world's shipping fleet.[146] Currently, there are 96 state parties representing 92.53% of the gross tonnage of the world's merchant fleet.[147]

The BWM Convention sets out a two-step procedure to address the issue of ballast water management. Section D "Standards for Ballast Water Management" is key here as it provides two possible approaches to ballast water management.[148] The first is Regulation D-1, which stipulates: "Ships performing Ballast Water exchange in accordance with this regulation shall do so with an efficiency of at least 95 percent volumetric exchange of Ballast Water".[149] Regulation D-2 sets a "Ballast Water Performance Standard", which details specific concentrations of organisms that are required in order for the ballast water to be effectively treated and discharged.[150] These two regulations represent contrasting approaches. One is focused on ballast water exchange as a solution to this particular issue while the other is focused on ballast water treatment. The intention is for Regulation D-1 to act as a temporary solution for existing ships until 8 September 2024. Once this deadline has passed, all

143 GEF-UNDP-IMO GloBallast Partnerships, *The GloBallast Story: Reflections from a Global Family – Partnerships to catalyze transformational innovations in marine biosafety – GloBallast Monograph Series No. 25* (Report, 2017) 13.

144 *Guidelines for Preventing the Introduction of Unwanted Organisms and Pathogens from Ships' Ballast Water and Sediment Discharges*, IMO Res A 18/Res. 774, adopted 4 November 1993.

145 *Guidelines for Preventing the Introduction of Unwanted Organisms and Pathogens from Ships' Ballast Water and Sediment Discharges*, IMO Res A 20/Res. 868, adopted 27 November 1997.

146 *BWM Convention* (n 16) art 19(1).

147 International Maritime Organization, *Status of Treaties* (n 125).

148 *BWM Convention* (n 16) Section D.

149 Ibid reg D-1.

150 Ibid reg D-2.

new and existing ships will be required to adhere to the treatment standards of Regulation D-2.[151]

This delay is partly because, at the time of the BWM Convention's adoption in 2004, there was no commercially viable technology for ship owners to achieve the strict standards for ballast water treatment under Regulation D-2.[152] As such, the treaty was supposed to encourage innovation. However, actual innovation has been slow.[153] It was initially expected that the technology would be ready by 2014, but the adoption of the treaty was further delayed until 2017, with the ultimate date of transition in 2024.[154] The BWM Convention also requires new treatment technologies to be approved by the IMO.[155] At this stage, China, the Republic of Korea, and Japan are leading the way in terms of national approvals of ballast water treatment systems.[156] However, while Japan and the Republic of Korea have achieved 9 and 16 IMO final approvals, respectively, China has only had 2 approvals by the IMO.[157]

While ballast water management does not have direct relevance to the prevention of GHG pollution from ships, it is an important part of the existing IMO regime for vessel-source pollution. The next section examines how the current regime has begun to deal with GHG emissions from ships and some future directions that may be necessary in light of the ITLOS Advisory Opinion.

Future challenges: the IMO and the regulation of GHG emissions from ships

Having laid out an overview of the current international legal framework regarding vessel-source pollution, it can be argued that the current regime has been effective at dealing with more traditional vessel-source pollution to this point. This section addresses the key challenge facing the future of the green shipping transition – the reduction of GHG emissions from shipping.

As mentioned previously, shipping emissions have increased from 977 million tonnes in 2012 to 1076 million tonnes in 2018, meaning that shipping emissions make up approximately 2.89% of global GHG emissions.[158] The IMO has been at the forefront of developing international measures to reduce

151 *Draft Amendments to Regulation B-3 of the BWM Convention*, MEPC 71/17/Add.1, adopted 7 July 2017.

152 Michael Tsimplis, 'Regulatory Systems Supporting Innovation: Lessons from the Development of the 2004 Ballast Water Management Convention' (2020) 36 *The International Journal of Marine and Coastal Law* 59, 61.

153 Ibid 82–83.

154 Ibid 73.

155 *BWM Convention* (n 16) reg D-3.2.

156 International Maritime Organization, *BWM Technologies* (Web Page, 2024) <https://www.imo.org/en/OurWork/Environment/Pages/BWMTechnologies.aspx>.

157 Tsimplis (n 153) 76–77.

158 International Maritime Organization, *Fourth IMO Greenhouse Gas Study* (n 4) 1.

GHG emissions from shipping since 1997. Several initiatives under MARPOL Annex VI have sought to address ship design, including the Energy Efficiency Design Index and the Ship Energy Efficiency Management Plan.[159] Both the EEDI and SEEMP were adopted in 2011. The EEDI is a series of mandatory measures for newly built ships in order to improve their energy efficiency. It aims to eventually reach a 30% reduction in GHG emissions compared to the average efficiency for ships built between 2000 and 2010.[160] Specifically, the EEDI initially applied to new vessels that are 400 gt or more of energy-intensive types such as tankers, bulk carriers, gas carriers, general cargo ships, container ships, refrigerated cargo carriers, and combination carriers.[161] An amendment in 2014 broadened the scope so that it would now apply also to "LNG carriers, ro-ro cargo ships (vehicle carriers), ro-ro cargo ships; ro-ro passenger ships and cruise passenger ships having non-conventional propulsion".[162] This is expected to cover ships responsible for up to 85% of carbon emissions.[163] These measures also gradually get stronger as the CO_2 reduction amount is set at 10% initially and then increases by 10% every five years, hence reaching a 30% reduction level by 2025.[164] The technology that shipbuilders use to achieve this efficiency improvement is not specified; rather it is measured on performance to encourage compliance and innovation.[165]

The SEEMP applies to both new and existing ships, acting as a method for managing fleet energy efficiency.[166] The accompanying Energy Efficiency Operational Indicator (EEOI) acts as a method of monitoring the performance of vessels in order to allow operators and owners to plan for more energy efficiency measures.[167] In this way, operators can determine the effect that various measures have on energy efficiency. The usage of new technologies is also encouraged by SEEMP.[168]

159 *Amendments to the Annex of the Protocol of 1997 to Amend the International Convention for the Prevention of Pollution from Ships, 1973, as Modified by the Protocol of 1978 relating thereto (Inclusion of regulations on energy efficiency for ships in MARPOL Annex VI)*, IMO Res MEPC.203(62), adopted 15 July 2011 ('*Inclusion of regulations on energy efficiency for ships in MARPOL Annex VI*').

160 Ibid reg 21.

161 Ibid.

162 *Amendments to the Annex of the Protocol of 1997 to Amend the International Convention for the Prevention of Pollution from Ships, 1973, as Modified by the Protocol of 1978 relating thereto (Amendments to regulations 2, 13, 19, 20 and 21 and the Supplement to the IAPP Certificate under MARPOL Annex VI and certification of dual-fuel engines under the NO_X Technical Code 2008)*, IMO Res MEPC.251(66), adopted 4 April 2014.

163 International Maritime Organization, *Improving the energy efficiency of ships* (Web Page) <https://www.imo.org/en/OurWork/Environment/Pages/Improving%20the%20energy%20efficiency%20of%20ships.aspx>.

164 *Inclusion of regulations on energy efficiency for ships in MARPOL Annex VI* (n 160).

165 Ibid.

166 Ibid.

167 Ibid.

168 Ibid.

In June 2021, the MEPC adopted more energy efficiency measures under MARPOL: the Energy Efficiency Existing Ship Index (EEXI) and the Carbon Intensity Indicator (CII).[169] The EEXI acts in much the same way as the EEDI, but it applies to existing rather than new ships.[170] These requirements came into force in 2023 for all vessels 400 gt and above.[171] Meanwhile, the CII is a system for measuring the performance of vessels 5000 gt and above in practice by taking mandatory reporting data and giving ships a rating from A to E for energy usage.[172] These ratings became stricter from 2023, and ship operators receiving a D or E will have to revise their SEEMP to demonstrate how they intend to improve.[173]

In addition to these energy efficiency measures, the IMO arrived at its Initial Strategy for GHG Reduction in shipping in 2018.[174] The Initial Strategy was envisioned as a starting point for a continually evolving series of measures that aim to reach the targets set by the 2015 Paris Agreement. To achieve this, the IMO set a target of a 40% reduction in GHG from 2008 levels by 2030 and a 70% reduction by 2050.[175] The first short-term phase was from 2018 to 2023.[176] Currently, they are in the medium-term phase (2023–2030), with long-term (2030–2050) measures to be put in place from 2030.

In the process of negotiating the Initial Strategy, there was debate over the principles to be included. The principle of common but differentiated responsibilities recognises that while all states have the obligation to address the issue of climate change, some states are much less responsible for it and, because of their economic situation, may be required to take on less of the burden.[177] This is a common principle in climate change law; however, it was seen to clash somewhat with the fundamental IMO principle of no more favourable treatment, found in several instruments including MARPOL.[178] This principle mandates that vessels flying the flag of a state that is not party to a convention will be treated no differently than a vessel with the flag of a party state.[179] In

169 International Maritime Organization, *Further shipping GHG emission reduction measures adopted* (Web Page, 17 June 2021) <https://www.imo.org/en/MediaCentre/PressBriefings/pages/MEPC76.aspx>.

170 Ibid.

171 Ibid.

172 Ibid.

173 Ibid.

174 *Initial IMO Strategy on Reduction of GHG Emissions from Ships*, IMO Res MEPC 72/17/Add.1, adopted 13 April 2018.

175 Ibid para 3.1.2.

176 Ibid art 4.1.

177 Charlotte Epstein, 'Common but differentiated responsibilities', *Encyclopaedia Britannica* (Web Page, 2023) <https://www.britannica.com/topic/common-but-differentiated-responsibilities>.

178 See, e.g. *MARPOL* (n 13) art 5(4).

179 Rosalie P Balkin, 'The IMO and Global Governance: Past, Present and Future' in David Joesph Attard, Rosalie P Balkin and Donald W Greig (eds) T*he IMLI Treatise On Global*

other words, vessels are not able to avoid regulation by simply changing their registry. These two principles were seen as incompatible by some negotiating states and this proved a stalling point within the negotiations.[180] However, the final instrument reconciled these points of view by including both principles, given that one applied to individual vessels specifically whereas the other was focused on state obligations.[181]

In 2023, the IMO adopted its second strategy.[182] The IMO's increased ambitions are clearly showcased in the 2023 GHG Strategy, aiming for (1) carbon intensity (grams of carbon dioxide released to produce a kilowatt-hour of electricity) of ships to decline through further improvement in energy efficiency for new ships; (2) carbon intensity of international shipping to decline by at least 40% compared to 2008 by 2030; (3) uptake of zero or near-zero GHG emission technologies, fuels, and/or energy sources to increase by at least 5%, while striving for 10% by 2030; and (4) GHG emissions from international shipping to reach net zero by or around 2050. While the IMO has proposed short-, mid-, and long-term measures to fulfil its ambitions, the 2023 IMO GHG Strategy is not a legally binding document. Without effective national implementation, the proposed measures "risk becoming broad ambitions with little action".[183] Moreover, the IMO has decided to set legally binding technical and economic measures to reduce GHG emissions in 2025.[184] Such measures include the goal of reducing the GHG intensity of marine fuel as well as pricing mechanisms to incentivise the transition to net-zero. This bodes well for the development of enforceable regulations that can address GHG emissions specifically. Indeed, given the timing of aiming to put these measures in place by 2025, the obligations outlined by the ITLOS Advisory Opinion can be taken into consideration.[185]

However, there are divergent proposals among countries about what these measures should entail. For example, the European Union and China have

Ocean Governance: Volume III: The IMO and Global Ocean Governance (Oxford Public International Law, 2018) 24.

180 Aldo Chircop, 'The IMO Initial Strategy for the Reduction of GHGs from International Shipping: A Commentary' (2019) 34 *The International Journal of Marine and Coastal Law* 482, 494–497.

181 Ibid.

182 *2023 IMO Strategy on Reduction of GHG Emissions from Ships*, IMO Res MEPC 80/17/Add.1, adopted 7 July 2023.

183 Beatriz Garcia, Anita Foerster, and Jolene Lin, 'Net Zero for the International Shipping Sector? An Analysis of the Implementation and Regulatory Challenges of the IMO Strategy on Reduction of GHG Emissions' (2021) 33(1) *Journal of Environmental Law* 8.

184 International Maritime Organization, *Marine Environment Protection Committee 81st session (MEPC 81), 18–22 March 2024* (Web Page, 2024) <https://www.imo.org/en/MediaCentre/MeetingSummaries/Pages/MEPC-81.aspx>.

185 *ITLOS Advisory Opinion* (n 17).

put forward separate proposals for a goal-based fuel efficiency standard.[186] While their structures are similar, the EU proposes that this standard should apply throughout the life of the fuel or "well-to-wake".[187] China's proposal, on the other hand, excludes any emissions prior to direct usage of the fuel within the vessel, instead preferring an assessment of fuel sustainability as "a condition of rewarding surplus emission reductions".[188] Ultimately, the 2023 GHG Strategy did not align with China's proposal as it requires a well-to-wake assessment of GHG emissions in its fuel efficiency standard.[189] Meanwhile, Pacific Island states have pushed for a carbon levy as part of the "economic element" of the GHG emissions pricing mechanism.[190] A number of countries have opposed this measure, including Brazil, Argentina, Chile, Uruguay, Guatemala, Ecuador, China, and South Africa, arguing that it will disproportionately harm developing countries by distorting trade and increasing the price of food.[191] China, in particular, has been reported as arguing that such a levy is "overly ambitious", "unrealistic", and "a disguised way by developed countries to improve their own market competitiveness" while encouraging developing countries to oppose it.[192] Further, the EU, China, and Pacific Island states have all suggested different ways to use any funds raised by such a levy.[193]

This divergence in positions has also been reflected in actions outside of the IMO. Since January 2024, the EU has unilaterally extended its emissions trading system (ETS) to cover CO_2 emissions from all large ships of any flag (of 5000 gross tonnage and above) entering EU ports.[194] Shipping companies are required to purchase and surrender (use) EU ETS emission allowances (or international credits, subject to limitations) for each tonne of reported CO_2 (or CO_2 equivalent) emissions within the scope of the EU ETS system.[195] The EU unilateralism in the regulation of GHG emissions from shipping will no

186 Andrew Friedman, 'The International Maritime Organization's Revised Greenhouse Gas Strategy: A Political Signal of Shipping's Regulatory Future' (2024) *The International Journal of Marine and Coastal Law* 1, 12–13.

187 Ibid 13.

188 Ibid.

189 Ibid.

190 Ibid 15.

191 Joe Lo, 'Latin America leads resistance to global shipping emission tax', *Climate Home News* (Web Page, 2023) <https://www.climatechangenews.com/2023/06/29/shipping-imo-brazil-tax-levy-emissions-shipping/>.

192 Gary Dixon, 'China urges rejection of emissions levy as it blasts 'unrealistic' wealthy nations', *TradeWinds* (Web Page, 2023) <https://www.tradewindsnews.com/esg/china-urges-rejection-of-emissions-levy-as-it-blasts-unrealistic-wealthy-nations/2-1-1479115>.

193 Friedman (n 187) 17.

194 *Directive (EU) 2023/959 of 10 May 2023, amending Directive 2003/87/EC establishing a system for greenhouse gas emission allowance trading within the Union and Decision (EU) 2015/1814 concerning the establishment and operation of a market stability reserve for the Union greenhouse gas emission trading system* [2023] OJ L 130/134.

195 Ibid.

doubt generate significant costs for shipping companies and concerns from other shipping powers (such as China, Japan, and South Korea), some of whom have previously expressed support for different approaches.[196]

Another challenge for the mitigation of GHG emissions from shipping is the mitigation of other types of airborne emissions. Annex VI of MARPOL has imposed very strict limits on sulphur (SOx) emissions, namely at 0.5% m/m and 0.1% m/m in designated special areas.[197] SOx is very harmful to human health, with this cap resulting in an estimated prevention of 570,000 premature deaths.[198] However, the cap has resulted in the search for fuels that burn more cleanly or exhaust cleaning "scrubber" systems as an alternative.[199] Both of these methods are anticipated to result in comparatively higher GHG emissions. Ships using scrubbers, for example, are expected to have higher fuel consumption, resulting in more GHG emissions.[200] The manufacturing process behind low-sulphur fuels also utilises more energy, resulting in further emissions.[201] Also, while an alternative fuel such as liquid natural gas may be used, which would result in a 100% reduction in SOx, a 20%–23% reduction in CO_2, and an 85% reduction in nitrous oxides, it would also be accompanied by an increase in emissions of unburnt methane or methane "slip".[202] Methane has been found to result in 86 times worse warming over a 20-year period than equivalent carbon emissions and hence, is a highly undesirable side effect of a potential change to low-sulphur fuels.[203] Other types of "ultra-low" sulphur fuels have been found to result in a 10%–80% increase in the production of black carbon, a substance that is extremely hazardous to human health and is also a GHG.[204]

Furthermore, atmospheric sulphur has been found to act as a cooling agent, reducing the warming effects of climate change by reflecting sunlight. One study has argued that the loss of this effect would be the equivalent of increasing shipping CO_2 emissions by 30%.[205] There is also some concern that the costs of these new measures may incentivise road transport, a far greater source of GHG emissions, although this seems unlikely given the other advantages of shipping.[206] Ultimately, it is somewhat of a regulatory oversight that these

196 Friedman (n 187) 12–18.
197 *MARPOL* (n 13) Annex VI reg 14.
198 Vasiliki Zisi et al., 'The impact of the 2020 sulfur cap on maritime CO_2 emissions' (2021) 6(4) *Maritime Business Review* 339, 340.
199 Ibid.
200 Ibid 340–341.
201 Ibid.
202 Ibid.
203 Paul Gilbert et al., 'Assessment of full life-cycle air emissions of alternative shipping fuels' (2018) 172 *Journal of Cleaner Production* 85–866.
204 Zisi et al. (n 199) 341.
205 Christos A Kontovas, 'Integration of air quality and climate change policies in shipping: the case of sulfur emissions regulation' (2020) 113 *Marine Policy* 103815, 8.
206 Zisi et al. (n 199) 342–343, 353–355.

two highly intertwined emission types are dealt with by separate regimes at differing stages of development. A focus for the IMO going forward will likely be upon harmonising these regimes lest the attempt at solving the problem of one type of emission exacerbates the other.

Concluding remarks

The regulation of vessel-source pollution is complex, wide-ranging, and vital for the health of the marine environment and the planet. The IMO, as the designated responsible body by UNCLOS for pollution prevention from shipping, has proven active in this space. However, the advent of climate change and the development of new technologies have ensured that the IMO and the broader shipping industry cannot rest on their laurels. Tackling vessel-source GHG emissions has been a difficult goal fraught with competing priorities and economic conditions. Because the nature of the shipping industry is inherently international, states prefer legally binding international rules and standards.

Nevertheless, the challenge lies ahead regarding the type of mechanism that will eventually be agreed upon by the IMO. The ITLOS Advisory Opinion has increased the urgency of these efforts and clarified states' obligations in relation to vessel-source GHG emissions. Ultimately, as UN Trade and Development stated in its annual review of maritime transport: "The maritime sector now stands at a pivotal moment, facing the daunting challenge of decarbonisation while navigating economic and geopolitical headwinds".[207] It is important that the IMO and its member states stay the course in the face of these challenges in order to do their part in addressing the planetary crisis of climate change.

207 UN Trade and Development, *Review of Maritime Transport 2023* (Web Page, 2023) <https://unctad.org/publication/review-maritime-transport-2023>.

9 Institutional compliance mechanisms for International Maritime Organization treaties

Regime building for the next crisis

Rebecca Prentiss Pskowski

Introduction

This chapter analyses the adoption of novel institutional treaty compliance mechanisms by the International Maritime Organization (IMO) as a case of ongoing international legal regime building necessary to defend the IMO's preeminent role in the international regulation of shipping. In the face of climate change, marine pollution, and other uncertain ocean futures we cannot today predict, further development of the IMO's compliance competencies may be needed in order for the organisation to retain its position as the preeminent forum for the development and refinement of international maritime treaties. An organisation that started as a "rich men's club" for the traditional maritime states to coordinate maritime safety standards transformed over the second half of the twentieth century into a universal organisation with a strong environmental mandate.[1] Now the climate crisis is forcing the IMO back into the limelight in the twenty-first century, with new expectations of international organisation transparency and accountability. Therefore, it is hoped that a better understanding of how the IMO comes to accept new compliance mechanisms will better equip the organisation's stakeholders to confront not only today's debates over international shipping's greenhouse gas (GHG) emissions but whatever the uncertain futures of the law of the sea may bring tomorrow.

1 For reference to the "rich men's club" moniker see, e.g. Yoshio Sasamura '34 Years of IMO' [1993] (4) *IMO News* 17, 18. For more on the history and transformation of the IMO during the twentieth century, see Ademun-Odeke 'From the "Constitution of the Maritime Safety Committee" to the "Constitution of the Council": Will the IMCO Experience Repeat Itself at the IMO Nearly Fifty Years On? The Juridical Politics of an International Organization' (2007) 43(1) *Texas International Law Journal*, 55; Agustín Blanco-Bazán, 'Implementation of IMO Conventions by Flag and Port States' in Alastair Couper and Edgar Gold (eds) *The Marine Environment and Sustainable Development: Law, Policy, and Science* (Law of the Sea Institute, University of Hawaii, 1991) 448, 468–475; Kaldone G Nweheid 'The International Maritime Organization: A Venezuelan Perspective' (1986) 6 *Ocean Yearbook* 171.

DOI: 10.4324/9781003518570-9

The IMO's treaty system is substantively comprehensive and enjoys an exceptionally high level of ratification.[2] The IMO plays a pivotal role in the international law of the sea regime, as the generator and custodian of "generally accepted international rules and standards", incorporated by reference into the United Nations Convention on the Law of the Sea (UNCLOS).[3] However, the IMO has been significantly slower than comparable specialised agencies such as the International Labour Organization (ILO) and the International Civil Aviation Organization (ICAO) in adopting institutionalised or centralised treaty compliance mechanisms.[4]

Recent decades have seen challenges to the legitimacy of the IMO as the forum for international shipping regulation. Critics have questioned whether the IMO's treaties and the law of the sea jurisdictional principles undergirding those treaties are adequate to protect seafarers, the marine environment, and the climate.

2 See, e.g. Laurent Fedi, 'International Maritime Regulation: Closing the Gaps Between Successful Achievements and Persistent Insufficiencies' in Roger Vickerman and Edoardo Marcucci (eds), *International Encyclopedia of Transportation* (Elsevier, 2021) vol 5, 600, 603; Frederick J Kenney, 'Global Regulation of Ships: The Future of Development and Implementation at the International Maritime Organization' (2018) 42(2) *Tulane Maritime Law Journal* 259, 261; André Nollkaemper, 'Improving Compliance with the International Law of Marine Environmental Protection: The Role of the European Union' in Jonathan Golub (ed), *Global Competition and EU Environmental Policy* (Routledge, 1998) 85, 86.

3 Craig H Allen, 'Revisiting the Thames Formula: The Evolving Role of the International Maritime Organization and Its Member States in Implementing the 1982 Law of the Sea Convention' (2008) 10(2) *San Diego International Law Journal* 265, 288–290; *United Nations Convention on the Law of the Sea*, opened for signature 10 December 1994, 1833–1835 UNTS 3 (entered into force 16 November 1994).

4 Hooghe and Marks analysed 72 international organisations for evidence of "delegation" – "conditional grant of authority by member states to an independent body", and "pooling" – joint decision-making by member states. Liesbet Hooghe and Gary Marks, 'Delegation and Pooling in International Organizations' (2015) 10(3) *Review of International Organizations* 305, 307. This definition of IO "delegation" would include my concept of institutional compliance mechanisms. Hooghe and Marks identified the IMO as an organisation with "extensive pooling and weak delegation" – "delegation to independent non-state bodies is minimal". Ibid 309. The ICAO, the ILO, and 52 other studied organisations displayed *more* delegation than the IMO, while only 8 organisations displayed *less* delegation (9 organisations displayed the same degree of delegation as the IMO). Ibid Figure 1. "The mobilization of shame is an established compliance tactic in UN-related agencies… IMO is not nearly as bold in using it as is ILO." Frederic L Kirgis Jr, 'Shipping' in Oscar Schachter and Christopher C Joyner (eds), *United Nations Legal Order* (Cambridge University Press, 1995) 715, 744–746. "When it comes to global safety oversight of its own members and despite all differences between the two transport modes, the IMO is still lagging behind the ICAO." Henning Jessen and Ling Zhu, 'From a Voluntary Self-Assessment to a Mandatory Audit Scheme: Monitoring the Implementation of IMO Instruments' [2016] (3) *Lloyd's Maritime and Commercial Law Quarterly* 389, 394. "Like the ILO, the IMO should start by keeping a closer eye on the behaviour of its members… Second, the IMO should have the same authority to investigate accidents as [ICAO] has when an air disaster occurs." Philippe Boisson, 'New Dispensation for Safety at Sea: Reasons and Conditions' (1994) 25(2) *Journal of Maritime Law and Commerce* 309, 316.

In response, the IMO has borrowed from other international legal regimes to develop and adopt novel institutional compliance mechanisms, including the International Convention on Standards of Training, Certification and Watchkeeping for Seafarers (STCW) 95 List of Confirmed Parties and the IMO Member State Audit Scheme.

This chapter asks what lessons these processes hold for future challenges to the IMO's legitimacy in combatting vessel-source pollution, including the ongoing IMO negotiations over the regulation of greenhouse gas emissions. In the face of uncertain futures, can institutional compliance mechanisms give the IMO the adaptability and dexterity it will need to continue to fulfil its role as shipping's global regulator?

IMO and compliance

The IMO was conceived, and still functions today, as a forum for the international negotiation of maritime treaties and standards. In the traditional maritime treaty model, the IMO's role is that of a negotiating forum and depository. Implementation, compliance, and enforcement are the responsibilities of sovereign member states who, after ratifying an IMO convention, must then incorporate that convention's standards into domestic law and exercise enforcement authority in their capacities as flag, port, and coastal states.[5]

An institutional compliance mechanism is a treaty compliance provision that, contrary to the "traditional model" just described, vests executive authority with an international organisation (e.g. the IMO).[6] In the international maritime law context, institutional compliance mechanisms can be contrasted with other treaty compliance functions executed by flag, coastal, or port states. Port state control (PSC) memoranda of understanding (MOUs), for example, are an institutional compliance mechanism external to the IMO. While the PSC MOUs apply standards developed and maintained by the IMO, they do so by exercising their sovereign port state authority. There is no role for the IMO

5 Allen (n 3) 290–299.

6 This article's definition of "institutional compliance mechanism" builds upon broader definitions of treaty "compliance mechanisms" developed by scholars including Oran Young, Nils Goeteyn, and Frank Maes. Oran R Young, *International Cooperation: Building Regimes for Natural Resources and the Environment* (Cornell University Press, 1989) 20–21. Nils Goeteyn and Frank Maes, 'Compliance Mechanisms in Multilateral Environmental Agreements: An Effective Way to Improve Compliance?' (2011) 10(4) *Chinese Journal of International Law* 791, 797. The terms "institutional compliance mechanisms" and "institutionalised compliance mechanisms" appear in international relations and international law scholarship, but are not yet well defined. Tanja A Börzel et al., 'Obstinate and Inefficient: Why Member States Do Not Comply with European Law' (2010) 43(11) *Comparative Political Studies* 1363, 1383; Goeteyn and Maes (n 6) 814. See also James Harrison, 'Compliance Mechanisms Under Treaties Relating to Protection of the Marine Environment' in Rosemary Rayfuse, Aline Jaeckel, and Natalie Klein (eds), *Research Handbook on International Marine Environmental Law* (Edward Elgar, 2023) 104.

or any IMO subsidiary body in evaluating flag state performance as MOUs maintain their own secretariats, which are not IMO bodies, for this purpose.[7]

The IMO has always had an institutional compliance mandate, albeit a limited one. From the organisation's inception, various reporting requirements incorporated into most twentieth-century IMO treaties obliged state parties to inform the IMO Secretariat regarding implementation and enforcement.[8] State performance in meeting these reporting requirements has been poor.[9]

Traditional treaty reporting requirements are ineffective at promoting compliance because they impose no negative or positive consequences – they have no teeth. The primary obstacle in establishing more rigorous institutional compliance mechanisms for IMO treaties is the consensual nature of the treaty-making process, as IMO member states are reluctant to delegate any of their sovereign enforcement powers to the IMO. As a member of the IMO Secretariat once trenchantly put it: "Where other countries are concerned, we would wish greater powers for IMO, but of course not for our own country".[10]

So, how does a new IMO institutional compliance mechanism come into being?

The STCW 95 List

One major industry transformation that took place during the tenure of the IMO, which led to a major challenge to the organisation's legitimacy, is the globalisation of the maritime labour force. At the time of the organisation's founding, merchant vessel crews largely shared the nationality of the vessel on which they served. Given the composition of the global fleet at mid-twentieth century, this meant that most seafarers were nationals of one of the Western "traditional maritime states". The training and certification of seafarers were governed by domestic law; each flag state educated and evaluated its deck and

7 For a more detailed review of the role of PSC in IMO treaty compliance, see Erik Jaap Molenaar, 'Port State Jurisdiction: Toward Comprehensive, Mandatory and Global Coverage' (2007) 38(1–2) *Ocean Development and International Law* 225.

8 Yoshifumi Tanaka, 'Reflections on Reporting Systems in Treaties Concerning the Protection of the Marine Environment' (2009) 40(2) *Ocean Development and International Law* 146, 156.

9 Ibid 157; Felicity Deane, Anna Huggins, and Md Saiful Karim, 'Measuring, Monitoring, Reporting and Verification of Shipping Emissions: Evaluating Transparency and Answerability' (2019) 28(3) *Review of European Community & International Environmental Law* 258, 266.

10 OHJ Dijxhoorn, 'Port and Shipping Management: The Role of IMO' (1993) 17(5) *Marine Policy* 363, 366. Dijxhoorn, and other commentators, note that finances are the other major limiting factor to the development of more rigorous IMO institutional compliance mechanisms. This paper focuses on the negotiations leading to incremental cessions of sovereignty and not substantively address the question of financing for institutional compliance mechanisms. See also Boisson (n 4) 316: "In the IMO, these measures are at present blocked by two major obstacles, politics, and money. The political problem requires redefinition of the sovereignty of each member State within the Organisation, while the economic difficulty relates to the budget of an institution whose main contributors are not necessarily the most anxious to strengthen standardisation requirements, even in order to reduce accidents".

engineering officers according to its specific standards. Similarly, these states established the certification and documentation criteria for ratings (unlicensed crew members such as ordinary and able-bodied seamen). In the traditional maritime states, maritime labour unions were strong, and wages were relatively high.

The rise of open registries with liberal regulations on crew nationality meant that vessel operators were free to hire whomever they chose. The concurrent forces of decolonialisation and rapid industrialisation in the Global South provided a seemingly endless supply of workers willing to work for far less than the standard wage of a seafarer from the traditional maritime states of Northern Europe.

By 1971, there was sufficient concern about the quality of global maritime training for the IMO to initiate negotiations on a binding international instrument.[11] The result was the International Convention on Standards of Training, Certification and Watchkeeping for Seafarers, 1978, the first international treaty to set standards for the education and licencing of merchant mariners.[12]

The STCW entered into force in 1984. It was widely adopted and, by the late 1980s, it covered more than 97% of world merchant tonnage.[13] But as additional parties signed on, and the STCW coverage extended, the treaty's credibility paradoxically diminished.[14] The STCW laid out the essential capabilities for seafarers of various ranks. However, by its terms, the treaty only required that those standards of training be met "to the satisfaction of the [national] Administration". As membership of the STCW grew and diversified, vessel operators, port states, and coastal states alike started to doubt the value of "STCW-compliant" seafarers' papers.

Suspicion was especially high among the "traditional maritime states", particularly those of Northern Europe. Highly unionised seafarers from the traditional maritime states perceived new sources of maritime labour as a threat to their job security and the relatively high collectively bargained wages

11 EO Agbakoba, 'The International Convention on Standards of Training, Certification and Watchkeeping for Seafarers, 1978' in *The Development and Implementation of International Maritime Training Standards: A Contribution to the Revision of the STCW Convention, 15–16 March 1994* (World Maritime University and the Nautical Institute, 1994) 13, 13. The IMO and the ILO had collaborated as early as 1964 to develop a voluntary instrument, the Document for Guidance, which made recommendations regarding the education and training of officers and ratings. Ibid.

12 *International Convention on Standards of Training, Certification and Watchkeeping for Seafarers*, opened for signature 7 July 1978, 1361–1362 UNTS 2 (entered into force 28 April 1984).

13 Mario Valenzuela, 'Enforcing Rules Against Vessel-Source Degradation of the Marine Environment: Coastal, Flag and Port State Jurisdiction' in Davor Vidas and Willy Østreng (eds), *Order for the Oceans at the Turn of the Century* (Kluwer Law International, 1999) 485, 501.

14 Ibid.

and benefits.[15] The International Transportation Workers' Federation (ITF) was keen to stoke fears of allegedly underqualified seafarers from developing countries.[16]

A proposal to revise the STCW, to incorporate "modern training and certification arrangements", was submitted to the IMO Maritime Safety Committee (MSC) in 1991 by the International Shipowners' Federation (ISF). In October 1992, the United States proposed that the pending agenda item related to the ISF submission be expanded and clarified as a "comprehensive review" of the entire treaty.[17] By the time that the US submission came up for discussion, two major oil spills in European waters had dramatically shifted the political situation.

In foul weather on 3 December 1992, the Greek-flagged double-hulled tanker *Aegean Sea* ran aground off the Galician coast, near A Coruña, Spain. One month later, on 5 January 1993, the Liberian-flagged single-hulled tanker *Braer* grounded in a similar incident in the Shetland Islands. Both spills had major impacts on the marine life and local fishing communities. The *Braer* spill, in particular, had a major impact on public opinion as it occurred in a remote, beautiful, and culturally significant archipelago. A long-standing risk of harm to the Shetlands due to the surrounding North Sea oil exploitation had now materialised.[18]

The *Aegean Sea* and *Braer* wrecks came weeks before the January 1993 meeting of the MSC that was to consider the US proposal to conduct a

15 Nathan Lillie, *A Global Union for Global Workers: Collective Bargaining and Regulatory Politics in Maritime Shipping* (Routledge, 2006), 97–98.

16 Ibid.

17 United States, *Development of Amendments to the STCW Convention,* 61st Maritime Safety Comm, IMO Doc MSC 61/4/3 (16 October 1992) 1. In addition to the mentioned concerns regarding uniformity, other limitations were technological – the 1978 treaty was drafted before the broad adoption of simulator training in maritime education – and pedagogical – the 1978 treaty assumed a traditional mode of maritime education, where classroom instruction paired with arbitrary lengths of sea service was presumed to impart competence. By the late twentieth century, crews were far smaller than they had been, limiting the opportunity for the nominally "certified" newcomer to learn on the job, and there were growing calls for a more "functional" approach that would attempt to evaluate the seafarer's competence based not on classroom performance, but on actual task performance.

18 It should be noted that the impact of the *Braer* on the IMO, on international politics, and indeed on this author, was magnified by its occurrence in the UK. The IMO is, of course, based in London, and British shipping interests are over-represented, if only by virtue of their proximity. Additionally, maritime as well as general press coverage of the *Braer* was extensive, Anglophone, and, judging by the press clippings collected by the IMO Maritime Knowledge Center, both well attended and well preserved by maritime policymakers. The *Aegean Sea* received less international press coverage by comparison, but both spills took place in Europe, and therefore received relatively outsized coverage and attention, as compared to oil spills in, for example, the Middle East and Africa. See generally David I Little, Stephen R J Sheppard, and David Hulme, 'A Perspective on Oil Spills: What We Should Have Learned about Global Warming' (2021) 202 *Ocean & Coastal Management* 105509.

comprehensive STCW review. Public and governmental anger over the casualties increased the pressure on the IMO to take action. While there were legitimate questions about the decisions made by the masters of both vessels, it remained unclear as to whether inadequate training or certification was in any way responsible for the losses. This did not prevent the ITF and others from capitalising on the attention. It did not help that in both cases, the ships' entire crews were saved by daring helicopter rescues. A letter writer to *Lloyd's List*, identifying himself as Odd S Pettersen, master mariner, summarises this view:

> Shame on the tanker manager/owner and *Braer*'s senior officers for allowing the Shetland disaster to happen…
>
> We are talking about good professional seamanship. Also, a master doesn't leave his ship before the ship leaves him.
>
> Why are many managers/owners trying to save money at the cost of safety by choosing low-paid, less qualified, inexperienced senior officers and letting the best Scandinavian, British, and others go idle because they request a salary they so rightly deserve?[19]

The MSC approved the US proposal and delegated the project to the Sub-Committee on Standards of Training and Watchkeeping (STW), with a target completion date of 1996.[20]

Across the Channel, in Brussels, the *Aegean Sea* and *Braer* spills served as an accelerant to European Community/European Union efforts to develop a common maritime policy.[21] The European transport commissioner was motivated to rush the publication of the Common Policy for Safe Seas in February 1993.[22]

The Common Policy was shortly followed by a commission proposal for a directive on the minimum level of training for seafarers in May 1993.[23] The proposed directive would limit the crew of EU-flagged vessels by requiring that seafarers be certified either by an EU member state or by a non-EU state (a so-called "third country") whose STCW compliance had been ratified by

19 Odd S Pettersen, 'Letter to the Editor: Saving Money at the Cost of Safety', *Lloyd's List*, 13 January 1993.

20 *Report of the Maritime Safety Committee on its Sixty-First Session*, 61st Maritime Safety Comm, IMO Doc MSC 61/21 (20 January 1993) para 4.19.

21 The Maastricht Treaty entered into force on 1 November 1993, and from that date the modern European Union came into being.

22 European Commission, *Communication "A Common Policy on Safe Seas" COM(93)66 final,* 62nd Maritime Safety Comm, IMO Doc MSC 62/INF.14 (1 April 1993); Athanasios A Pallis, *The Common EU Maritime Transport Policy: Policy Europeanisation in the 1990s* (Ashgate, 2002) 104.

23 *Proposal for a Council Directive on the Minimum Level of Training for Maritime Occupations* [1993] OJ C 212/1.

the EU. Prior to this proposal, the status quo was that individual EU member states, like all STCW parties, had the right to make their own determinations as to which nations' STCW certificates to accept as adequate and compliant.[24]

At the next STW meeting, IMO Secretary General William O'Neil made clear that the organisation would prioritise the revision with an accelerated timetable and the unprecedented use of a group of "independent consultants" to develop the amended text, which would be approved by member states.[25]

The really novel measure of STCW 95, regarding the IMO's involvement with implementation, is the institution of a "List of Confirmed Parties" which is often, though never officially, referred to as the STCW 95 "White List".[26]

Under Regulation I/7 of the convention, states parties are required to submit, within one year after entry into force for the party concerned, a comprehensive initial implementation report detailing, *inter alia*, the identity of the governmental agency, ministry, or department responsible for the STCW 95 administration, the domestic legislative and administrative measures taken to effectuate treaty standards, and details of domestic training, licensing, and certification requirements.[27] Regulation I/8 and related provisions of the mandatory STCW Code provide that subsequent reports, including an independent evaluation of training and assessment activities and the administration of certification systems, be submitted at least every five years.

So far, this is just a procedural reporting requirement. However, Regulation I/7, through Section A-I/7 of the mandatory STCW Code, further requires the secretary general to maintain a list of "competent persons", approved by the Maritime Safety Committee, to review the STCW 95 party submissions.

24 Pallis (n 22) 114.

25 *Proposed Timetable for Revision of the STCW Convention*, 24th Sub-Comm on Standards of Training and Watchkeeping, IMO Doc STW 24/WP.1 (8 March 1993); *Ninth Session of the Joint IMO/ILO Committee on Training (JCT9)*, 63rd Maritime Safety Comm, IMO Doc MSC 63/4/2 (11 February 1994).

26 Even IMO Secretariat members have been observed to use the "white list" designation. See, e.g. Lawrence D Barchue, 'The Voluntary IMO Member State Audit Scheme: An Accountability Regime for States on Maritime Affairs' (2009) 8(1) *WMU Journal of Maritime Affairs* 61, 70 ('VIMSAS: An Accountability Regime'). The terminology was presumably borrowed from the various regional port state control memoranda of understanding (MOUs), whose members pool their annual port state inspections data to develop risk-based "white", "grey", and "black lists" of flag states. See, e.g. Paris Memorandum of Understanding on Port State Control, *White, Grey and Black List*, (Web Page) <https://www.parismou.org/detentions-banning/white-grey-and-black-list>. Stan Morrison provides a diplomatic account of why the "white list" terminology is officially disfavored in the IMO context: "Regulation 1/7 was drafted intentionally to have positive rather than negative implications. The term white list is used by some as a contrast to black list. However, this terminology is not necessarily the most suitable because it implies disapproval of those Parties not so listed. Any use of the list must take into account the fact that an evaluation based strictly on a written report prepared by the Party concerned can only be a limited evaluation". WSG Morrison, *Competent Crews = Safer Ships* (World Maritime University, 1998) 287.

27 Morrison (n 26) 287.

Panels of competent persons, composed of either three or five members, shall meet, at the discretion of the secretary general, to evaluate state party implementation reports. The panel then provides its opinion to the secretary general, who then prepares a report for submission to the MSC. If the MSC deems that a party has demonstrated "that full and complete effect is given to the provisions of the Convention", the committee will add that party to the list of confirmed parties. States parties are entitled to have a representative present at any meeting of competent persons evaluating their reports, for the purposes of clarification, and, prior to submitting a report to the MSC, the secretary general is also required to seek further clarification from the party, where necessary.

This provision remains unique among the IMO conventions, and commentators have termed it the leading edge of "the creeping erosion of sovereignty".[28] Looking forward, senior IMO Secretariat staffer Lawrence Barchue wrote:

> the notion of sovereignty, through which states had benefited economically from the registration of ships and their use of the freedom of the high seas, had been breached by the aforementioned amendment to the 1978 STCW Convention. It then fell squarely to the IMO to develop this new regulatory space further and demonstrate that its work over five decades to regulate international shipping would not continue to be questioned.[29]

IMSAS

Even during the adoption of the STCW reforms in 1995, a simultaneous and more extensive reform of the IMO treaty compliance monitoring was underway, primarily within the organisation's Sub-Committee on Flag State Implementation (FSI).[30] While the STCW 95 List focused on reforming a single instrument, the ongoing reforms within the FSI had a much broader scope, aiming to introduce new accountability measures for flag state compliance not only with the STCW but also with the IMO's other key instruments like the International Convention for the Prevention of Pollution from Ships 1973, as modified by the Protocol of 1978 (MARPOL) and the International

28 Michael Ekow Manuel and Raphael Baumler, 'The Evolution of Seafarer Education and Training in International Law' in Proshanto K Mukerjee, Maximo Q Mejia and Jingjing Xu (eds), *Maritime Law in Motion* (Springer, 2020) 471, 284.

29 Lawrence Barchue, 'The IMO, the Audit Scheme, and Its Role in Global Ocean Governance' in David Joseph Attard, Rosalie P Balkin and Donald W Greig (eds), *The IMLI Treatise on Global Ocean Governance* (Oxford University Press, 2018) 250, 256 ('The IMO, the Audit Scheme, and Its Role').

30 This sub-committee was succeeded, in 2014, by the Sub-Committee on Implementation of IMO Instruments (III).

Convention for the Safety of Life at Sea (SOLAS), alongside significant instruments such as the Convention on the International Regulations for Preventing Collisions at Sea (COLREG) and conventions governing load lines and tonnage measurement.[31]

In 1994, the UK proposed independent and mandatory audits of every flag state registry, including an audit of any organisation to which a sovereign nation had delegated responsibility for its registry.[32] The UK further proposed that major incidents should be investigated by an (unidentified) independent organisation, which should then make a public report. The dry language of the sub-committee report indicates that this proposal was rather controversial: "Some delegations were of the opinion that the United Kingdom paper was very useful and provocative, but others felt that it must be considered very carefully as it raised certain legal issues".[33]

In 1999, the FSI developed a flag state self-assessment form (SAF).[34] The SAF was intended to aid individual member states in their internal improvements of implementation measures. Additionally, states were invited to bring problems identified to the IMO for technical assistance and submit the results to the IMO with the hope of developing an anonymised data source for the use of IMO committees and other member states.[35]

The SAF was not a great success. In June 2004, the IMO had received SAF submissions from 58 member states, in addition to 14 subsequent updates.[36]

31 *Protocol of 1978 Relating to the International Convention for the Prevention of Pollution from Ships*, opened for signature 17 February 1978, 1340–1341 UNTS 61 (entered into force 2 October 1983); *International Convention for the Safety of Life at Sea*, opened for signature 1 November 1974, 1184–1185 UNTS 2 (entered into force 25 May 1980); *Convention on the International Regulations for Preventing Collisions at Sea*, opened for signature 20 October 1972, 1050 UNTS 16 (entered into force 15 July 1977). These are the IMO's "three main regulatory international conventions". Agustín Blanco-Bazán, 'The IMO: Working within the UNCLOS Framework and Global Ocean Governance' in David Joseph Attard, Rosalie P Balkin and Donald W Greig (eds), *The IMLI Treatise on Global Ocean Governance* (Oxford University Press, 2018) vol 3, 27, 29.

32 *Responsibilities of Governments Under Safety and Pollution Prevention Conventions*, 3rd Sub-Comm on Flag State Implementation, IMO Doc FSI 3/3/5 (30 December 1994).

33 *Report to the Maritime Safety Committee and the Marine Environmental Protection Committee*, 3rd Sub-Comm on Flag State Implementation, IMO Doc FSI 3/17 (23 March 1995) para 3.4; Keith Hindell, 'Strengthening the Ship Regulating Regime' (1996) 23(4) *Maritime Policy & Management* 371, 379–80.

34 *Self-Assessment of Flag State Performance*, IMO Assembly Res 881, IMO Doc A 21/Res.881 (4 February 2000, adopted 25 November 1999), revoked and replaced by *Self-Assessment of Flag State Performance*, IMO Assembly Res 912, IMO Doc 22/Res.912 (22 January 2002, adopted 29 November 2001).

35 Jessen and Zhu (n 4) 396; John NK Mansell, *Flag State Responsibility: Historical Development and Contemporary Issues* (Springer, 2009) 142.

36 Jessen and Zhu (n 4) 396–397.

More than 100 IMO member states did not submit any SAF, including 7 of the 30 largest flag states by registered tonnage.[37]

Meanwhile, in June 2002, the IMO Council approved a member state proposal to develop an IMO Model Audit Scheme, using the ICAO Universal Safety Oversight Audit Programme (USOAP) as a model.[38] The council remained closely involved with the development of a Voluntary Member State Audit Scheme (VIMSAS) over the next several years, and a joint working group (JWG) was established for that purpose in June 2003.[39] Pilot audits were conducted in 2004, and VIMSAS was finalised and adopted by the assembly in 2005.[40]

VIMSAS included the provisions of SOLAS, MARPOL, tonnage and load line conventions, along with various mandatory protocols.[41] A total of 75 VIMSAS audits were carried out between September 2006 and December 2015, after which time it was replaced by the IMO Member State Audit Scheme (IMSAS).[42] Those audits represented flags registering 94% of world tonnage.

In November 2009, the IMO Assembly adopted Resolution A.1018(26), calling for VIMSAS to transition into a mandatory audit scheme.[43] This endeavour required the amendment of the relevant substantive IMO treaties.[44]

As with the STCW 95 List, aggressive strengthening of European Union maritime safety law and policy is one possible "trigger" for the acceleration of audit proposals that had been slow to catch on when proposed by the UK in 1994. Two major European oil spills, the *Erika* in 1999 off Brittany, France, and the *Prestige* in 2002 off Galicia, Spain, marked a distinct turning point in the EU's response to maritime disasters. For the first time, the decision to take a unified response was not controversial.[45] By the time of the third proposed round of EU reforms, the "Erika III package", EU member states were directed to subject themselves to a VIMSAS audit once every seven years.[46]

37 Ibid 397.

38 Ibid.

39 Barchue, 'VIMSAS: An Accountability Regime' (n 26) 64.

40 Ibid 65–66; *Code for the Implementation of Mandatory IMO Instruments,* IMO Assembly Res 973, IMO Doc A 24/Res.973 (19 December 2005, adopted 1 December 2005); *Framework and Procedures for the Voluntary IMO Member State Audit Scheme,* IMO Assembly Res 974, IMO Doc A 24/Res.974 (21 December 2005, adopted 1 December 2005).

41 Barchue, 'VIMSAS: An Accountability Regime' (n 26) provides a comprehensive list at 66.

42 Barchue, 'The IMO, the Audit Scheme, and Its Role' (29) 261–262.

43 Ibid; *Further Development of the Voluntary IMO Member State Audit Scheme,* IMO Assembly Res 1018, IMO Doc A 26/Res.1018 (18 January 2010, adopted 25 November 2009).

44 Barchue, 'VIMSAS: An Accountability Regime' (2009 n 26) 62; Jessen and Zhu (n 4) 405.

45 Nengye Liu and Frank Maes, 'The European Union's Role in the Prevention of Vessel-Source Pollution and Its Internal Influence' (2009) 15 *Journal of International Maritime Law* 411, 414.

46 Alexander Proelss, 'The 'Erika III' Package: Progress or Breach of International Law?' in Hans-Joachim Koch et al. (eds), *Climate Change and Environmental Hazards Related to Shipping: An International Legal Framework* (Brill, 2013) 129, 132.

The package was adopted in April 2009, months before VIMSAS transitioned into IMSAS.

IMSAS has two major shortcomings, shared with VIMSAS: it lacks both enforcement and transparency.[47] While IMSAS contains detailed provisions for corrective action plans, including an audit follow-up, there is no compulsory element to this aspect of the scheme. There is no mechanism, in IMSAS or elsewhere in mandatory instruments, to mandate state action in response to a negative audit report. In theory, it seems that a delinquent member state could fulfil its obligation to submit to an audit, prepare a minimally adequate corrective action plan, and then take no corrective action, resigning itself to a near-identical performance in its next audit seven years later.

Regarding transparency, audit reports are confidential and only distributed to other member states.[48] Member states are free to release the results of their audits to the public, but a recent visit to the public Global Integrated Shipping Information System (GISIS) database reveals that no mandatory audit reports have yet been released.[49]

The public output of IMSAS comes in the form of anonymised consolidated audit summary reports (CASRs). To date, five CASRs have been released, as well as a meta-analysis of the first four CASRs.[50] The meta-analysis identifies various "main findings", or common points of concern, including, for example, "the lack of continual improvement of the measures taken to give effect to those mandatory IMO instruments" and failings in "the Administration's oversight programme of recognized organizations (ROs) [and] agreement between the Administration and the RO".[51]

47 Robin Churchill, 'Compliance Mechanisms in the International Law of the Sea: From the Individual to the Collective' in Holger P Hestermeyer et al. (eds) *Coexistence, Cooperation and Solidarity: Liber Amicorum Rüdiger Wolfrum* (Martinus Nijhoff, 2012) vol 1, 777, 797; Jessen and Zhu (n 4) 392, 409–411.

48 "One authorized person from each Member State has full access to the audit reports from other Member States, including executive summary reports (ESR), corrective action plans (CAP) and each Member State's comments on the progress of the implementation of its corrective action plans (CPICAP). Member States can designate an authorized person following the procedure specified in Circular Letter No. 3587, dated 15 September 2015." International Maritime Organization, *Member State Audit Scheme* (Web Page) <https://www.imo.org/en/OurWork/MSAS/Pages/Default.aspx>.

49 International Maritime Organization, *GISIS: Member State Audits, Reports Overview* (Web Page) <https://gisis.imo.org/Public/MSA/ReportsOverview.aspx>. A number of voluntary audit reports, conducted under VIMSAS, have been publicly released by the audited states, but that probably reflects a desire among some of the states who submitted to VIMSAS to advertise their relatively high levels of compliance.

50 Available for download at International Maritime Organization, *Analysis of Consolidated Audit Summary Reports (CASR)* (Web Page) <https://www.imo.org/en/OurWork/MSAS/Pages/CASRs.aspx>.

51 *Analysis of Four Consolidated Audit Summary Reports Under the IMO Member State Audit Scheme (IMSAS)*, 7th Sub-Comm on Implementation of IMO Instruments, IMO Doc III 7/INF.27 (6 May 2021) annex, paras 22, 31.

These reports have considerable value, both to the interested public and to the IMO, in that they identify common shortcomings and may, over time, reveal positive and negative trends in state implementation. However, they are rather weak in comparison to the transparency provided by the ICAO USOAP on which IMSAS was initially modelled. The USOAP does not release full audit reports, but it provides country-by-country implementation level data, and the ICAO even provides an interactive data display platform, where individual countries' relative performance, on eight elements of implementation, can be compared.[52]

Unlike the STCW 95 List, which has not seen significant development in the years since its approval, IMSAS is still very much a mechanism in development. At the time of writing, the IMO Council is currently considering a secretariat-led proposal to update the scheme in advance of the second audit cycle.[53] Notably, the proposal includes the potential "prioritisation" of the second round of audits to make best use of limited IMO resources. Prioritisation would entail a "risk-based" approach where each state would be assigned a "risk profile" based on the outcome of the first round of audits and audit follow-ups.[54] "High-risk" states could then be prioritised and scheduled for audit relatively early in the audit cycle to allow for more time and resources to be dedicated, while "low-risk" states could be scheduled for "late" audits towards the end of the audit cycle. As the audit schedule has been public, at least up to this point, this prioritisation proposal has the potential to disclose the identities of the presumably low-performing states that have been designated "high risk", bringing a new element of transparency to the scheme. The joint working group on the Member State Audit Scheme, dormant since 2012, met again in October 2023 to discuss this proposal.[55]

Negotiation of institutional compliance mechanisms at IMO: a proposed deliberative process

How did IMO member states agree to cede some fraction of their sovereign rights and adopt both the STCW 95 List and IMSAS? Drawing on the work of Louis and Maertens, this chapter theorises that both successful negotiations resulted from conflicts of institutional IMO norms. Member states were willing to expand the organisation's executive authority into jurisdictions traditionally held only by states in order to resolve this conflict.

52 International Civil Aviation Organization, *Safety Audit Results: USOAP Interactive Viewer* (Web Page) <www.icao.int/safety/Pages/USOAP-Results.aspx>. See also Jessen and Zhu (n 4) 391–393.

53 *Further Development of the Scheme,* 128th Session of IMO Council, IMO Doc C 128/7/1 (25 October 2022).

54 Ibid annex, paras 11–14.

55 *Provisional Agenda*, 7th Joint Working Group on Member State Audit, IMO Doc JWGMSA 7/1 (26 April 2023).

The identified IMO norms are global uniformity, procedural equality, and technical decision-making:[56]

1. IMO stakeholders[57] uphold the ideal of global uniformity: regulation of international shipping ought to be global, to maintain a "level playing field" and allow ships (and shipping) companies to operate worldwide. A corollary to this global-uniformity norm is the belief that the IMO is the (only) proper forum for the development of global standards.
2. IMO stakeholders are committed to procedural equality of all member states. This derives from the underlying international law principle of sovereign equality and can most succinctly be phrased as "one nation, one vote". However, voting is not the most relevant context for the reinforcement of this norm. While decision by majority vote is authorised by the organisation's parliamentary rules, in practice, decisions are almost always made by consensus. Consensus decision-making, where any member can veto any decision, can be used by international organisations to maintain the "narrative" of sovereign equality.[58] Collaterally and reinforcing the value placed on procedural equality, IMO stakeholders are sensitive to historical and contemporary economic and political inequities in international relations. This recognition can be seen in the insistence on regional representation in small-group deliberations.
3. IMO stakeholders believe in technical decision-making. Agreements should be reached based on consideration of acknowledged technical expertise, not political bargaining. This is a common norm among international organisations, especially "specialised" organisations like the IMO.

When, in the face of IMO inaction, an advantaged maritime state or group of states enacts unilateral or regional regulation, the IMO norms of global uniformity and procedural equality come into conflict. The unilateral or regional regulation challenges the global uniformity norm. To re-establish global uniformity and reassert the IMO's regulatory preeminence, global standards must be brought into line with the unilateral or regional regulation. Nevertheless, for the plenary of member states to embrace a new global standard solely due to the preemptive and unilateral adoption by a powerful state or group of states would contravene the norms of procedural equality and technical expertise.

56 Marieke Louis and Lucile Maertens, *Why International Organizations Hate Politics: Depoliticizing the World* (Routledge, 2021) 36–40.
57 IMO member states and the non-governmental and inter-governmental organisations with consultative status at the IMO.
58 Vincent Pouliot, *International Pecking Orders* (Cambridge University Press, 2016) 100.

In the cases of both the STCW 95 and IMSAS, to resolve the conflict between the IMO's norms of uniformity and sovereign equality, IMO stakeholders engage in a process of depoliticisation, whereby the offending unilateral or regional standard is technicised, diluted, and delayed[59]:

1. A proposal to strengthen compliance, modelled on an existing or proposed non-IMO compliance mechanism, is introduced to an IMO deliberative body by an influential state or group of states.
2. Other states object that the proposal will impinge on their sovereignty and is of a political character. There is no possibility of consensus in the plenary debate (stalemate).
3. IMO leadership (elected committee chairs, the secretary general, secretariat staff) propose moving the discussion to an expert intersessional group discussion for further development.
4. Plenary agrees to an expert group (or intersessional working group, correspondence group, etc.), conditioned on regional representation to maintain the norm of procedural equality.
5. The actual composition of the expert group is, predictably, not very equitable, given the disparate resources of state delegations. The expert group includes heavy industry participation, with representatives of private firms contributing both via industry non-governmental organisations (NGOs) in consultative status and via direct and indirect industry participation in member state delegations. This industry participation facilitates the "technicisation" of the proposal, and the expert deliberation proceeds on "technical" lines.
6. The coalition of influential states, industry, and leadership presents the expert-developed proposal to the plenary and represents the revised proposal as an industry-approved technical product justified by the needs of the global shipping trade, rather than a political product put forward by a powerful member state.
7. Finally, the depoliticised product returns to the plenary, where it can be presented as consistent with IMO norms and accepted by consensus.

This process preserves the IMO's institutional norms and institutional identity. Recognising and further developing a model of this process can facilitate efficient IMO decision-making and the development of new institutional compliance mechanisms and competencies. Efficient negotiation and institutional innovation can enable the IMO to address new and unforeseen problems, thereby preserving, strengthening, and hopefully improving international shipping regulation and the broader law of the sea regime.

59 Ibid 3–6.

Institutional compliance development in action? – IMO and GHG regulation

The negotiation of the two compliance mechanisms discussed above, the STCW 95 List and IMSAS, are established historical facts. Although the mechanisms, especially IMSAS, are not static, the entire chain of events from proposal to the successful adoption of the novel institutional compliance mechanism can be traced comprehensively. Is it possible to observe and document this type of negotiation in real time? This section attempts to map the proposed process onto an ongoing IMO negotiation.

GHG regulation is the most visible, most political, and most consequential policy issue currently under consideration at the IMO.[60] The evolving international climate change governance regime recognises that emissions control for international shipping and aviation cannot be accomplished at a strictly national level. Pursuant to the Kyoto Protocol, signatories to the UN Framework Convention on Climate Change (UNFCCC) explicitly designated the IMO as the forum in which nation states should pursue limitations on future greenhouse gas emissions from international shipping.[61] The ICAO was assigned an analogous role in regard to international aviation.

Considering the historical and present-day inconsistency of flag state enforcement of the IMO environmental and safety standards, and the limitations of PSC, there is reason to question the effectiveness of any future IMO limits on GHG emissions, absent improved compliance mechanisms.[62]

At present, the IMO data collection system (DCS) is strictly information gathering and cannot be considered a treaty compliance mechanism. However,

60 Matt Apuzzo and Sarah Hurtes, 'Tasked to Fight Climate Change, a Secretive UN Agency Does the Opposite' *New York Times* (online, 3 June 2021) <https://www.nytimes.com/2021/06/03/world/europe/climate-change-un-international-maritime-organization.html>; Aldo Chircop and Desai Shan, 'Governance of International Shipping in the Era of Decarbonisation: New Challenges for the IMO?' in Proshanto K Mukerjee, Maximo Q Mejia and Jingjing Xu (eds) *Maritime Law in Motion* (Springer, 2020) 97, 98–99; Craig Shaw and Zeynep Şentek, 'Black Trail: The Shipping Industry Is a Massive Climate Polluter. Is It Committed to Change?' *The Black Sea* (online), 30 April 2021 <https://theblacksea.eu/black-trail-project/black-trail/>.

61 *Kyoto Protocol to the United Nations Framework Convention on Climate Change*, opened for signature 11 December 1997, 2303 UNTS 162 (entered into force 16 February 2005), Article 2(2); *United Nations Framework Convention on Climate Change*, opened for signature 9 May 1992, 1771 UNTS 107 (entered into force 21 March 1994). Beatriz Martinez Romera, *Regime Interaction and Climate Change: The Case of International Aviation and Maritime Transport* (Routledge, 2018) 11.

62 Felicity Deane, Anna Huggins, and Md Saiful Karim, 'Measuring, Monitoring, Reporting and Verification of Shipping Emissions: Evaluating Transparency and Answerability' (2019) 28(3) *Review of European, Comparative & International Environmental Law* 258, 266.

its potential future utility as a compliance tool is recognised by IMO member states, industry, environmental NGOs, and academics.[63]

The IMO DCS is already used by two linked voluntary compliance regimes, both called the Poseidon Principles, one of which pertains to financial institutions and one to marine insurers.[64] The European Union Regulation for the monitoring, reporting, and verification of CO2 emissions from maritime transport (EU MRV) is a regional mandatory reporting regime that currently operates in parallel with the IMO DCS. The EU MRV is more rigorous than the IMO DCS and illustrates the potential utility of a strengthened DCS for future compliance applications.[65]

Policy development at the IMO, as at other international organisations, is slow moving and accretive. This process can result in path dependency.[66] Hence, a reporting structure, once embedded in MARPOL, will tend to remain there, and its availability will affect future policy decisions and developments. If the IMO DCS is an emergent or nascent IMO institutional compliance mechanism, further study of the ongoing debate on the scope and application of the IMO DCS can illuminate the larger forces at work in the expansion of the IMO's compliance mandate.

Concluding remarks

Despite its somewhat stodgy reputation, the IMO has made major changes to its operations before, such as the widespread adoption of the tacit acceptance procedure to speed the amendment of the technical annexes of IMO treaties.[67] In recent years, the organisation has taken steps towards increased deliberative transparency, most notably by relaxing the limitations placed on

63 BHP Group Limited et al., *Carbon Levy Evaluation: Could a Carbon Levy in Shipping Be an Effective Way to Help Reach the IMO Greenhouse Gas Reduction Goals?* (White Paper, October 2019) 8; Deane et al. (n 62) 265–266; Elanchezhian Manoharan, 'Emission Data Reporting Requirements' (2021) *Thome Group News* 8.

64 See generally *Poseidon Principles, Version 5.0* (PDF File, October 2023) <https://www.poseidonprinciples.org/finance/wp-content/uploads/2019/07/Poseidon_Principles.pdf>; *Poseidon Principles for Marine Insurance, Version 1.1* (PDF File, May 2023) <https://www.poseidonprinciples.org/insurance/wp-content/uploads/2021/12/Poseidon-Principles-for-Marine-Insurance-Technical-Guidance.pdf>; Pia Rebelo, 'Poseidon Principles: Legal Directions for Implementation and Enforcement' (2020) 26(2) *Journal of International Maritime Law* 109.

65 Deane et al. (n 62) 265–266; Jonathan Lonsdale et al., *A Study to Estimate the Benefits of Removing Market Barriers in the Shipping Sector* (Final Report, March 2019) 31.

66 See generally Tine Hanrieder, 'The Path-Dependent Design of International Organizations: Federalism in the World Health Organization' (2015) 21(1) *European Journal of International Relations* 215.

67 See generally Lei Shi, 'Successful Use of the Tacit Acceptance Procedure to Effectuate Progress in International Maritime Law' (1999) 11(2) *University of San Francisco Maritime Law Journal* 299.

journalists attending IMO meetings.[68] There were calls for the live streaming of IMO meetings during these reform discussions of 2019,[69] but the COVID-19 pandemic changed the equation as travel to London became impractical if not impossible, and the IMO rapidly adopted a remote video meeting modality that included live streams to registered non-participants. Even with travel restrictions lifted and in-person meetings back in session, the sessions are now formally "hybrid" meetings, with the limited-access live stream continued. Discussions of truly public live streaming are ongoing, with the IMO Council agreeing in principle that at least some meetings should be publicly broadcast.[70]

The IMO has been uniquely slow to establish institutional compliance mechanisms for its treaties; its member states have done so only in times of acute institutional stress, when the organisation's foundational norms have come into conflict.

When this author suggested to IMO insiders that the IMO DCS could become the foundation of a future marine fuel emissions compliance regime, she was met with laughter and disbelief. However, while the climate change crisis unfolds more slowly compared to the oil spills of the twentieth century, the strengthening European model of emissions monitoring indicates that the IMO may soon face an internal crisis. It will need to address the conflict between its norm of institutional uniformity and its norm of procedural equality.

This chapter finds that member states agree to cede compliance authority to the IMO in explicitly political circumstances where the IMO's own legitimacy is threatened. However, the IMO's strong norms of "technical", non-political debate require member states to first engage in a process of depoliticisation, wherein the political issue is technicised, diluted, and delayed. It is hoped that a further study of this phenomenon can encourage efficient negotiation of future IMO treaty instruments, to include institutional compliance mechanisms, and that this added efficiency will help the IMO and the broader law of the sea regime to confront, and adapt to, both present-day crises and uncertain ocean futures.

68 In spring 2019, the IMO first gave journalists pre-meeting access to meeting documents. Michelle Wiese Bockmann, 'Open-Mouthed at IMO Openness', *Lloyd's List* (online, 10 May 2019) <https://www.lloydslist.com/LL1127443/Open-mouthed-at-IMO-openness>. Later that year, the IMO Council made the long-awaited and highly controversial move of allowing observing journalists to quote delegation statements made during plenary meetings. *Summary of Decision*, 30th Extraordinary Session of IMO Council, IMO Doc C/ES.30/D (22 November 2019). These reforms are limited to the nominally public plenary meetings of the major IMO organs, including the assembly, council, and committees, and do not extend to sub-committees or working groups, where most of the "work" of negotiation gets done.

69 Anastassios Adamopoulos, 'IMO Facing Renewed Calls for Transparency Reform', *Lloyd's List* (online, 11 July 2019) <https://www.lloydslist.com/LL1128336/IMO-facing-renewed-calls-for-transparency-reform>.

70 *Public Live Streaming of IMO Meetings*, 128th Session of IMO Council, IMO Doc C 128/4(b) (29 September 2022).

10 Developing Ocean Regimes for an Uncertain Future

Shirley V. Scott and Nengye Liu

The chapters in this book have offered insights into the complexities of developing legal and regulatory responses within ocean law to the triple challenges of climate change, biodiversity loss, and pollution. While each chapter stands in its own right, the concluding chapter draws out key themes that have emerged from the set as a whole.

The triple challenge that ocean law and governance seeks to address presents as a number of specific issues, including vessel-source greenhouse gas emissions, ocean acidification, seabed mining, the management of multiple offshore activities, and the loss of marine biodiversity. In addition to investigating such issues, the chapters have also provided insights into the generic dimensions of regime design, including creating a regime that is robust, effective, flexible, and sufficiently resilient to respond in near real time to a dynamic context. As the complexity of environmental issues and the web of existing laws become ever more complex, planning for and managing the intricate interactions between and among the respective regimes have become more important than ever before.

One of the strengths of this collection is the diverse range of theoretical and methodological approaches employed by the authors, all of which have proven worthwhile for studying regime dynamics and interaction. The approaches include global experimentalist governance as initially developed by Grainne De Búrca, Robert O. Keohane, and Charles F. Sabel[1]; Elinor Ostrom's scholarship on robustness and adaptive governance[2]; Ellen Hey's work on regime interaction[3]; and the theorising of Lucile Maertens and Marieke Louis on the dynamics of depoliticisation within international organisations.[4]

As the authors have effectively demonstrated in their analyses, it is extremely difficult to design and implement a regime that is simultaneously effective, robust, flexible, and resilient. The juxtaposition of analytical approaches in this

1 See above, ch 2
2 See above, ch 5.
3 See above, ch 6.
4 See above, ch 9.

DOI: 10.4324/9781003518570-10

collection has also illuminated that progress in knowledge-building in relation to robustness and any other dimension of regime dynamics and interaction would likely be accelerated if there were greater uniformity in the usage of key terms.

The need for regimes to be robust was perhaps the most emphasised theme throughout the volume. Kristine Elfrida Dalaker explained that the biodiversity beyond national jurisdiction (BBNJ) negotiations foregrounded a widespread desire to create a robust regime, although just what was meant by "robust" was rarely specified with any precision. The desire for a robust regime concerning marine biodiversity can be interpreted as a call for a regime well able to protect biodiversity. Here, the meaning of "robust" is something akin to "effective". However, in everyday language, robustness refers to the quality of strength, more so than to effectiveness in the sense of success; thus, the two terms are not interchangeable.

Drawing an analytical distinction between the two provides scope for analysing the relationship between robustness and effectiveness. In this respect, it is important to note the tendency of regimes to prioritise robustness – their own institutional strength, over effectiveness.[5] This would seem reasonable to the extent that if an institution ceases to exist, it cannot be expected to achieve very much. To the extent that conflating the two terms is reasonable, it may be because robustness is likely a key component of an effective regime.

The triple environmental crisis of climate change, biodiversity loss, and pollution underscores the importance of ensuring that an initiative designed to address any one of these challenges does not do so at the expense of another environmental issue. David Leary illustrated that the production and use of electric vehicles have generated demand for specific minerals, including cobalt, that are found in the deep seabed and whose extraction could be anticipated to harm associated ecosystems.

In a similar vein, as explored by Gabriela Argüello, offshore wind power generation in the exclusive economic zone may disturb species and generate change to the seabed and marine habitats. It may also give rise to tensions with users of offshore waters from the fishing and shipping sectors. The possibility that negotiation of the BBNJ might interrupt the operation of existing regimes, including regional fisheries organisations, was a concern during the BBNJ negotiations. Ethan Beringen helpfully traced how this concern was managed and minimised in the resulting agreement.

When robustness refers to institutional strength, combining robustness with flexibility seems particularly challenging. However, as Frosch has discussed, solutions have been found. The outcome is often referred to as resilience. The need for an international institution to adapt in the face of

5 Shirley V. Scott, 'Comparing the Robustness and Effectiveness of the Antarctic Treaty System and the UNFCCC Regime' (2019) 11(2) *Australian Journal of Maritime & Ocean Affairs* 94, 94–106.

changed circumstances is not new to the current negotiating context. Even the International Convention for the Regulation of Whaling, concluded as long ago as 1947, included an institutional mechanism for adjusting catch limits as necessary without the need to revise the treaty text itself.

Rebecca Prentiss Pskowski has explained that although it began with a certain compliance mandate, the International Marine Organization (IMO) originally left most implementation, compliance, and enforcement to states. Having adapted, the IMO is now expected to undergo further evolution in its compliance and enforcement mechanisms. Contrary to some expectations, Pskowski believes that these developments will enhance the IMO's ability to fulfil its responsibilities while adapting to a complex and unpredictable environment. She explains how this evolution might unfold based on her analysis of the IMO's evolution so far.

However, it remains problematic if, despite long-term efforts to address the concerns of all negotiating states, the procedural mechanisms established by a treaty still allow powerful states to legitimately detract from the success of the instrument in addressing the issue. Area-based management likely plays an important role in achieving the BBNJ's effectiveness. Yet, the process of establishing, implementing, monitoring, and enforcing marine protected areas is complex, with the potential to result in longer than optimal timeframes and to introduce political trade-offs and ambiguity into outcomes.[6]

Ultimately, the bottom line must be effectiveness. There seems little point in having a wealth of ocean regimes that are robust, flexible, and resilient if they are also ineffective; indeed, such regimes could potentially do more harm than good if they are inadequate to address environmental crises while giving the illusion of progress. Moreover, if their design leaves too much scope for power and unrelated politics to detract from the ambitions of states and other political actors, progress in protecting the environment might be further diminished.

The evolution of the climate change mitigation regime, including the attempts at top-down and bottom-up governance approaches, suggests that there is no universal agreement on how to enhance effectiveness as a single dimension of regime design, particularly in respect of a multifaceted issue central to the functioning of the contemporary global economy. At the same time, in a narrower and perhaps more technical issue area, Beringen and Nengye Liu found the IMO to have been quite effective in addressing "traditional" as opposed to climate-related vessel-source pollution. In this sense, flexibility and resilience might be considered crucial mainly because they are prerequisites for effectiveness.

The climate change regime also illuminates the contemporary difficulty, if not impossibility, of achieving an effective regime on a global environmental

6 See Nengye Liu, 'Establishing Marine Protected Areas in the Southern Ocean, Lessons for the BBNJ Agreement' (2024), 165 *Marine Policy*, 106216.

issue should the substantive provisions specified in the treaty be deemed unfair. In the climate change regime, the heavy conceptual lifting to ensure perceived fairness has been accomplished through the concept of common but differentiated responsibilities and respective capabilities. The equivalent concept in the 1982 Law of the Sea Convention was the common heritage of mankind (CHM). However, as discussed in the chapter by Carina Costa de Oliveira, Harvey Mpoto Bombaka, and Ana Flavia Barros-Platiau, the legal significance of the CHM principle within the law of the sea was diminished in the early 1990s with the conclusion of the 1994 Implementing Agreement.

De Oliveira, Bombaka, and Barros-Platiau provided valuable insights into how the principle, updated to the common heritage of humankind (CHH) in the BBNJ Agreement, might contribute to the conservation of marine biodiversity in the context of seabed mining. The authors noted the difficulty of reconciling the four elements of the CHH principle: joint management, non-appropriation, benefit-sharing, and the peaceful use of resources. Nevertheless, they advocated for more widespread applications of the principle and to it being treated as a general principle of international law.

This rich collection of chapters should significantly contribute to the debate among scholars of regime design and of the law of the sea, which is crucial for effectively addressing the triple planetary crises of climate change, biodiversity loss, and pollution.

Index

FSC
www.fsc.org
MIX
Papier | Fördert
gute Waldnutzung
FSC® C083411

Kolibri 360 GmbH
Ferdinand-Jühlke-Straße 7
99095 Erfurt, Deutschland
produktsicherheit@kolibri360.de